Early and Medieval Christianity

The Collected Papers in Church History of Roland Bainton

The Collected Papers in Church History

SERIES ONE

Early and Medieval Christianity

By Roland H. Bainton   77793

Beacon Press   Boston

Acknowledgments

Grateful acknowledgment is made to the following for permission to reprint the articles comprising this volume:

Yale University Press: *The Idea of History in the Ancient Near East;* The Society of Biblical Literature and Exegesis: *Journal of Biblical Literature;* National Council of the Churches of Christ: *International Journal of Religious Education;* The Metropolitan Museum of Art; *The Journal of Religious Thought;* Harper & Brothers and The American Association of Theological Schools: *The Ministry in Historical Perspectives;* Abingdon Press: *Religion in Life; Church History;* Harvard Divinity School: *Harvard Theological Review;* University of Chicago Press: *Journal of Modern History;* The American Society for Reformation Research: *Archiv für Reformationsgeschichte;* H. D. Tjeenk Willink & Zoon: *Autour de Michel Servet et de Sebastien Castellion; Theology Today; Die Religion in Geschichte und Gegenwart.*

Foreword

In the autumn of the year 1417 the masons had finished their work on the church of St. Nicholas in the village of Lynn in Norfolk, England. The carpenters were already working on the roof and the glaziers had started to install the windows. The masons at daybreak on a September morning assembled to hear mass before the great altar of their own construction before going their separate ways in search of other employ. The scene is reconstructed by G. G. Coulton. Among the most taciturn of the masons, he tells us, was Roger Pigott, but as he surveyed the completed work and singled out his own mark on the arches, he was moved to speech. In a hoarse whisper and almost to himself he muttered:

"Aye, they will mount up at the Day of Doom." "Mount up whither, man?" "Mount up to my reckoning, William Hindley. There's nothing heavier than stones in a common way; and I guess there must be some twenty or thirty hundredweight of mine here in this church, all cut as honestly as a man can cut them. So the blessed St. Nicholas will see to it that every stone goes into my scale at Doomsday; and the Devil may pull as hard as he will at the other, yet I trust that mine shall weigh him down." So he passed his hand lovingly over the nearest pillar; and all men streamed out silently, marvelling that Roger could talk like a clerk when it came to saying farewell to his own work.[1] This charming picture of a medieval mason taking

[1] G. G. Coulton, *Medieval Faith and Symbolism* (Torchbooks, N.Y., 1958), pp. 224–225.

v

leave of his labors in the confidence that his well carven
stones would by the favor of St. Nicholas weight the scales
in his favor at the day of Judgment affords a certain parallel
to any leave taking from long labors in any time. But
greater than the similarity is the contrast between the
ancient mason and the modern historian making the last
revision of his articles. Between them lies the Reformation
and he who has drunk from Luther will never suppose that
any work of man will tip the scales at Doomsday, nor can
he invoke the intercession of St. Nicholas or peradventure
St. Luke, the historian. Another difference is not of time
but of material. The worker with ideas can never enjoy the
same satisfaction as the worker with solid stuff. The mason
can stroke his stones and affirm without fear of contradiction that they are well cut. The scholar can never be so sure
that he has wrought well. He may be pleased to leaf through
his book, because the book itself is something concrete, and
being well printed may give the illusion that something has
been said.

Again the mason may feel that his work will endure.
That church at Lynn has lasted over five hundred years,
whereas the glory of scholarship, however excellent, is only
the splendor of autumn leaves. Yet perhaps at this point the
difference is not so great. Stones also have no permanence,
nor did the medieval mason expect it of them. He looked
forward to the *Dies irae, dies illa, Solvet saeculum in favilla,*
just as today the craftsman and the author alike live in
foreboding of the Armageddon of man's own devising. The
medieval mason built not for eternity but to the honor of
St. Nicholas and of our Lady, and the modern builder in
whatever medium labors not for perpetuity but *ad majorem
gloriam Dei.* Why, in any case, should worth be measured
in terms of time? A biographer of Erasmus has rendered the
erroneous judgment that his greatest achievement was
The Praise of Folly, because this alone of all his works is
read today. As if that were a supreme distinction! The
greatest work of Erasmus was the edition for the first time
of the Greek text of the New Testament in print. Today it

is a museum piece. As an edition it has long since been superseded and should much sooner have ceased to be the *textus receptus*. The purpose of scholarship is to feed scholarship, and that is the reason for garnering the fruits of the years into a single basket, that they may be the more readily accessible and may perchance a little longer serve till better work is done.

The present collection of papers aims at completeness for material not in books. Those essays which have appeared in other of my volumes are not included, here with the exception of "Michael Servetus and the Trinitarian Speculation of the Middle Ages" (which appeared without the full critical apparatus and footnote citations in *Hunted Heretic*, Beacon Press, 1953). Papers not reprinted here can be traced through the complete bibliography.

R.H.B.

Abbreviations

Used in footnotes and bibliographies.

ANF	*Ante-Nicene Fathers*
ARG	*Archiv für Reformationsgeschichte*
BKGMAR	*Beiträge zur Kulturgeschichte des Mittelalters und der Renaissance*
c Cels	*Contra Celsum* (Origen)
CIL	*Corpus Inscriptionum Latinorum*
CSEL	*Corpus Scriptorum Ecclesiasticorum Latinorum*
DB	Hasting's *Dictionary of the Bible*
DCB	*Dictionary of Christian Biography*
EA	Erlangen ed. (Erlangen Ausgabe)
EE	*Opus Epistolarum Des. Erasmi*
Ep	Epistle
HE	*Historia Ecclesiastica*
HRE	Herzog's *Realencyclopaedie*
NH	*Naturalis Historia*
PG	Migne, *Patrologia graeca*
PL	Migne, *Patrologia latina*
PNF	*The Nicene and Post-Nicene Fathers*
R	*Restitutio* of Servetus
Trin. Err.	*De Trinitatis Erroribus* of Servetus
T.u.U.	*Texte und Untersuchungen*
VC	*Vita Constantini*
WA	Weimar Ausgabe (*Luthers Werke*)

Contents

To

Erich and Erika Dinkler
and to the memory of her father
Hans von Schubert

I. Patristic and Medieval Christianity

1 Ideas of History in Patristic Christianity

The concept of history is usually employed as embracing the entire span of man's life in time upon this earth with the obvious sequence of birth, begetting, and death. The idea of history seeks to disclose other more elusive sequences, and possibly laws, to comprehend the meaning of the whole. This may be done by deductions from observation, but the Christian can never rest content to interpret events by events, nor will he essay to understand man's terrestrial course without invoking the celestial. The idea of history must encompass the origin and destiny of man.

Our concern in this paper is with early Christian thinking in the first five centuries after the New Testament and primarily in the East. This geographical delimitation for this period, however, is largely fictitious, for truly the twain did meet. To which, for example, would one assign Jerome writing in Latin at Bethlehem or Irenaeus writing in Greek at Lyons?

I. Christ the End of History

The point of departure for any such study must, of course, be the New Testament, because Christian thinking

First published under the title "Patristic Christianity," in *The Idea of History in the Ancient Near East* (ed. R. C. Dentan; Yale University Press, New Haven, 1955). Only the first sentence, which originally referred to the series of essays published with this one, has been revised.

3

was simply an elaboration, interpretation, and application
amid the course of ongoing events of New Testament concepts. With regard to the significance of the New Testament
for the idea of history two assertions have been made,
apparently contradictory. The first is that Christ marked the
end of history. The second is that Christianity for the first
time supplied a meaningful philosophy of history. The first
of these statements can be understood in more than one
sense. If it means that Christ ended the sequence of births,
begettings, and deaths, then obviously it is not true. What
we can say is only this: that the early Church expected
Christ to be the end of history. The assumption was that he
would come again to inaugurate a new order in which there
should be no marrying or giving in marriage, but this expectation was never realized, and in the words of II Peter
3:4, "All things continued as they were from the beginning
of the world."

In another sense Christ may be said to have been the
end of history in that he elevated men into a new dimension
of living in which the immediacy of the vertical relationship
to God superseded and almost obliterated the horizontal relationship of man to man. Paul affirmed that he no longer
lived, but Christ lived in him.[1] And John asserted that they
alone truly live who eat and drink of the Son of Man.[2] This
view was amplified in the early Church into the doctrine of
the deification of man, who in Christ becomes so truly a new
creature as to put off corruptibility and mortality and to
share in the very nature and being of God. According to
Irenaeus, God became man in order that man might become
God. The change was assumed to be effected particularly
through the sacrament of the Lord's Supper, for just as the
bread and wine after consecration are no longer common
elements, so also is the believer altered, divesting himself of
the distinctively human and putting on the divine nature.[3]
He who thus becomes God with God is indifferent to and

---

[1] Gal. 2:20.
[2] John 6:53.
[3] Irenaeus, *Adv. Haer.*, III, 18, 7; IV, 18, 5.

above space and time. Such thinking was congenial especially to the theologians of the East from Irenaeus to Athanasius and John of Damascus and explains why to this day the Eastern liturgy concludes the mass not with the cross but with the resurrection and the assurance of newness of life.[4]

Yet, not here is one to find the essence of the Christian concept of history. To begin with, this view is not specifically Christian. Did not the mystery cults also aspire to make man divine and immortal? Did not Plotinus pray for the experience of ecstasy in which the spatial and the temporal become unreal? Cannot one in fact say that mysticism spells the end of history? At the same time mysticism does not end history. He who experiences ecstasy experiences it in the body. He who becomes oblivious to time will be snapped back by the crying of a babe or the burning of the toast, and even if the raptures of the mystic were continuous, which is never the case, he would be living two lives, in the spirit and in the flesh. The reader becomes vividly aware of this in perusing Bunyan's *Pilgrim's Progress*, for in the beginning, when Christian is distraught as to his destiny, his family seek to cure his distemper by "harsh and surly carriage," and he is compelled in consequence to set out upon his pilgrimage alone, but after the trumpets have sounded for him on the other side, we discover that his family have been with him in the flesh all the time, and he with them. The Christian, then, though not of this world, is not out of this world. He may be at times beyond time, but he lives in time. We may perhaps say that though he transcends history, he is enmeshed in history.

II. Delay of the Parousia

The early Christian fathers became increasingly aware of their involvement as time passed without the coming of the Lord. They began to consider when he would appear and why he delayed. Speculations with regard to his

[4] Cf. the works of Bauer, Bornhäuser, Butterworth and Lot-Boradine in bibliography at end of chapter.

coming entailed a theory of history which was constructed
by a combination of two Old Testament ideas. The first was
that of the Sabbath rest, after the work of the week was
done, on the seventh day. The other was the statement of
Psalm 90:4: "For a thousand years in Thy sight are but as
yesterday when it is past." The assumption, then, was the
course of world history would run for six thousand years. To
calculate the end one must first have determined the beginning. This might be done by constructing a chronology for
the Old Testament and thus arriving at the date of creation.
This computation many of the early Christians attempted,
but others preferred a much more fundamental mode of
reckoning in terms of the amount of time required between
the first and the second comings of Christ. Some time was
plainly needed, because the Lord had distinctly said that
before the end "The Gospel must be preached to all nations,"[5]
and the Apostle Paul had envisaged the gathering in of the
Jews.[6] Many of the fathers held that the denouement was
being deliberately held back by God to provide time for the
world mission of the Church. Some even interpreted the
expression in II Thess. 2:7, "The power which restrains," as
referring to the great missionary commission.[7]

How long would this take? Hippolytus answered that
the work would require one half of a day of a thousand
years. The incarnation of Christ was thus assumed to have
fallen exactly in the middle of the sixth period and the end
would be around 500 A.D. Since Hippolytus flourished at the
beginning of the third century, this would leave close to
three hundred years. Lactantius, in the days of Constantine,
employed the same scheme, but since he was a century later
than Hippolytus, the time before the coming of the Lord was
reduced to approximately two hundred years. Such speculations continued in the West until St. Augustine broke with
all millenarianism and projected the coming indefinitely into
the future. In the East the development was not essentially

          [5] Mark 13:10.
          [6] Rom. 11.
          [7] Cullmann, "Le Caractère eschatologique" and "Quand Viendra le Royaume
de Dieu?" (See Bibliography for complete references.)

different from that in the West. In the second century in Asia Minor Papias indulged in the lush imagery of Jewish apocalyptic and described the new imminent age in crassly materialistic terms; but these chiliastic expectations speedily declined. The Alexandrians spiritualized eschatology, and Gregory of Nyssa performed the same function as Augustine when he rejected the scheme of the Sabbath in the seventh millennium. Instead, for him, the seven thousand years embraced the whole of time without a break, and the Sabbath was the eighth period of eternity.[8]

Thereafter, alike in the East and the West, the established churches centered attention more on the day of judgment than on the return of the Lord. Recurrently, however, the masses, stimulated by some natural calamity, some unusual conjunction of the planets—for astrology was admitted to the courts of the Lord—would flare up in apocalyptic reveries. The year 1000 in the West in certain circles inspired such speculations, and in the East, curiously, the year 1492 was assumed to be the seven thousandth year from the creation of the world. In the West in the late twelfth century Joachim of Fiore revived primitive eschatology by manipulations of the figure 1,260, the number of days spent by the woman in the Apocalypse in the wilderness, and these days converted into years. Even in Bolshevist Russia the authorities have been disturbed by popular agitations inspired through proclamations of impending cataclysms.[9] But the great established churches, perhaps precisely because they were established, have been less disposed to look for the end of the world, and even the church of the martyrs early grew dubious as to whether the end was soon to be desired, since the coming must be preceded by an accumulation of woes. Should the Christian then pray "Come quickly, Lord Jesus"[10] or for a delay of the end, *pro mora finis?*[11]

[8] Daniélou, "La Typologie millenoriste," and Frick.
[9] Vasiliev.
[10] *Didache* X.
[11] Tertullian, *Apology*, XXXII and XXXIX. Cf. Bainton, n. 72.

III. *Not Cycles but Successive Creations*

The distinctive contribution of Christianity to the idea of history, then, was not the view that Christ had ended history. In a literal sense it was not true; and in a spiritual sense the life in the spirit was lived and was expected to be lived in the ongoing framework of events in time. The distinctive element lay rather in the flat rejection of the cyclical theory of the Greeks. A Christian could never have behaved like Scipio Africanus who, when he committed Carthage to the flames, wept not out of pity for the fifty thousand survivors whom he was about to enslave but only from the reflection that the revolving wheel of time would at long last bring the same fate to Rome.[12] The Christian could never say of Christ what Aristotle said of Plato: that in another age there might be another Plato. The Christian could not think of himself as living prior to the incarnation of God in Christ as Aristotle said that he was living prior to the fall of Troy quite as much as afterward, since in the recurrent cycle Troy would fall again.[13] "Once and for all Christ died unto sin." [14] "Once and for all He entered into the holy place." [15] "Once and for all we are sanctified by the offering of His body." [16] Only one early Christian author was ever so much as suspected of a cyclical view of history, and he did not entertain it. This was Origen, who said that life on earth is a purgation and for this purpose one life may not suffice. In other words, he suggested the idea of purgatory. Moreover when the purgation is complete, said he, inasmuch as man is free, there is the possibility of retrogression, and the whole process may have to start over again. Yet this is not to say that in each life there will be another Redeemer, because there is no foundation other than that which has been laid for us once and for all in Christ Jesus.[17]

[12] Polybius, *Hist.* VI.
[13] Cf. Puech.
[14] Rom. 6:10.
[15] Heb. 9:12.
[16] Heb. 10:12.
[17] Koch, p. 92.

The affirmation that Christ was at once new and definitive was an assertion about the course and the nature of history. The possibility of something new is involved, and this concept is rooted in the picture of God the Creator, the Lord of Life, bound by no ineluctable sequence, able by a supreme act of His omnipotent will to summon being out of nonbeing.[18] This He did at the creation, and the statement of the Creed, "I believe in God, the Father Almighty, the Creator," was an assertion not only about God but also about history. God created, in the Christian view, not in the sense of shaping up previously existing materials as in Plato's *Timaeus* but by saying, "Let there be," and there was. "Let there be light," and the universe was suffused with radiance before ever the suns were sent hurtling upon their courses.[19]

The Creator God is forever creating, for "He who commanded the light to shine out of darkness hath shined in our hearts to give the light of the knowledge of the glory of God in the face of Jesus Christ." [20] The incarnation is a new creation, and the Christian is a new creature. Gregory of Nyssa declared that history "goes from beginnings to beginnings by means of beginnings which have no end." [21] That which is new can therefore be definitive, in no need of repetition. Christ is thus the beginning and the end, truly the alpha and the omega, the pivot of all history, as our chronology has eventually recognized by dating not forward from the creation of the world to Christ, but backward from Christ to the creation.[22]

Yet this does not mean that history is simply a series of disjointed episodes. There are sequences, first the blade, then the ear, and then the ripened corn. God has a plan for the ages. For the early Church the first practical question was to know the significance in the divine plan of the interval

[18] Frank, p. 57.

[19] Daniélou, "The Conception of History in the Christian Tradition."

[20] II Cor. 4:6.

[21] *Hom. Cant.* VIII. *PG*, vol. 44, col. 1043b. Cited in Daniélou, "The Conception of History," p. 68. Does not check.

[22] Cullmann, *Christus und die Zeit.*

between the first and the second comings. The Church was all the more driven to give some meaningful content to this period because of the judgment of the Gnostics that time itself is a calamity. The Gnostic exclaimed: "In this world of darkness I have lived for a million myriad of years and no one knew that I was there. The years succeeded to the years, the generations to the generations. I was there, and they did not know that I was there, in their world." A Gnostic prayer declared: "Now our gracious Father, innumerable myriads of years have passed by since we have been separated from Thee." The Gnostic was bound to regard time on earth as a calamity because life in time is spent in the flesh, which is an impediment and an imprisonment. Marcion spoke brutally of the ignominy of existence, engendered in obscenity and brought forth in impurity. The body is a sack of excrements which death will turn into a stinking cadaver.[23]

No Christian ever talked that way. The Apostle Paul might desire to depart and be with Christ. Ignatius might hope that his martyrdom would not be impeded; but even Origen, who was closest to the Gnostics, did not stigmatize life in the body as an imprisonment. God gave us bodies for a good purpose: that in them we might receive our instruction, perfect our training, and complete our probation.[24] The interval, then, between the first and second comings had a twofold purpose: to gather in the Gentiles and to effect the purgation of the Christians. The Shepherd of Hermas remarked, for example, that for the heathen there is always repentance, and for the Christian who has lapsed there is one more chance.[25]

IV. Historical Sequence: The Church and the Pre-Christian Dispensation

The above expressions all apply to individual Christians, but these individuals were not isolated, and history was re-

---

[23] Quispel, p. 93.
[24] Koch, p. 37.
[25] Hermas, *Vis.* II, ii, 5.

garded as something more than the progress of particular persons in the way of salvation. They are members of the Church and the Church has her role in the divine economy. She is called the bride of Christ,[26] and thus she is affirmed to be in intimate communion with her unique source. She is the new Israel of God.[27] In early Christian literature she was called the new Eden, the restorer of paradise.[28] Thus to relate the Church to Israel was to connect her with the course of Jewish history prior to the coming of Christ. Here a most difficult problem confronted the early Christians, both to assert the continuity of Christianity with Judaism against the Gnostics and to assert the superiority of Christianity to Judaism against the Jews. The Gnostics, because they condemned the creation, condemned also the Creator and His chosen people together with their sacred book. Since the world is evil, said they, He who made it must be evil. He is not, then, the God and Father of our Lord Jesus Christ but a malevolent demiurge, and all those in the Old Testament who regarded him as evil and all those who defied him are to be considered good, such as Cain, Seth, Dathan, Kore, and Abiron. The whole scale of values was reversed, and the coming of Christ in consequence was considered to have been absolutely new, a complete break in history. Until that time the supreme God was hidden in obscurity. Truly he was an unknown God. Then with shattering suddenness he stepped into the course of time in the fifteenth year of Tiberius.

The Christian Church on the contrary affirmed the goodness of creation and the identity of the Creator God with the Redeemer God. The Old Testament was then retained, but only with qualifications. How, then, could this previous development be related to the revelation of God in Christ? Several devices were employed to integrate the new covenant with the old. One was the device of dispensations, that is to say, God dealt with his chosen people by

---

[26] Eph. 5:32.
[27] Gal. 6:16.
[28] Irenaeus, *op. cit.*, V. 20. Cf. Bainton, n. 99.

stages. From the side of man's behavior the course was marked not so much by progress as by deterioration. First Adam fell, then the human race was so perverse as to incur the Flood. The covenant with Abraham was only with a saving remnant, and Moses because of the hardness of men's hearts had to give a bill of divorce. The fathers stoned the prophets and when the Son came, He was slain upon a tree.

From God's side, however, there was a progressive self-disclosure culminating in the cross and the resurrection. The dispensations were linked together by certain anticipations cast according to a similarity of pattern. The Old Testament was interpreted in terms of typology. "As Moses lifted up the serpent in the wilderness, so should the Son of Man be lifted up." The sacrifice of Isaac prefigured the sacrifice of Christ; the four-winged creatures in the vision of Ezekiel, namely the man, the eagle, the lion, and the ox, foreshadowed the four evangelists; and so on. This is not a cyclical theory of history because the new covenant did not repeat precisely the old. The sacrifice of Christ was not a repetition of the sacrifice of Isaac. As a matter of fact Isaac was not sacrificed, and no one would pretend that the four gospels repeated the four creatures of the prophet's vision. The point was rather that a certain identity of meaning, a similarity of structure linked each dispensation with that which was to come. The more so was this the case because of the assumption that the pre-existent Christ in the form of Wisdom or Logos was on occasion partially disclosed even in the Old Testament. He it was who appeared to Abraham at the oak of Mamre. He it was who stood before Moses in the burning bush. The uniqueness of the incarnation was at times almost imperiled by this projection backward of the work of Christ.[29]

This was obviated by assuming a progressive revelation culminating in the Incarnation. In the realm of ethics, God led his people through successive stages to a more advanced level. In former times acts were condoned or enjoined by God which are no longer allowed. Polygamy was conceded to the patriarchs, says Tertullian, because of the need at

[29] Daniélou, *Sacramentum Futuri.*

that time to replenish the earth more rapidly, though even then it was contrary to God's preferred intent, since he used only one rib to make a helpmate for Adam.[30] Other discrepancies from the Christian code, such as the despoiling of the Egyptians, the suicide of Samson, or the extermination of the Canaanites, were explained sometimes as due to a special revelation no longer valid, or allegorized and thus denuded of any literal meaning.[31]

The Old Testament era, in general, however, was assigned to the period of the fall, and the Christian Era marked a new dispensation, a restoration of the state of the garden of Eden prior to the transgression of Adam. The Church was described as the new Eden of God whose mission it was to restore the lost splendor. In her fellowship the lion and the lamb should lie down together. This idea, incidentally, readily lent itself to combination with a similar concept prevalent particularly among the Stoics of a golden age in the past without war, without property, without slavery, progressively lost in deterioration through the ages of Silver, Bronze, and Iron. The Christians did not appropriate the whole of this program. War alone should be repudiated. Slavery, however, was simply to be Christianized. The attitude toward property is the most interesting as an illustration of discriminating borrowing and adaptation. The Church did not espouse a communal ownership of all goods, but at the same time often echoed Cynic-Stoic praises of poverty. A drink, said the Cynic, is no more refreshing because from a silver or a golden cup, and sleep is no sweeter on an ivory bed.[32] The Christian would make the same observation and then inquire whether Christ came from heaven with a silver footbath to wash the disciples' feet.[33] Note that Christ came from heaven and not from the lost Atlantis. The motivation for poverty was also different. The

---

[30] Tertullian, "Exhortation to Chastity," *ANF* *4, 53*. Cf. "To His Wife," *ibid.*, p. 39.

[31] Cf. chapter 7.

[32] Lovejoy, *Primitivism*, pp. 142–143.

[33] Clement of Alexandria, *ANF*, *2*, *247*, Tertullian, *ibid.*, *4*, 16–17; Cyprian, *ibid.*, *5*, *279–280*.

Cynic sought to insure inward tranquility by divesting himself in advance of everything of which by Fortune he might be despoiled. When Diogenes saw a boy drinking out of his hands, the sage smashed his cup, saying, "Fool that I am to have been so long encumbered with superfluous baggage."[34] The Christian Tertullian inquired rather whether a neck adorned with a necklace would bow before the ax of the executioner.[35] For the Christian poverty was a part of the discipline necessary to maintain morale for martyrdom. The point was not reinforced by assuming such simplicity to have been the original condition of mankind. Only Lactantius referred to the Church as the restorer of the age of Saturn.[36] Ambrose made much of poverty but little of the theme of the lost paradise, though he did borrow from the philosophers the view that the accumulation of private wealth is against nature.[37]

All such appropriations from classical theories are noted mainly to emphasize the way in which the Church transformed in borrowing. The main point in the whole concept of the Church as the New Eden was not that the external conditions of the garden were recovered but rather the condition of man. The Christians were new creatures who exemplified in their behavior the love, joy, peace which are the fruits of the spirit.

V. Secular History

Thus far in our discussion the Christian theory of history has been delineated solely from the point of view of God's plan for man's redemption. Have, then, the Christians no conception of a secular history? Basically, no, but still as the Christian Church found itself operating within the framework of the empire, attention was devoted to the relations of the Church to the state and to society, and re-

[34] Seneca, *Ep.* XC.
[35] Tertullian, "On the Apparel of Women," II, 13, *ANF*, 4, 25.
[36] Lactantius, "Divine Institutes," *ANF*, 7, 140–142, cf. 219.
[37] Lovejoy, "The Communism of Saint Ambrose."

flections emerged as to the course of empires. The Church was in the anomalous position of being persecuted by an emperor who claimed to be god and of being assisted by an empire which rendered accessible to the Gospel the remotest corners of the known world.

Diverse attitudes developed. They are all adumbrated in the New Testament. The most favorable attitude to the empire is to be found in the Lukan writings, which note the coincidence of what one might call sacred and secular chronology. Christ was born under Augustus and baptized under Tiberius. In the Book of Acts the Roman magistrates are represented on the whole as curbing the fanaticism of the Jews. The most hostile attitude is that of the Book of Revelation, which portrays Rome as Babylon drunk with the blood of the saints. The intermediate position is that of Paul and the Pastorals. For Paul, in II Thessalonians, the man of sin who sets himself forth as God appears to be the deified Roman emperor, but the power which restrains the chaos of the apocalyptic woes may be the Roman Empire. At any rate, in the succeeding period, whereas some interpreted "the power that restrains" as the missionary activity of the Church, others saw in it a reference to the empire.

In the period between the New Testament and the age of Constantine these three general positions recur. The most favorable was that which saw in the empire a providential provision for the dissemination of the Gospel (so Origen) and rejoiced that the roads were open and the seas were clear (so Tertullian). The most hospitable to Rome was Melito of Sardis, who looked upon Christianity and the empire as two conjoint works of God for the benefit of mankind. At the other extreme was Commodianus, who would welcome an invasion by the Goths to overturn the empire.

The main line followed the thought of Paul. The deified emperor should be resisted until death, but the empire was viewed as a force restraining disorder. The judgment on the empire was qualified. The encomia of the Roman panegyrists were blended with the execrations of the conquered. The exigencies of polemic drove Christian apologists to deprecatory views of Rome. When the pagans charged that Christianity was responsible for whatever calamities befell, the reply was first of all that the calamities antedated Christianity and must therefore have some other source. Roman literature itself supplied the refutation in the view that a virus of corruption had infected the blood stream of Rome from the very outset of her history. When the founding fathers, the twins, were suckled by a wolf, and when Romulus slew Remus, then Rome was established by fratricide. This theme is to be found in Horace and was avidly appropriated by Tertullian and Minucius Felix. Another similar theme went back to a speech made by Scipio Nasica in the Roman Senate at the time when the fate of Carthage was under debate. He opposed destruction on the ground that a great state needs a rival to keep her from internal dissension. When, then, Carthage was actually demolished and Rome subsequently succumbed to civil wars, Sallust reverted to this prediction as the explanation of Roman degeneration. This note recurs in the apologetic of Lactantius.[38] The Christians also were not unwilling to burrow in the anti-imperial literature of the East, even though some of it may have become traditional and comparatively devoid of animus. Older even than Daniel was the theory of the four monarchies which should pass away to be superseded by a fifth. The application to an empire of either the number four or the number five was thus both a judgment and a prediction. If the empire was called the fourth, then its collapse was imminent; if it was the fifth, it was about to overthrow and succeed its predecessors. A note of hostility, then, is observable in that chronology which declares that Assyria was followed by Rome in the position of the fourth monarchy. This sequence runs through not a few of the fathers, though perhaps they merely perpetuated a tradition without being altogether aware of its implications.[39]

With the accession of Constantine Christian theologians in the first flush of enthusiasm for their victorious champion

[38] Bainton, pp. 203–205.
[39] Swain.

reverted to the view of Melito of Sardis, arguing that coincidentally Rome had pacified the world and Christianity had overcome the demons and tamed belligerent peoples. The Roman peace and the Christian peace together had turned swords into plowshares. Christ was therefore made into a Roman citizen, and Augustus almost into a Christian. The close affiliation of Christianity and the empire received a theological undergirding. The argument was advanced mainly by the Antiochian theologians with their strong emphasis upon the divine unity. They contended, notably Eusebius of Caesarea, that polytheism had been appropriate to a congeries of city-states inspired by demons to incessant turmoil, but now monotheism and monarchy called for each other: one God, one Lord, one faith, one baptism, and one Constantine.[40] Hear the words of Eusebius:

> The wars of antiquity were due to polytheism. Then the demonic gods were overcome by Christ, then divergent governments and wars ceased as one God was proclaimed to all mankind. At the same time one universal power, the Roman empire, arose and flourished, while the enduring and implacable hatred of nation against nation was now removed: and as the knowledge of one God, and one way of religion and salvation, even the doctrine of Christ, was made known to all mankind; so at the self-same period, the entire dominion of the Roman empire being vested in a single sovereign, profound peace reigned throughout the world. And thus, by the express appointment of the same God, two roots of blessing sprang up together for the benefit of men; the Roman empire and the teaching of the Christian religion.[41]

This attitude toward the empire was to run through a long line of Eastern theologians.

But the West was confronted with a new situation. Rome was sacked by the troops of Alaric in the year 410 A.D. The shock was profound. *Roma aeterna* was no longer impregnable. The pagans revived the ancient reproaches and ascribed calamity to the neglect of the old gods. Augustine retorted by a recital of all the crimes and all the calamities

---

[40] Peterson.
[41] "Oration on Constantine," XVI, *PNF*, 1, 606.

from the fall of Adam to the fall of Rome. "Great cities
without justice are but robbery on a large scale." Well did
the anti-Roman historian Pompeius Trogus trace the succession of robber states from Assyria to Rome. Was she not
founded on fratricide and extended by the rape of the
Sabines and the demolition of Carthage? What then of the
benefits conferred by Rome; what of the one language and
the bond of peace? Yes, but by how many wars, how much
bloodshed, were they achieved? Had it not been better that
such benefits be conferred with the consent of the peoples?
Talk not of glorious victories. Look at naked deeds, at the
lust of dominion with which Sallust reproached mankind.
The glory of the empire rests on lust and blood. Thus all
the imprecations of the vanquished reverberate through the
pages of Augustine, and when he comes to Augustus and the
founding of the empire, he is no more favorable. There is no
talk here of Christ as a Roman citizen. Roman history first
reaches a point of turning with the conversion of Constantine, and if there be Christian emperors like Constantine
and Theodosius, then may their sway increase.[42]

By this conclusion Augustine appears to have wrecked
his argument. He seemed to be contending that Rome had
fallen because of her sin. Why, then, should she collapse
precisely at the time when some measure of improvement
had been introduced by the Christianizing of her ruler? The
real answer is that Rome no more fell because of her sins
than rose because of her virtues. She was quite as bad, and
indeed much worse, in the days of her ascent. The point is
rather that empires rise and fall according to the economy
of God. He can use even the Assyrian as the rod of his anger
and is dependent on none for the achievement of his ends.
Ultimately, the only history is the history of God's great
plan.

Modern writers somewhat divide when they come to
deal with the outworking of this philosophy of history in
which we do observe a difference between the East and the
West. How do the lines run from Eusebius and Augustine to

[42] *Civ. Dei*, Bks. I–V, XVIII–XXII.

the Caesaro-papism of the East and the papal theocracy of the West? A recent writer[43] contends that the East provided the political and historical thinking for the West, that not Augustus but Eusebius is the father of the *Sacrum Imperium* of the Middle Ages. Augustine is held in no sense to have endorsed the empire. The mere conversion of an emperor did not mean for him the Christianizing of the empire. Now to be sure, Augustine was not naive, but certainly he did not, like Tychonius, place all kings on the side of the devil. The empire enshrined for him values not lightly to be relinquished, and when Boniface, the general of Rome, proposed on the death of his wife to become a monk, Augustine remonstrated, "For God's sake, not now!" [44] The empire must be defended. Moreover, under the guidance of the Church, the empire might achieve some semblance of justice. In the indeterminate period of man's life to come on earth, Church and state in collaboration might accomplish, if not a restoration of paradise, at least something better than demonic chaos.

Moreover, the thinking of the Easterners came in time more nearly to approximate that of Augustine. The age of exuberance was succeeded by disillusionment with regard to the sons of Constantine when they embraced heretical Arianism and persecuted the orthodox. Then Hilary, Hosius, and Athanasius reminded the ruler that "The purple makes emperors not priests." [45] In the East almost more than in the West the idea took root of Rome transplanted to the East and destined to be eternal by reason of consecration at the hands of the Holy Orthodox Church.

Neither in the East nor in the West did Christians ever contemplate an ideal consummation on earth. Never did they forget that life is but a pilgrimage and man's eternal blessedness and supernal rest lie beyond this veil of tears.

Such a conclusion validates the apparently contradictory judgments that Christ is the end of history and that Chris-

[43] Kamlah.
[44] *Ep.* 189.
[45] Setton.

tianity offers the first meaningful philosophy of history. If history be defined as a chain of events, each linked to the other in causal sequence, then Christ makes plain to us that in this sense there never was any history because God is Lord of all events. He can break all sequences with that which is altogether new. Yet there is in events a sequence arising solely from the purpose of God to culminate the drama of redemption. This, rather than either the wickedness or the goodness of man, explains the rise and fall of empires, and this enables man to survive the rise and the fall of empires because hope is fixed upon Him who sitteth above the circle of the earth.

Selected Bibliography

BAINTON, ROLAND H., "The Early Church and War," *Harvard Theological Review*, 39, No. 3 (July 1946), 189–212.

BAUER, LUDWIG, "Untersuchungen über die Vergöttlichungslehre in der Theologie der griechischen Väter," *Theologische Quartalschrift*, 98 (1916), 467–491; 101 (1920), 28–64, 155–186.

BIETENFELD, HAND, "The Millenial Hope in the Early Church," *Journal of Scottish Theology*, 6, No. 1 (Mar. 1953), 12–30.

BORNHÄUSER, K., "Die Vergöttungslehre des Athanasius und Johannes Damascenus," *Beiträge zur Förderung christlicher Theologie*, 7, No. 2 (1903), 7–198.

BREHIER, EMILE, "Quelques traits de la philosophie de l'histoire dans l'antiquité classique," *Revue d'histoire et de philosophie religieuses*, 14 (1934), 38–40.

BUTTERWORTH, G. W., "The Deification of Man in Clement of Alexandria," *Journal of Theological Studies*, 17 (1915–1916), 157–169.

CAMPENHAUSEN, HANS, "Weltgeschichte und Gottesgericht," *Lebendige Wissenschaft*, vol. 1, 1947.

CULLMANN, OSCAR, "Le Caractère eschatologique du devoir messianique et de la conscience apostolique de S. Paul," *Revue d'histoire et de philosophie religieuses*, 16 (1936), 210–245.

———, "Quand viendra le Royaume de Dieu? " *Revue d'histoire et de Philosophie religieuses*, 18 (1938), 174–186.

———, *Christus und die Zeit*, Zollikon-Zurich, 1946.

DANIÉLOU, JEAN, "La Typologie millenoriste de la semaine dans le Christianisme primitif," *Vigiliae Christianae*, 2 (1948), 1–16.

———, "*Sacramentum futuri*, Études sur les origines de la typologie biblique," *Etudes de théologie historique*, Paris, 1950.

———, "The Conception of History in the Christian Tradition," *Papers of the Ecumenical Institute*, 5 (1950), 67–79. This paper appears also in *The Journal of Religion*, 30 (1950), 171–179.

DÖLGER, FRANZ, "Rom in der Gedankenwelt der Byzantiner," *Zeitschrift für Kirchengeschichte*, 56 (1937), 1–42.

Ecumenical Institute, Papers of, vol. 5 (1950), "The Meaning of History."

EGER, HANS, "Kaiser und Kirche in der Geschichtstheologie Eusebs von Caesarea," *Zeitschrift für die Neutestamentliche Wissenschaft*, 37/38 (1938–1939), 97–115.

FRANK, ERICH, *Philosophical Understanding and Religious Truth*, New York, 1945.

FRICK, ROBERT, "Die Geschichte des Reich-Gottes-Gedankens in der alten Kirche bis zu Origenes und Augustin," *Beihefte zur Zeitschrift für die Neutestamentliche Wissenschaft*, vol. 6 (1928).

FUCHS, HARALD, *Der geistige Widerstand gegen Rom in der antiken Welt*, Berlin, 1938.

——, "Augustin und der antike Friedensgedanke," *Neue philologischen Untersuchungen*, vol. 3, Berlin, 1926.

GOGUEL, M., "Eschatologie et apocalyptique dans le Christianisme primitif," *Revue de l'histoire des religions*, 106 (1932), 381–434, 489–524.

GUITON, JEAN, *Le Temps et l'éternité chez Plotin et St. Augustin*, Paris, 1933.

KAMLAH, WILHELM, *Christentum und Geschichtlichkeit*, Stuttgart, 1951.

KAMPERS, FRANZ, "Roma aeterna und sancta Dei ecclesia rei publicae Romanorum," *Historisches Jahrbuch*, 44 (1924), 240–249.

KOCH, HAL, "Pronoia und Paideusis, Studien über Origines," *Arbeiten zur Kirchengeschichte*, vol. 22, 1932.

LEWALTER, ERNST, "Eschatologie und Weltgeschichte in der Gedankenwelt Augustins," *Zeitschrift für Kirchengeschichte*, 53 (1934), 1–51.

LOT-BORADINE, M., "La Doctrine de la 'déification' dans l'Eglise grecque jusqu'au XI siècle," *Revue de l'histoire des religions*, 150 (1932); 5–43, 525–574.

LOVEJOY, ARTHUR O., *Primitivism and Related Ideas in Antiquity*, 1935.

——, "The Communism of Saint Ambrose," *Journal of the History of Ideas*, 3, No. 4 (October 1942), 458–468.

LÖWITH, KARL, *Meaning in History*, Chicago, 1949.

MOMMSEN, THEODORE, "St. Augustine and the Christian Idea of Progress," *Journal of the History of Ideas*, 12, no. 3 (June 1951), 346–374.

NESTLE, WILHELM, "Griechische Geschichtsphilosophie," *Archiv für Geschichte der Philosophie*, 41 (1932), 80–114.

OPITZ, HANS-GEORG, "Euseb von Caesarea als Theologe," *Zeitschrift für die Neutestamentliche Wissenschaft*, 34 (1935), 1–19.

PETERSON, ERIK, *Der Monotheismus als politisches Problem: Ein Beitrag zur Geschichte der politischen Theologie im Imperium Romanum*, Leipzig, 1935.

PUECH, HENRI, "La Gnose et le temps," *Eranos Jahrbuch*, 20 (1951), 57–113.

QUISPEL, G., "Zeit und Geschichte im antiken Christentum," *Eranos Jahrbuch*, 20 (1951), 115–118.

SETTON, KENNETH M., *Christian Attitudes toward the Emperor in the Fourth Century*, New York, 1941.

SWAIN, JOSEPH WARD, "The Theory of the Four Monarchies: Opposition History under the Roman Empire," *Classical Philology*, 35 (January–October 1940), 1–21.

VASILIEV, A. A., "Medieval Ideas of the End of the World: West-East," *Byzantion*, 16 (1942–1943), 462–502.

WERNER, HELMUT, "Der Untergang Roms," *Forschungen zur Kirchen und Geistesgeschichte*, vol. 17, 1939.

2 The Origins of Epiphany

The origins of the Christian feast of Epiphany on the sixth of January are still obscure.[1] There is no trace of its celebration during the age of the martyrs.[2] In the West it must have arisen later than the Donatist schism in 311 A.D., because the Donatists retained whatever they had in common with the Church up to the time of the division and this feast they did not observe.[3] In the East it must have been earlier than the Council of Nicaea in 325 A.D., because the

The following material is extracted from my doctoral dissertation "Basilidian Chronology and New Testament Interpretation," published in the *Journal of Biblical Literature*, XLII, Pts. I and II (1923), and reprinted by permission. The assignment was to study the dates to which Basilides assigned events in the life of Christ to see whether they might have any validity. I speedily came to the conclusion that they had none, and the question then was to determine whence they were derived. I was led to think that they were borrowed from contemporary Greek and Egyptian cults. As far as the New Testament was concerned the findings were negative, but one point of interest emerged bearing on the date of Epiphany. This point has gone without notice because it was submerged beneath material comparatively inconsequential; it is here brought to the fore, omitting the rest.

[1] The present state of the problem is described by L. Fendt, "Der heutige Stand der Forschung über das Geburtsfest Jesu am 25 XII und über Epiphanias," *Theologische Literaturzeitung* LXXVIII (1953), 1–10. The literature used originally in the paper was: A. Meyer, *Das Weihnachtsfest*, pp. 7–29. Usener, *Das Weihnachtsfest*, in *Religionsgeschichtliche Untersuchungen*, 1–2, pp. 187–213. Lagarde, *Mitteilungen*, 3, 4. *Altes und Neues über das Weihnachtsfest*, p. 241 ff. Nilsson, *Griechische Feste*, pp. 275 and 293. Duchesne, *Christian Worship*, pp. 257–265. Rohde, *Psyche*, 295 ff. Articles on Epiphany in *Catholic Enc.*, V, p. 504, Cyril Martindale, *Enc. of Rel. and Ethics*, K. Lake, *HRE.*, 3, vol. V, p. 414, Caspari, *Bingham's Antiquities of the Christian Church*, vol. II, p. 1141 ff.

[2] Albert Ehrhard, *Die Kirche der Martyrer.*

[3] S. *Augustini Episcopi Sermo CCII in Epiphania Domini IV*, Migne, PL, XXXVIII, p. 1033.

Arian Emperor Valens observed it in the year 372 A.D. If this festival had been only orthodox and not also Arian Gregory of Nazianza,[4] who relates the episode, would have been bound to call attention to so great an accommodation to orthodoxy on the part of the heretical emperor and this he does not do. Hence one may infer that the observance of the day was common to the Nicene and the Arian parties and must in that case have antedated the Council of Nicaea at which time they definitely diverged.

If then the feast arose somewhere between 311 and 325 A.D. where did it come from? There are two possible sources. The first is the heretical sect of the Gnostic Basilidians. Clement of Alexandria says: "The followers of Basilides celebrate the day of his baptism also, spending the night before in reading. They say that it was the fifteenth year of Tiberius Caesar, the fifteenth of the month Tybi, but some the eleventh of the same month." [5] Now the eleventh of the Egyptian month Tybi was January 6.

One observes, however, that the celebration was of the baptism rather than of the birth. As a matter of fact they were identical, for these Basilidians held with the Adoptionist Cerinthus that Jesus was a man like others until at the baptism Christ came into him in the form of a dove.[6] The baptism thus constituted his birth as the Son of God. There is evidence to show that the Basilidians took the same view. Clement says, "the dove was seen as a body, which some call the Holy Spirit, but the Basilidians the minister." [7] Clement accused these Basilidians of making ignorance the source of salvation and then inquired, "Was this ignorance of good things? If so the *minister* and the *preaching* and the baptism are rendered superfluous to them." [8] From this it would seem that the dove was the

---

[4] *S. Gregorii Theologi Oratio XLIII. In Laudem Basilii Magni*, §52. Migne, PG, XXXVI, p. 561. See Usener, *op. cit.*, p. 192.

[5] Clement of Alexandria, *Stromata*, 1 Cap. XXI, 145, 1–146, 4, ed. Stählin, p. 90.

[6] Irenaeus, *op. cit.*, 1, 21, 1.

[7] *Excerpta ex. ser. Theodoti*, §16.

[8] *Str.*, II, 8, 38, 1.

minister by which Christ entered Jesus at his baptism, so
that at this time he was really born as the Son of God.

But in any case those who followed the Lukan chronology, according to which Jesus was thirty years of age
when he came to his baptism, assumed that he was baptized
on his birthday. Consequently, without any theory of adop-
tionism, the day of the baptism and the day of the birth
were the same. We may therefore assume that the Basilidians observed January 6 as the day of the baptism and also
of the birth. And here is a possible source for the later
orthodox festival of Epiphany. But that the Church should
borrow from the heretics even after a lapse of two hundred
years does not appear probable, because even in the fourth
century the controversy had not ceased to be bitter.[9]

The other possible source is heathen. Among the
pagans January 6 was the epiphany or manifestation of the
glory of the god Dionysus. On that day he was born as the
aeon by Kore, the virgin.[10] The event was celebrated by
carrying torches.[11] On that day he turned water into wine,[12]
which led to a rite of the storing of waters.[13] In the Church
later on we have similarly a veritable epiphany or manifestation of the glory of Jesus. To January 6 was assigned most
commonly the baptism;[14] sometimes the baptism and the
birth;[15] sometimes the birth without mention of the baptism
because of the adoptionist nature of the feast;[16] in one case

[9] Eusebius, *VC*, III, 64–65.

[10] Epiphanius, *Haer.*, II, 51, 22, ed. Dindorf, p. 482.

[11] *Ibid.*

[12] *Diodori Siculi*, Lib. III. Cap. LXVI, §1–2. *Pausanias*, 6, 26, §1–2, ed.
Carolus Godofredus Siebelis. *C. Plinii Secundii N. H.*, II, 106, ed. Gabriel Brotier,
cf. XXXI, 13. For further evidence and a discussion of the chronology, see A.
Meyer, *op. cit.*, pp. 15–16, and the notes.

[13] Epiphanius, *Haer.*, II, 51, §30, Dindorf, *Aristides Rhaetor*, Oxford, 1730,
II, 573 (p. 341) and 612 (p. 361), cited by K. Lake in the *Enc. of Rel. and Ethics*,
cf. Plutarch, *De Iside et Osiride*, 36.

[14] Jerome on *Ezech.*, 1:3, Migne, PL, XXV, p. 18.

[15] *Joannis Cassiani Collationes*, X, 2. PL, XLIX, 820. Date 418–427 A.D.

[16] So in a papyrus published by G. Bickell in *Mitteilungen aus der Sammlung
der Papyrus Erzherzog Rainer*, 1887, Bd. 2, 83–86, cited by Usener, *op. cit.*, p. 189,
note 1. So also in the *Peregrinatio Silviae*. Geyer, *Itinera Hierosolymitana Corpus
Scriptorum Eccl. Lat.*, 39, pp. 37–101. G. Krüger in *HRE*, 3, 18, p. 345 ff. gives
394 A.D. as the latest possible date of the document. The first leaf is missing, but
we can tell that Epiphany is the subject because the next feast is its quadragesima.

also the conception.[17] Soon the day served to commemorate
in addition the adoration of the shepherds,[18] the visit of the
Magi, the appearance of the star,[19] the miracle at Cana[20]
and the feeding of the five thousand.[21] We find also a storing
of waters[22] and a feast of lights.[23] The Church and the
heathen temple had thus in common the turning of water
into wine, the storing of waters and the feast of lights as
well as the birth of the Savior and of the aeon. The co-
incidences are so great as to suggest that we look here for
the source, rather than to the Basilidian practice. And the
very number of the diverse events attached to Epiphany
better comports with a festival of the manifestation of the
whole glory of the God than with an adoptionist baptism.
The probability appears greater that the Church borrowed
directly from the heathen. The Basilidians may of course
have done precisely the same thing.[24] And the problem still

---

The account of the visit to the cave at Bethlehem is also lost, but the story is re-
sumed with a return to Jerusalem. We may infer that the procession came from
Bethlehem, because we are told that a journey was made there every day (p. 77,
1.9) and that the rites preceding Epiphany were similar to those leading up to
Easter, which began with a visit to the cave at Bethlehem (p. 93, §42).

[17] The Armenians commemorate the baptism, birth and conception on the
same day. Usener, *op. cit.*, p. 208.

[18] Ephraem Syrus († 373 A.D. G. Bickell, *Ephr. Syri Carmina Nisibena*,
Lips., 1866, p. 9 note 1). Usener, *op. cit.*, 195–198, cites the editions of Lamy and
Benedictus, neither of which is accessible to me.

[19] Ephraem Syrus and Epiphanius, who is dependent upon him. *Haer.*, II,
51. It is worthy of note that Epiphanius put the baptism back sixty days from
Jan. 6 to Nov. 8, probably to avoid an adoptionist interpretation, see §§16, 22, 24
and 27.

[20] Ephraem Syrus and Epiphanius, *loc. cit.*

[21] *S. Augustini Sermo CXXXVI*, Migne. PL, XXXIX, p. 2013, *in Epiphania
Domini*, VI, *Missale Gothicum in Vigiliis Epiphaniae*. Neale and Forbes, *Gallican
Liturgies*, p. 49 ff.

[22] See note 13.

[23] *Peregrinatio Silviae*, *S. Gregorii Theologi Oratio XXXIX in Sancta Lumina*,
Migne, PG, XXXVI, p. 336.

[24] The assumption that they did has been based on: Epiphanius, *Haer.*,
11, 51, 22, ed. Dindorf, p. 482. Usener assumed that Epiphanius was describing a
Gnostic rite because of the mention of crosses (*op. cit.*, p. 28) but the cross was not
peculiar to the Christians. Socrates, *HE*, V, 17, Migne. PG, LXVII, p. 608, cf.
Sozomen 7, 15, Ruf., *HE*, II, 29. The Dusares, who is born in Petra, is the Arabian
equivalent of the Greek Dionysus. A. Meyer, *op. cit.*, p. 19, note 27. Cf. Macrobius,
Saturnaliorum, Lib. I, cap. XVIII, ed. Ludovicus Janus, p. 171, §8. On Dionysus
and Kore, see Nilsson, *op. cit.*, pp. 279 and 289.

remains why the Church should have waited so long to
borrow from either of them. Perhaps after Constantine,
when so many poorly instructed pagans came into the
Church, the danger was greater that they would lapse on
the days when their former coreligionists celebrated festivals
and that therefore the Church felt a greater need for counter
attractions than in the age of the martyrs when the cate-
chumens were better grounded.

The institution of the festival will not have been so
abrupt, however, if the novelty consisted only in the institution of a feast rather than also in the introduction of a calculation. To celebrate the birth of Jesus on January 6 was one
thing, to assign it to that date was another. The thesis here
propounded is that the ascription of the birth to this date
actually goes back to the beginning of the second century.
The demonstration consists in converging evidences. Data
will be adduced to show that the birth of Christ was set on
January 6 not only by the Basilidians but also by the
Montanists and Marcionists as well as by an orthodox source
of Clement of Alexandria. Since they would scarcely have
borrowed from each other this dating must be prior to the
Gnostic split and consequently must go back to the beginning
of the second century.

But before citing the evidence certain preliminary
points on which the argument hinges must be established.
The gospels supply no specific information as to the time of
the year when Christ was born. If anything one would suppose that it would not have been in the winter because
"shepherds were abiding in the fields watching their flocks
by night." But there is definite information with regard to
the death and the resurrection because these occurred at the
time of the Passover. Jesus died on the fourteenth of the
Jewish month Nisan according to John's gospel and on the
fifteenth according to the Synoptics. From this fixed point it
was possible to arrive at an approximate date for the birth
through the assumption that the passion occurred on the
anniversary of the conception. By adding, then, to the date
in Nisan the period estimated for the gestation one arrived
at the birth.

Our evidence for such calculations commences only in the fourth century. We begin with Ephraim Syrus, who said:[25]

In Nisan the Lord of Thunder weakened his heart through sympathy, and entered into the womb of Mary that he might dwell there; in Nisan again he has shown himself strong, and after loosing the womb of hell is risen.

Augustine gives us some equally illuminating information:[26]

Not without reason did the Lord, speaking of the building of his body, in whose figure the temple was destroyed by the Jews, say that he would raise himself up in three days; the number six itself is known being placed before the year, for they said (Jo 2:20), "Forty and six years was this temple in building," and forty six by six give two hundred and seventy six, which makes nine months and six days, so, since ten months are reckoned to child-bearing women, (not that all come to birth on the sixth day after the nine months, but because in so many days the perfection of the Lord's body was learned, as the authority of the church guards the tradition received from the elders) so he is believed to have been conceived eight days before the calends of April—March 25, *on which day also he died.* And as he was buried in a new tomb, where no other mortal had been placed (Jo 19:41) neither before nor after, so it behooved that he should be conceived in the womb of a virgin, where no mortal had ever been generated. The tradition is that he was born eight days before the calends of January—December 25. Reckoning from the one day to the other then, there are two hundred and seventy six, which is six times forty six.

Chrystostom arrived at the same result by figuring forward from what he took to be the date of the conception of John in Luke, and backwards from December 25 as the birth.[27] The calculations are found in his sermon on Christmas. He commences by saying that it is only ten years since

[25] *Ephraim Syrii Hymnus*, XXI, *De Resurrectione Christi*, v. 10, Lamy 2, 774. I have translated the German of Usener, *Das Weihnachtsfest*, p. 200, which see for other references.

[26] Aug., *De Trinitate*, IV, 5, 9. Migne, PL, XLII, p. 894. Cf. Cyril of Alex. to Leo, Migne, *ibid.*, 54, p. 605, *quia codem die conceptus in utero est, et mortuus in cruce.*

[27] S. *Joannis Chrysostomi in Diem Natalem D. N. Jesu Christi*, Migne, PG, 49, pp. 357–358, §6.

the celebration of the birth of Christ on December 25 had been introduced into his church at Antioch. There had been a good deal of dispute about it in his congregation, some asserting that it was new, some that it was old, being celebrated from Thrace to Gadara. He attempts to establish its validity by three arguments. (1) If it were not correct it could not have spread so rapidly. (2) Any one who consults the Roman records will find the day of the census mentioned by Luke. (3) The exact day may be worked out from the notices in Luke. When Mary conceived, Elizabeth was in her sixth month (Lk. 1:36). There were thus three months between the births of John and Jesus. Zacharias could go into the Holy of Holies only once a year on the tenth of the seventh month (reckoning from Nisan, Lev. 16:29).

So it was then that the promise was made to Zacharias. The time of the promise was that of the feast of tabernacles and of the fasting, for this is that which was written, "Humble your souls" (Lev. 16:29). The feast was kept among the Jews about the last of the month of Gorpiaios, as ye witness (There were many Jews in Antioch) — — — The six months of the conception of Elizabeth are Hyperberetaios — October, Dios — November, Apellaios — December, Audynaios — January, Peritios — February and Dystros — March. After this sixth month came the commencement of the conception of Mary. Whence reckoning nine months we reach the present day (December 25th). April is the first month of the conception of the Lord, which is Xanthikos,[28] after which Artemisios — May, Daisios — June, Panemos — July, Lōos — August, Gorpiaios — September, Hyperberetaios — October, Dios — November, Apellaios — December, and this is the present month in which we keep the day.[29]

Chrysostom does not give the exact day of the conception, but he says that it fell in the month of March, nine months before the twenty-fifth of December. This would

[28] Montfaucon usually eliminates the Julian equivalents of the Macedonian months as later additions. Usener, p. 226, note 18, thinks that this should be done here also.

[29] The Antiochian months here used are the exact equivalent of the Julian. This is proved by the *Florentine and Leyden Hemerologia*, published together in 1809 by St. Croix, *Histoire de l'Acad. royale des Inscript. et Belles-lettres avec les Mémoires de littérature*, Paris, tome 47, pp. 66–84, cited in Ginzel, *op. cit.*, III, 31.

land him at the twenty-fifth of March, the day often chosen, as we shall see, for the crucifixion. We thus have the same coincidence of the conception, and the crucifixion or resurrection, which we found in Augustine.

Cosmas Indicopleustes gives us an even more precise section "on the conception of the Lord":[30]

Zacharias going into the temple according to the tradition of the law on the tenth of the seventh month and being told that he would beget John by Elisabeth, in her sixth month it was announced to the Virgin that this was the commencement of the first month; for since Zacharias was told on the tenth of the seventh month and Elisabeth conceived in that same month, it is clear that six months of the year were gone and six to come, minus ten days and another two or three or seven until Zacharias went to his house, so that there were 168 or 167 or 163 days. It is possible then to know the beginning of the conception of the Lord, that is the beginning of the first month—it was indeed the sixth to Elisabeth according to the tradition of the gospels, for God always has and does guard this order—since also all keep the birth of our Lord, the ninth month having been completed from the beginning of the first month, on Choiak 28 — December 25.

Cosmas was more precise and hence less consistent than Chrysostom. He reckoned a maximum of 168 days to the conception from September 1, the seventh month. (The Jewish and Antiochian year began with March.) This would land him at March 18. He reckoned back nine months from December 25, which would bring him to March 25. Which reckoning he preferred matters little for our purpose. March 18 was the date of the entrance of the sun into Aries. March 25 was the equinox. Both were dates to which the crucifixion was commonly assigned.[31] We see once more that the conception was placed on the day of the crucifixion and resurrection.[32]

When Easter was universally accepted as a movable feast the synchronism was lost because March 25 was re-

[30] *Cosmae Indicopleustae Topographiae Chr.*, V, 194. Migne, *PG*, LXXXVIII, 196.

[31] On March 18, see *Epiphanius*, II, 51, 1, Dindorf, p. 447.

[32] Cf. Cyril of Alex. to Leo, Migne, *PL*, LIV, p. 605.

tained for the conception.[33] As such it was widely regarded
as New Year's Day and remained such in England until
1751, when the Gregorian calendar was introduced.[34] The
annunciation falls to this day on March 25 in the Roman
church. The modern Egyptians celebrate it on Phamenoth
29, which is April 26 on the Gregorian basis, but March 25
on the Julian.[35] The Greek church too places on March 25
the εὐαγγελισμὸς τῆς θεοτόκου.[36] All of this is witness to the
earlier practice of placing the conception and the crucifixion
on the same day.

If then there was in the fourth century this means of
arriving by calculation at the date of the birth there is the
possibility that such reckoning had an earlier beginning.
And if the procedure was to reckon from the date of the
death we need to know how this was calculated. The dates
in the month Nisan were of course perfectly precise on the
Jewish calendar, but not on the Julian because the one was
lunar, the other solar. When the Jewish year was so far
behind the solar that the lambs would not be old enough to
kill for the fourteenth and the first fruits to be offered on
the sixteenth of Nisan, an intercalary month was inter-
polated by the high priest. During the years 26 to 35 A.D.
the fourteenth of Nisan ranged from March 19 to April
18.[37] As the Church became increasingly Gentile there was
an indisposition to allow the date of Easter to be determined by the high priest and a tendency to shift to the
Julian calendar.

But then other points of divergence arose. There was

[33] Cf. *Chron. Pasch.*, Dindorf 1, 22.

[34] Ginzel, *op. cit.*, III, p. 275.

[35] Lagarde, *Mitth.*, 3–4, p. 292. He quotes *Nilles*, 2, 643.

[36] Ginzel, *op. cit.*, III, p. 308.

[37] *The Journal of Theological Studies*, XII, 45 (October 1910). Fotheringham
proceeds on the assumption that the official Jewish year was still empirically determined in the time of Christ. The opposite view is defended by Turner, article
Chronology, DB, and Ramsay, *Expositor*, Nov. 1899. The case for the empirical
chronology is summed up and developed by Schürer, *The Jewish People in the
Time of Christ*, First Div. II, app. 3, *Jewish and Macedonian months*; Bacon,
Expositor, July, 1900; and Fotheringham, *Society of Historical Theology*, 1901–1902,
Journal of Theology, vol. XXIX and in the article cited above. This view seems to
me sufficiently established to require no further discussion.

the initial difference as to the particular date in Nisan, whether the fourteenth or the fifteenth. The churches of Asia Minor, following John's gospel held to the fourteenth and hence were called Quartodeciman. The Roman church was not so much concerned to insist on the fifteenth with the Synoptics as to observe always the same day of the week, since Christ appeared risen from the dead on a Sunday. The Quartodecimans did not place the same stress on the appearance to the disciples, which for them did not so much constitute the resurrection as did the victory over death by the death on the cross which immediately released spirits of the departed from Hades and enabled them to appear in the temple prior to Sunday.[38] Hence the passion and the resurrection tended to coincide and the period of fasting was reduced.[39] Among those so minded, then, a date for Easter was also a date for the passion and this might also be a date for the conception.

The primary concern of the Quartodecimans was not, however, as their name implied, to observe the fourteenth of the Jewish month Nisan[40] as to observe a fixed date regardless of the day.[41] Some of them shifted to the Julian calendar. But then which fixed date was to be taken as the equivalent of the fourteenth of Nisan? The range of its incidence made it oscillate around the vernal equinox which on the Julian calendar was March 25. But the choice of this day was probably not reached by direct calculation from the incidence of the fourteenth of Nisan. There was an intrinsic appropriateness. That day of the year when day began to be longer than night was fitting for the celebration of a resurrection and this symbolism was not lost upon the

[38] Matt. 27:52–53.

[39] Drummond, *The Character and Authorship of the Fourth Gospel*, p. 471, discusses the letter of Basilides to his brother Dionysius of Alex. Routh, *Reliq. Sac.* III, p. 223. See Preuschen, art. *Easter Controversy*, in *New Schaff-Herzog Enc.*, vol. IV, 1910.

[40] As Schürer supposed, *Zts. f. d. hist. Theol.*, 1870, p. 251, art. *Passastreit.* He is corrected by Bacon, *The Fourth Gospel in Research and Debate*, p. 413.

[41] Apollinaris of Hierapolis. *Chronicon Paschale*, cited in *Canonicity*, A. H. Charteris, p. 194. Cf. Bacon, *The Resurrection in Primitive Tradition and Observance*, Am. *Journal of Theol.* p. 383.

Church Fathers. Clement of Rome said that the resurrection came at that point in the year when the day triumphs over night and the flowers blossom in newness of life.[42] Theophilus of Antioch compared the death and resurrection to the dying and rising of seasons and days, of seeds and fruits, and to the waning and waxing of the moon.[43] For Pseudo-Cyprian, Jesus was the "sun of righteousness with healing in his wings." [44] Such imagery was of course also appropriate to Christmas when the date came to coincide with the birthday of the *sol invictus*.[45]

In addition to intrinsic appropriateness there was the coincidence that the mystery cults had already made the same sort of conjunction. March 25 was at Rome the date for the official celebration of the resurrection of Attis.[46] This confronts us with the larger question whether in general the dates of Christian festivals were borrowed from the heathen to provide counter attractions or were reached by calculation. Both processes may have been at work. March 25 could have been calculated as the mean date for Nisan 14 and could have been taken from the resurrection of Attis. December 25 might have been calculated from March 25 as the date of the conception and might have been borrowed from the birthday of Mithras. And if both the equinox and the solstice were taken from the heathen, the interval between them would at once be seen to be nine months and this could give rise to the calculations as to the conception.

But now for the evidence that Easter, as the commemoration conjointly of the passion and the resurrection, was celebrated on March 25. Our evidence applies to Asia Minor and to Gaul. In Cappadocia the Quartodecimans celebrated the crucifixion on March 25.[47] For Gaul there are several witnesses. The first is a document of about the fourth

[42] 24.

[43] *ANF*, II, p. 93.

[44] Hartel, p. 266.

[45] For passages see A. Meyer, *Das Weihnachtsfest*, notes 54–55.

[46] Mommsen, *CIL*, 1, 2, p. 338 and 390. Frazer, *Adonis, Attis, Osiris*, p. 199, ed. 1906. Bacon, *The Resurrection in Primitive Tradition*, p. 385.

[47] Epiphanius, *Haer.*, II, 50, 1. Dindorf, p. 447.

century[48] which asserts that the Gauls (1) observed Easter on a fixed date regardless of the day *quacunque die*, (2) the passion and the resurrection were celebrated on the same day *quando Christi resurrectio tradebatur, semper Pascha celebrant*, (3) and the day was March 25. This statement cannot be universally true for Gaul because Irenaeus of Lyons agreed with Victor of Rome that the resurrection should always be celebrated on the Lord's day, but Irenaeus strenuously opposed the excommunication of the Quarto-decimans and may well have been prompted in part by their presence in his congregation consisting in part of emigrés from Asia Minor.

For Gaul there is further evidence. Duchesne cites the following passage from S. Martinus Dumiensis:[49]

Until recently many of the Gallican bishops have observed the custom of celebrating the day of the Pascha on March 25, when, according to the tradition, the resurrection took place.

Note that the Pascha and resurrection are assigned to the same day. Duchesne thought that this must be an error.

We are indebted to Krusch for further examples.[50] The following passage is taken from the spurious *Tractatus S. Adthanasi episcopi Alex. de racione pasche*, §1. The locality is mentioned only in the Cölner manuscript:

I know that many are accustomed to inquire with scrupulous accuracy why we keep the Pascha like the Jews at different times according to the moon. It would seem better to them, that, if we commemorate the Lord's passion, we should observe one day, namely the 25th of March, which many of the Gallican bishops are said to have observed until recently.

He gives another passage from the spurious *Prologus S. Cyrilli Alex. Episc. de ratione paschae*, c. 1, which is a witness to the practice, although nothing is said of the place.[51] Ginzel quotes a statement of Bede that such was the practice in Gaul.[52]

---

[48] *Mitteilungen*, 3, 4, p. 274 ff.

[49] *Christian Worship*, 263, *S. Martinus Dumiensis*, Migne, *PL*, LXXII, 50. Cf. Frazer, *Adonis, Attis, Osiris*, 199.

[50] *Der 84 jährige Ostercyclus*, p. 90, notes 4 and 6.

[51] I have not been able to check this citation.

[52] *Op. cit.* III, 219. Beda, *de temp. rat.* c. 47, Migne, *ibid.*, XC, 495.

We are ready now for the evidence that several groups
in the early Church assigned the birth of Christ to January 6.
The first instance is that of the Montanists. Duchesne
pointed out[53] that they observed the passion and the resurrection conjointly like the Quartodecimans on April 6. Now
this date is exactly nine months prior to January 6 following.
That the Montanists made any direct use of January 6 is
not affirmed. Duchesne thought that it was deduced from
April 6. But surely the reasoning must have gone the other
way. There is nothing else to account for the selection of
April 6. It is not a significant date on the solar calendar.
There is no evidence that it was a heathen festival, and
there is no other use made of it in Christian circles, where, as
we have seen, the prevailing date was March 25. But
January 6 was the Epiphany of Dionysus. It is hard to suppose that this date was not the point of departure and that
April 6 was reached by assuming that this was the day of
the conception and therefore of the passion, according to
the type of calculation already noted for a later period.

The second example is that of the Marcionites. The
following passage occurs in Tertullian's *Adversus Marcionem*:[54]

Anno XV Tiberii Christus Jesus de caelo manare dignatus est
spiritus salutaris Marcionis, salutis qui ita voluit quoto quidem
anno Antonini maioris de Ponto suo exhalaverit aula canicularis,
non curavi investigare, de quo tamen constat, Antoninianus
haereticus est sub Pio impius, a Tiberio autem usque ad Antoninum
anni fere centum quindecem et dimidium anni cum dimidio mensis,
tantumdem temporis ponunt inter Christum et Marcionem.

The passage is very difficult to construe. *Aura* is of
course to be substituted for *aula*, but what of *salutis?* Bill
enumerates the various conjectures,[55] *Marcionis salutem qui
ita voluit,*[56] *Marcionem saltem.*[57] His own suggestion is
"*salutis qui ita voluit (spiritum e caelo exhalatum esse, ipsum)*

---

[53] *Christian Worship*, p. 264, citing Sozomen VII, 18.
[54] 1, 19, Migne, PL, II, p. 267. I am indebted to Professor Bacon for this
reference.
[55] *T. u. U.*, 38, p. 69.
[56] Ursinus, Harnack.
[57] Lipsius.

quoto quidem anno, etc." The passage might then be translated:

In the fifteenth year of Tiberius, Christ Jesus was deemed worthy to descend from heaven, the saving spirit of Marcion. I do not care to investigate in what year of Antoninus, the Elder, the wind of the dog-star blew him from Pontus, who thus wished the Spirit to be blown from heaven. From this, however, it appears that he was a heretic under Antoninus; under Pius, impious. From Tiberius, moreover, to Antoninus there are about 115 years and a half year and a half month. So much time they place between Christ and Marcion.

It is evident that we are dealing here not with the interval between Tiberius and Antoninus on any basis, but with a Marcionite calculation of the time between Christ and Marcion.[58] Both termini can be determined almost exactly because we have the year in one case and the month in the other. Christ descended in the fifteenth year of Tiberius, i.e., 29 A.D. Marcion was blown from Pontus by the wind of the dog-star, which rose about the end of July. If then we add 115 years to 29 A.D. we get the year 144 A.D. for Marcion. And if from the end of July, 144 A.D., we subtract 115 years, six months and a half, we are thrown back to the first week of January, 29 A.D. Marcion, as an Adoptionist, will have reckoned the descent of Christ from the baptism, so this is the event which fell in the first week of January. And if in that week, it is difficult to suppose that any other day was intended than the sixth corresponding to the Epiphany of Dionysus.

The Marcionite calculation in itself leads us to the almost certain conclusion that the date was recognized equally by the church. A comparison was made between the saving work of Christ and Marcion.[59] What Christ taught the church had perverted, but Marcion had restored. His followers would bring the orthodox back to the teaching of the Master whom both revered by an appeal to a date which

[58] Harnack, *Chronologie*, I, pp. 297 ff., 306 f., and *T. u. U.*, 45, *Marcion*, Beilage 1, p. 18. Bill, *op. cit.*

[59] It matters little for our purposes whether the point of departure be Marcion's sailing from Pontus (Bill) or his breach with the Roman church (Harnack).

both recognized. "You, like us," they would say, "believe
that on the sixth of January 29 A.D. Christ was baptized
and the Spirit entered into him. We would teach you the
true significance of that event." The Marcionites were
reckoning the time of the restoration of the gospel from the
date to which the church assigned its inception.

The third item of evidence is the most direct. We find
an actual employment of January 6 for the birth of Jesus
by an orthodox writer before the composition of the first
book of the *Stromata* of Clement of Alexandria[60] (202–
203 A.D.). This may be inferred from the fact that Clement
here employs different chronological systems. In 140:7 he
says that between the captivity under Vespasian and the
death of Commodus on December 31, 192 A.D., there are 121
years, six months and 24 days, but in 145:5 the sum given
is 121 years, ten months and 13 days.[61] Again in 145:1 the
birth of Christ is assigned to the twenty-eighth year of
Augustus—3/2 B.C., but 194 years, one month and 13 days
before the death of Commodus, which according to the
Julian calendar gives November 18, 4/3 B.C.[62]

These discrepancies can be explained only if Clement
employed sources based on different chronological systems.
One will have been the Augustan, which differs from the
Julian only in that it employs the Egyptian months. The
other will have been the era of Nabonassar, which loses a
day every four years so that the months go wandering
through the year. It is, therefore, called the *annus vagus*.
We shall expect to discover that the longer intervals were
calculated according to the vague year and the shorter according to the fixed. This assumption may serve also to
explain why Origen placed only 42 years between the passion
and the destruction of Jerusalem, which he assigned rightly

[60] Harnack, *Chronologie*, vol. 2, p. 11.

[61] Stählin, whose text I have given before in translation (p. 81), follows
Usener in giving 122 years, but Usener's correction is designed to make Clement
agree with history according to the Julian calendar. We must seek rather to justify
Clement's arithmetic. 30 years plus 42 years and 3 months from 194 years, 1 month
and 13 days, give 121 years, 10 months and 13 days.

[62] This date is accepted as that of Clement by Ginzel, III, p. 196, note 1,
and by A. Meyer, *Das Weihnachtsfest*, p. 6, note 4.

to the Passover,[63] but wrongly to 71 A.D.,[64] whereas Clement made the interval 42 years and three months.

If the dates are worked out in this dual fashion there are some very surprising results.[65] The first discrepancy was between the sums given for the interval from the destruction of Jerusalem to the death of Commodus. The shorter is 121 years, six months and 24 days, which on the Julian basis gives June 6–7, 71 A.D. for the destruction. If then the 42 years and 3 months to the passion be reckoned back on the movable basis, we arrive at March 18–19, 29 A.D., a date to which the crucifixion was frequently assigned. The longer sum is 121 years, 10 months and 13 days. On the movable basis this will bring the destruction of Jerusalem to March 23, the equinox of 72 A.D. The year is wrong, but the day is significant, because Origen reckoned an even number of years between the destruction and the passion, which was commonly assigned to the equinox.

But the most surprising results are obtained for the birth, when we calculate the 194 years, 1 month and 13 days from the death of Commodus on the movable basis. I give the calculations in full according to Schram's tables, pp. 186–187:

$$\text{Dec. 31, 192 A.D.} = 1791520 + 31 = 1791551$$
$$1791551 - 522 = 29 \text{ Mechir } 940 \text{ Nab.}$$

$$\begin{array}{rl}
940 \text{ Mechir} & 29 \\
194 \text{ 1 month} & 13 \\
\hline
746 \text{ Tybi} & 16 = 1720682 \\
 & 16 \\
\hline
 & 1720698 \\
 & 692 \\
\hline
\end{array}$$

6 January 2 B.C.

[63] Lewin, *Fasti Sacri*, 2116.

[64] *Hom. in Jer. XIV*, cf. *Cels.*, IV, 22.

[65] Most of them have been worked out by H. Browne in the *Journal of Classical and Sacred Philology* (Cambridge), 1–2, 1854–1855, *S. Clemens Alex. on New Testament Chronology*, p. 327 ff.

In other words if we use the movable calendar, Clement agrees with himself as to the year of Christ's birth, and the day turns out to be the very Epiphany which we are considering.

The source will scarcely have been heretical. We may, therefore, conclude that an orthodox writer later than the death of Commodus (192 A.D.) and earlier than the first book of the *Stromata* of Clement (202–203 A.D.) assigned the birth of Jesus to January 6. We thus discover that this date was recognized not only by the Basilidians, Montanists, and Marcionites, but also somewhere in the church at the very height of the heretical controversies. Mutual borrowing is scarcely credible. One is, therefore, forced to the conclusion that January 6 as a Christian dating for the birth of Christ antedates the schisms and hence goes back to the beginning of the second century. The festival of the fourth century will then have been built upon a traditional calculation.

3 Saint Augustine's Methods of Religious Teaching

The most outstanding and epoch making method of Saint Augustine was that of religious autobiography. His Confessions inaugurate an era in Christian literature. Nowhere previously do we find anything so intimate save in the letters of Paul, and these are but occasional and fragmentary. The account which Justin Martyr gives of his conversion is stiff and probably a mere literary stereotype. The apologies and refutations in the hands of a Tertullian are spirited and mordant, but scarcely intimate. The Confessions mark a new type.

Wherein lies the appeal? To begin with, in the impression of naked truthtelling. But is the impression merely an illusion? Augustine himself raised the question—what question did he not raise? "How shall men know that I speak the truth when they hear from myself about myself?" He answers, "To thee, Lord, I so confess that men may hear to whom I cannot prove whether I confess the truth, but they believe me whose ears charity opens to me" (Conf. X, iii). Our age has substituted higher criticism for charity and has very seriously impugned the reliability of the Confessions on the ground that the picture of the conversion written a

First published under the title "Methods of Great Religious Teachers: Saint Augustine," in *International Journal of Religious Education* (September 1932), as the first of four essays on the methods by which great religious teachers have sought to commend their way of life to men.

dozen years after the event is not corroborated by the tracts
composed in the months immediately following. The Confessions portray moral upheaval and emotional turmoil. The
almost contemporary tracts disclose a philosophic calm and
even a bantering lightness. Some have gone so far as to
assert that in 385 A.D. Augustine was not converted to
Christianity but to Neoplatonism. Not until several years
later when he became a priest, did he embrace Catholic
orthodoxy. Criticism of late, however, has been veering
toward a rehabilitation of the Confessions. A minute comparison with the tracts shows the earlier and later accounts
to be complementary rather than antithetical. Or if there is
a conflict it is not always between the tracts and the Confessions, but between one statement in the tracts and another.
For example, Augustine says in the tracts that he gave up
his profession of teaching rhetoric because of an illness of
the lungs. In the Confessions, on the other hand, the primary reason was the religious conversion. This same motive,
however, appears also elsewhere in the tracts, and in the
Confessions Augustine says that he welcomed the sickness
as an excuse for retirement (IX, ii). Oh! So then he did not
wish to declare his full mind at the time. Here is a clue to
the evident difference in tone. The purpose in writing was
different. In the tracts Augustine was not ready for complete
self revelation. Moreover he was constricted by Ciceronian
forms. He had won the assurance of salvation, but had not
attained his literary stride.

Nor need we be surprised that immediately after the
turmoil of the conversion Augustine should be occupied with
philosophic problems. He always was. In the very midst of
writing the Confessions he starts philosophizing about con-
fessing. How can he relate God's dealings without recollec-
tion? But what is memory? How is it that we remember
forgetfulness when forgetfulness blots out what we remember? (X, xvi). Incorrigible analyst! Such an incontrovertible
example makes plausible the account of the conversion in
the Confessions. Here Augustine tells us (VIII, viii–ix) that
in the garden he tore his hair, struck his forehead, and

clasped his knee. Then in the very midst of this upheaval he reflects, "The mind commands the body (in these movements) and is obeyed. The mind commands itself and is resisted."

There is a sense, however, in which the Confessions do create a false impression. They move too swiftly. Eight chapters survey thirty years. The moments of tension are selected. After a consecutive reading one exclaims, "How can he maintain such emotional strain and keep his mind?" It is a relief to turn to the early tracts and to discover leisurely discussion and genial repartee. On the other hand the Confessions are truer than the jottings of a journal. The past must always be rewritten in the light of the outcome. If a man changes his profession or his fiancee, he immediately realigns his previous course. All of the elements of disquietude which produced the rupture now take on significance and the apparently trivial and hitherto unnoticed circumstances impelling the new choice now assemble themselves like the dry bones and the four winds of a new insight breathe upon them that they may live. But yet again autobiography is always misleading. Hugh Walpole says that the Journal of Arnold Bennet is unsatisfactory because it leaves out the picture of his generosities. Not only saints, but even gentlemen portray themselves in too unfavorable a light.

A further element in the appeal of the Confessions is the indirectness or at least the unobtrusiveness of the intent to convert. If Augustine lapses from plain narrative it is to pray rather than to preach. The work is addressed to God even more than to the reader. Occasionally the author feels a measure of incongruity and breaks off: "To whom am I telling this? Not to thee, oh my God, but to my kind" (II, iii). Usually, however, the absorption in the narrative is so great and the sense of the immediacy of both God and the reader so real that the story proceeds without embarrassment.

A part of the indirectness is the feeling that conversion to Christianity must be a process rather than an event.

Augustine tells his story that others may be helped the sooner to pass through their difficulties, but at the same time there is at least the implication that it would be unfortunate to arrive without difficulties. Assurance is not so firm unless attained through doubt. Greater is the joy over one penitent than "over ninety and nine just persons which need no repentance." "The storm tosses the voyagers. Shipwreck threatens. All turn pale in the face of death. Sky and sea become calm, and they rejoice in the proportion to their fear" (VIII, iii). Much as Augustine regrets his tortuous course he implies at times that he would not have had peace on easier terms. He is glad that he fell upon Neoplatonic works before finding satisfaction in the Scriptures. Had the order been reversed he would not have been so convinced that Neoplatonism was powerless to satisfy (VII, xx). "Thou Lord, hast commanded the earth to bring forth thorns and thistles for me that with labor I should reach my bread" (IV, xvi).

Others too must struggle. Yet they can be helped, and best of all by being brought to see how some one else passed through precisely the same difficulty. Augustine achieves his purpose in part by relating how the stories of others helped him at crucial moments. When he was in an "almost persuaded" mood he bared himself to a spiritual counsellor, saying that he had been reading Neoplatonic works translated into Latin by Victorinus. The physician of the soul broke in at that point, congratulated him on having read these books and then told the story of that very Victorinus, who had made the attempt to be a Nicodemus, but found no peace until he had made public confession of his faith, spurning even the private confession which the church allowed to the timid (VIII, ii).

The Confessions again are effective because they are so probing. Augustine mercilessly exposes himself that the complacent reader may recognize shortcomings of which he is not aware. The weak is to be made strong by a disclosure of his weakness (X, iii). This is the justification of the frequent self analysis, in addition, of course, to the fact that

Augustine enjoyed it. Take his dissection of the love of praise. To desire the praise of men rather than the commendation of God is, of course, amiss. But it surely would not do to go to the other extreme and provoke the hatred of men. Moreover Augustine does not relish praise if it is unintelligent and misplaced. Does not this indicate that he is pleased not so much by the praise itself as by his neighbor's discrimination? On the other hand "I am not praised when my judgment of myself is not praised" (X, xxxvi). Or take again the famous instance in which Augustine confesses to two sins in his youth, sexual immorality and the stealing of green pears. He spends much more time probing the second than the first, and with good reason. The motives for sexual irregularity are obvious, but why should any one steal *green* pears? Part of the explanation Augustine finds in the fact that he certainly would not have committed the theft had he been alone. But why did the crowd make a difference? "We chuckled." Here is a clue. Why do men so seldom burst out laughing when alone? The theft was akin to humor, which requires an audience and depends upon incongruity. "We chuckled at the thought of fooling those who never suspected what we were up to" (II, iv–ix). Or take again Augustine's analysis of why we like to go to the theater and have a good cry. It is because we feel so sympathetic when there is an opportunity to grieve without the necessity to relieve (III, ii).

The mightiest appeal in the Confessions lies in the fact that the work is a song of triumph, "to stir up the heart that it sleep not in despair and say 'I cannot,' but that it awake in the love of Thy mercy and the sweetness of Thy grace" (X, iii). The story is the record of what God has done and can be counted on to do. Augustine breaks frequently into prayers like these. "Late have I loved Thee, whose fairness is so old and yet so new. Late have I loved Thee. And behold Thou wert within, and I without and there I sought Thee. Unlovely I broke upon the loveliness which Thou hast fashioned. Thou wert with me and I was not with Thee. Long was I held from Thee by those things which without

Thee are naught. Thou didst call and cry and burst my
deafness. Thou didst gleam and glow and dispel my blind-
ness. Thou didst exhale fragrance. I drew breath and I pant
after Thee. I have tasted and do hunger and thirst. Thou
hast touched me and I burned for Thy peace" (X, xxvii).
"Those who seek shall find Him, and those who find Him
shall praise Him" (I, i).

Even this account is sufficient to show that the Confessions are enthralling because they are the record of a
great man dealing with great themes. Life and death,
friendship, sex, the pursuit of honor and riches, the love of
mother and son, shame, renunciation, grief tinging every
object, despair, hope, the vision of God and peace. All these
pass before us. Let not lesser souls attempt Confessions. A
listless sinner makes a lifeless saint and neither knows how
to confess. Luther once ejaculated in a very different connection. "God does not save imaginary sinners. Therefore
be a sinner and sin for all you are worth!" The same advice
might be given to those who would write Confessions. Or at
least they must be able to say with Saint Augustine, "I
sought what I might love, in love with loving, and safety I
hated, and a way without snares, for within me was a famine
of that inward food, thyself, my God" (III, i).

4 The Ministry in The Middle Ages

No more compact summary of the view of the ministry
as it had developed in the patristic period is extant than
Chrysostom's tract *On the Priesthood*.[1] It was written to
justify the decision to remain a monk rather than to undertake the more onerous tasks of a parish minister. What a
reversal of values comes here to light! At first monasticism
was deemed the most rugged form of the Christian life, the
very successor to martyrdom. Now the priesthood had come
to be regarded as more arduous and monasticism was defended as the safest way to heaven, for though here one
might not rise so high, neither could one fall so low. Chrysostom proceeds in his tract to enumerate the many features
of the stupendous office.

The priest first of all, said he, has sacramental functions. He stands before the altar bringing down not fire from
heaven but the Holy Spirit. At his hands the Lord is again
sacrificed upon the altar and the people empurpled with
that precious blood. Only by eating of the flesh of the Lord
and drinking of his blood can man escape the fires of hell.
How tremendous then is the office of the priest through
whose hands alone this saving rite can be administered!
Vastly greater is he than an earthly parent who generates

First published in *The Ministry in Historical Perspectives* (ed. H. Richard
Niebuhr and Daniel D. Williams; Harper and Brothers, New York, 1956). Only
the first sentence has been revised. Reprinted by permission of The American
Association of Theological Schools.

[1] *PNF*, IX.

only unto earthly life, whereas the priest regenerates unto life eternal. To him has been given an authority exceeding that of angels and archangels.

He has likewise a disciplinary function, for he must excommunicate the unworthy, and whatsoever he shall bind on earth shall be bound in heaven. He is to serve likewise as a judge, and much of his time will be consumed in adjudicating the disputes of his flock. He is also an administrator of the property of the Church which is to be used for the entertainment of strangers and the care of the sick.

He is the instructor of his people through the pulpit; a skilled theologian, he must be able to refute the heretics and the pagans. As a preacher he will have to compete with tragedies and musical entertainments. He has a pastoral function and must be able to mingle with men in all walks of life. If he does not make a round of visits every day, unspeakable offense will ensue. He must distribute his smiles with utter impartiality and not beam inordinately upon anyone in particular. The virgins are under his care, and he must endeavor to confine them to their homes, save for inexorable necessity. The widows will try his patience, since they are garrulous and querulous. The married women he must visit when sick, comfort when sorrowful and reprove when idle, and in all of this scrupulously guard himself, recognizing that chaste women may be even more upsetting than the wanton.

Thus far Chrysostom. His picture is comprehensive and illuminating. It leaves out much which was to accrue to the priesthood in a later time. The distinction between the clergy and the laity is implied but is not spelled out. Already it had been made clear. Although Constantine as a layman was accorded a large share in the calling and direction of councils, yet when his son Constantius undertook to enforce decisions contrary to Nicene orthodoxy, he was roundly reproved by Bishop Hosius on the ground that emperors may not burn incense.[2] And the Emperor Theodosius was twice reproved by Ambrose, once when after the massacre of Thessalonica

---

[2] Shotwell and Loomis, *See of Peter* (New York, 1927), pp. 577–580.

he approached the church; secondly when, already absolved for the bloodshed, he ventured to go beyond the chancel and take his place among the priests.[3] Constantine had conferred special immunities upon the clergy, subsequently curtailed when they precipitated too great a rush for holy orders.[4] Still the clergy remained a caste.

Their functions and deportment differed from those of the laity. Not only the monk but also the minister had a code. Priests should not meddle in business and if they did, were to be shunned as the plague.[5] The bishop, of course, was responsible as an agent for the goods of the Church, and the Church, even before Constantine, held property as a corporation. The goods were not vested in the bishop personally and for himself he must abstain from all private commercial transactions. Again he must not be a magistrate, and when Paul of Samosata, in the late third century, became a Ducenarius of Zenobia of Palmyra, the very pronunciation of his title evoked a shiver of disapprobation.[6] The objection arose largely from the fear that the magistrate might have to pass sentence of death or torture. Consequently, to deter the mob from making him a bishop, Ambrose, at that time a Pretorian prefect, held an impromptu court and passed a severe sentence to show that one who so acted according to the law was disqualified for the service of the gospel.[7] The throng as a matter of fact was not deterred, and that in itself was a step toward the Middle Ages. Above all, the minister should never be a soldier. Ambrose was quite clear on that score, although he did not condemn soldiers and even exhorted the emperor to a campaign and almost a crusade against the Arian barbarians.[8] The minister then should not be a merchant, a magistrate, or a militiaman.

[3] Theodoret, "Ecclesiastical History," 17, *PNF*, Ser. 2, III, 143–145.
[4] Maude Aline Huttmann, "The Establishment of Christianity and the Proscription of Paganism," Columbia University, *Studies in History, Economics and Public Law*, LX, 2 (1914), 149–157 and 62–63.
[5] Letter 52, *PNF*, Ser. 2, VI, 91.
[6] Eusebius, *Historia Ecclesiastica*, VII, 30.
[7] F. Holmes Dudden, *The Life and Times of St. Ambrose* (Oxford, 1935), p. 66.
[8] The code of the just war is elaborated in the *De Officiis*. Exhortations to the emperor to fight the Arian Goths appear in the *De Fide*.

The monk, whose role appeared to Chrysostom relatively easier, was, however, acquiring enlarged functions
which blurred the differentiation. By St. Jerome scholarship
and monasticism were combined and the role of the Benedictines was thus foreshadowed. Likewise after the sack of
Rome, when refugees streamed into the East, Jerome's
monastery became a hostel. He tells us also of high-born
Roman matrons, who having embraced the religious life,
dedicated themselves to ministering in hospitals to sufferers
from the most loathsome diseases.[9] The cell had thus become
expanded to encompass the study, the hostel, and the
hospital.

The Church throughout the Empire had acquired a
high degree of universality and centralization which served
as a model to be surpassed in the high Middle Ages, but
only after a long period of obscuration. The bishop of Rome
enjoyed a certain presidency of love. His church was regarded as the purest custodian of the primitive tradition
because founded by the two pillar apostles, Peter and Paul.
The bishop of Rome by the middle of the fourth century
was deemed to have been the successor of Peter, not simply
as the founder but as himself the first bishop of Rome. His
successor in the see wielded the power of the keys to him
committed. Actually the early ecumenical councils were not
summoned by the bishops of Rome nor did they attend. At
the same time Rome exerted a preponderant influence upon
their decisions and when the orthodox were intimidated or
persecuted they looked to Rome as their protector and
asylum.

After the barbarian invasions in the West great changes
ensued. The traditional functions of the priest described by
Chrysostom all continued but the once forbidden tasks also
were added to his portfolio. In consequence, although in a
formal way the line between the laity and the clergy was
accentuated, in function the two more nearly approximated
each other, doubly so because the laity assumed a larger
role in the founding, supplying, and reforming of churches.

[9] Letter 77, *PNF*, p. 160.

The monks likewise extended their functions when many became priests. In the meantime, priests became celibate and thus the regular and secular clergy were less to be distinguished. The term "regular" was applied to the monastics because they followed the *regula* or rule, the term "secular" to the parish clergy because they served *in saeculo,* in the world. The word had not yet acquired the connotation of secular in the sense of worldly.

These great changes were occasioned by a vast alteration in the social structure as a result of the barbarian inroads.[10] Centralization and public order broke down. The invasions menaced goods and life. After the main incursions subsided, sporadic raids of pillaging Norsemen continued and even major thrusts from the Danes in the West and the Magyars in the East. When the barbarian kingdoms became established they warred upon one another and within them barons preyed upon barons. Security had to be sought on some walled promontory in the company of bellowing and offensive herds. The disorders interfered with commerce. A further and even more serious setback was occasioned by the Mohammedan invasion commencing in the sixth century which made of the Mediterranean an Islamic sea.[11] The decline of commerce meant also that there was a decline of cities and a reversion to an agricultural economy with exchange in kind rather than in coin.

The invaders were either Arian Christians or pagans, in neither case orthodox subscribers to the Nicene creed. This meant that they did not accept the leadership of Peter's successors. The Arians had no centralizing focus comparable to Rome and their missionaries had attached themselves in the north to the tribes. When these were converted to the Nicene faith they still retained or tended to retain the decentralized organization. An assertion of authority on the part of the Roman church was all the more difficult because

[10] Hans von Schubert, *Geschichte der christlichen Kirche im frühmittelalter* (Tübingen, 1921).

[11] Henri Pirenne, *Economic and Social History of Medieval Europe* (New York, 1937).

the city of Rome geographically was no longer at the center
of the Christian world, as in the days when the extremities
were Spain and Syria. After the Mediterranean was lost to
Islam, Rome came to be on the periphery of the new world
of the West. The center was at Metz in Germany and the
other extremity at Hadrian's wall in Scotland.

The task of converting and Christianizing the northern
peoples was stupendous in view of the disorder, hampered
communication, and nonviable currency. New methods were
imperative, and new functions, imperceptibly at first but
inevitably, accrued to the Church and to the clergy. Rome
could commission missionaries to the North but thereafter
they were on their own. No missionary boards could finance
them with bank drafts or postal money orders. They would
have to be self-sustaining and there was only one way by
which they could support themselves in a rural society and
that was on the land. They acquired ground already do-
mesticated or themselves undertook to fell the forests or
drain the swamps. No agency of the Church was so well
adapted to this task as the monastery and it can be no accident that whereas Christianity went into Ireland under
episcopal auspices, when the curtain rises for the second
scene, the form disclosed is monastic. Groups of monks
could form a community and establish a self-sufficient life
with their own fields, vineyards, graineries, fish ponds,
rabbitries, and orchards. As late as the high Middle Ages
the Cistercians profoundly affected the economic life of
Europe by their projects of reclamation. Waters were
gathered behind dikes into ponds stocked with fish, bogs
were transformed into "golden meadows," greenhouses
introduced new plantings, and forests were discriminately
cut with an eye to conservation.[12]

In all of this one sees much that was new in the functions of the clergy. Chrysostom had not enumerated among
the ministerial cares the maintenance of a suitable tempera-
ture in a greenhouse. The three activities which the Early

---

[12] James Westfall Thompson, *An Economic and Social History of the Middle
Ages 300–1300* (New York, 1928), pp. 614–615.

Church had forbidden to the clergy came to be appropriated. The first was business. To be sure, in the first centuries the bishop was the administrator of the Church's goods but in the Middle Ages he was more, and the Church's business was so enlarged, so intricate, and so geared into all of the property and commercial activities that the difference at this point between the cleric and the lay was no more than that the former was more successful.

The bishop of Rome became a great business administrator. In the days of Gregory I (590–604) vast possessions not overrun by the Lombards were still in the hands of the Church, timber and grain lands in Sardinia, Sicily, Calabria, and northern Italy. We find the bishop of Rome sending the churches lumber and lead, supplying the populace of Rome with grain, *panem* if not *circensem*, and supporting a great concourse of nuns presumably refugees in the city. In order to manage these huge estates an imposing bureaucracy had been developed with a whole hierarchy of managers, *rectores patrimonii*.[13] The letters of Gregory afford a striking contrast to those of Augustine, who was concerned with the cure of souls rather than with the care of estates. The epistles of Gregory read like the correspondence of a dean. Every letter renders a decision.

To the north in Gaul and later in Germany the secular clergy came in surprisingly short order to be endowed with fantastic estates, as much as one-third or one-half of the land in the kingdom. Frequent expropriations by rulers like Charles Martel were speedily recouped by fresh donations. These gifts were now vested not in the Church as a corporation but personally in the bishop or the abbot.[14] Of course, he still thought of himself as acting for the Church. In any case, immense amounts of his time would have to be devoted to oversight and collection.

The fate of the monasteries was not different. The

[13] Evelyn Mary Spearing, *The Patrimony of the Roman Church in the Time of Gregory the Great* (Cambridge, England, 1918).

[14] Emile Lesne, *Histoire de la Propriété ecclésiastique en France*, 8 vols. (Lille, 1910–1943).

Benedictines began with a regime of manual labor for each
of the brothers, but when lands were given with the laborers
thrown in, the monks did not drive them off in order to do
the work themselves but accepted the serfs with the soil.
The monk then became a squire or, if his tastes so dictated,
perchance a scholar with a lily hand. In the high Middle
Ages, when the new monastic orders produced wine, wool,
and grain beyond their needs, they began to dispose of the
surplus in the channels of trade, outfitted convoys on the
roads, and flotillas on the rivers. Altogether they were the
most enterprising businessmen of their day.[15]

Functions of government devolved upon churchmen.
There was no conspiracy for power, simply the discharge of
a job to be done. In Italy the popes reluctantly took over
the role of the Caesars. By reason of the invasions any control in Italy, even in the areas still free of the invaders, was
but tenuous when exercised from Constantinople or even
Ravenna. Gregory I, precisely because of his immense re-
sources, found himself doing what formerly government had
undertaken. The debilitating practice of feeding the Roman
populace went back to the days when rival contestants for
office distributed largesses of food to the public. In the end
the Empire was feeding the citizens. When then the sovereign
at Constantinople could no longer function in this way, the
Church of Rome wafted the wheat from the plains of Africa.
If Roman citizens were captured by the barbarians, who had
the gold for their ransom if not the bishop of Rome? And if
he thus dealt with the barbarians, how inevitable that he
should make agreements and even treaties with their rulers?
Little wonder that Pippin, the king of the Franks in 754,
recognized the actual conditions when he conferred upon the
pope the keys of ten cities that over them he might exercise
civil rule. This date is commonly taken to mark the beginning of the estates of the Church over which the pope was
temporal lord until 1870. His authority was restored in 1929
over the diminished area of Vatican City.

[15] George Gordon Coulton, *Five Centuries of Religion,* 4 vols. (1923–1950);
especially III.

In the north churchmen likewise assumed functions of government. Since the clergy were the only literate class the kings of the Franks drafted them as civil servants. The precedent was thereby laid for many a subsequent figure who combined the role of a high ecclesiastic and a prime minister or chancellor of the realm, men like Sully, Ximenes, Wolsey, and Richelieu. The amazement of Henry II can well be divined when his favorite Thomas à Becket refused to conform. Bishops and abbots became rulers in their own domains when the feudal system became established and taxes, military levies, and the administration of justice devolved upon the holders of land. So long as churchmen held vast estates they could not escape obedience and service to their overlords nor responsibilities and protection for the underlings. They had become prince-bishops and prince-abbots.

Under such circumstances they could scarcely obviate involvement in war. In the days of the invasions even abbots as well as bishops donned armor over their cassocks to repel raiders. Monasteries were begirt with walls. Sometimes even nuns entered the fray and in the conflict of baron with baron the churchman behaved like his neighbor. In the days of Henry II in Germany, for example, a robber baron so devastated the archdiocese of Treves that the archbishop fled. The Emperor thereupon selected a hardfisted young noble, raced him through the grades of the hierarchy until he was made the archbishop of Treves. He promptly distributed the goods of the Church to knights who formed a small standing army and repulsed the marauder.[16]

Such behavior at least prior to the year 1000 was looked upon as a defection from the Christian ideal. The view that the soldier could himself be esteemed as a servant of the Church, that the knight should be inducted with a religious ceremony and that churchmen might even participate in conflict with the sword as well as with the cross, was the outcome of a great peace crusade. In the first half

[16] James Westfall Thompson, *History of the Middle Ages* (New York, 1931), p. 172.

of the eleventh century churchmen sponsored the Truce of God and the Peace of God whereby the time for active hostilities was so restricted that warfare became a summer sport and the number of combatants so reduced as to make of it an aristocratic pastime. This was the intent, but many barons took the oath and did not keep it. Then churchmen raised a disciplinary army of enforcement, a peace militia. Here was the notion of the holy war, under the auspices of the Church in order to suppress war. This concept was basic for the Crusades. Urban II began his famous exordium with a plea for peace. "Let Christians," he urged, "stop shearing each other and go against the common enemy of the faith!" And all the assembly shouted, *"Dieu le veult!"* [17]

The prohibition of clerical participation broke down. An example is given in the case of a priest in the Frankish army on the first crusade. At Constantinople quarrels with the Greeks led to a skirmish between vessels in the Bosphorus. Anna, the daughter of the Greek emperor, relates with horror that a priest from the bow of his ship hurled missiles against her father's admiral till even stones were exhausted. When the Frankish vessel was captured this priest, severely wounded, embraced the opposing commander saying that with better weapons he would have won, then expired and went to hell, according to Anna, because as a priest he had taken weapons. [18] The West, however, did not condemn him. Even before the crusade, Leo X led his forces against the Normans. The aversion even of monasticism to war collapsed with the founding of the Hospitalers, Knights of St. John, and the Templars with the enthusiastic blessing of that great monk St. Bernard.

This change in clerical functions excites wonder but even more remarkable was the success of the papacy in uniting the diverse and warring factions of France in the first crusade: the knights of Langue d'Oui and Languedoc, the Normans of Normandy, and the Normans of Sicily and

---

[17] Carl Erdmann, *Die Entstehung des Kreuzzugsgedankens* (Stuttgart, 1935).

[18] Anna Comnena, *The Alexiad,* tr. Elizabeth A. S. Dawes (London, 1928), pp. 255–256.

southern Italy, Godfrey and Baldwin, the Roberts and
Tancred, Raymond of Toulouse, and Adhemar of Puy.
What united them was the conviction that *God* willed it.

How did the Church ever come to persuade them of
this? The attempt would hardly have succeeded had not the
Church been fired with a flaming zeal to Christianize the
very fabric of society and to accomplish this end first of all
by emancipating and purifying herself. The Gregorian reformers were deeply aware of all the corruptions inherent in
the very processes of Christianization. The Church had to
be of the people in order to win the people and in so doing
all too readily became like the people. The warring of
bishops and abbots was understandable enough in a disorderly society and might be condoned as self-defense. Yet
all too often it became predatory. The immense episcopal
baronies had originated innocently out of the very necessities
of the situation. Then they had become so lucrative as to
tempt the avaricious and the ambitious. The manning of
churches by lay patrons, at first a boon, had become a bane,
when through their power of lay investiture they consecrated
superfluous sons in order to enlarge their domains. The
centralizing of political authority in the hands of the emperor was stabilizing but if to this end he determined
episcopal appointments his eye might be less directed to
saintliness than to amenability. The marriage of the clergy
was supported by the sanction of eminent churchmen such
as St. Ambrose but introduced the possibility of a hereditary
episcopacy.

To cure all of these ills two drastic reforms were
launched. The one aimed at the independence, the other
at the purity of the Church. The clergy were to be emancipated from lay control. They were not to be subject to the
civil courts. Justice for churchmen should be administered
by the Church. The tonsured were to be exempt from lay
authority, and even though guilty of theft, rape, and
murder should enjoy benefit of clergy. The practice of
assigning all ecclesiastics to the bishop's court is discernible
in England only after the conquest and was a result of the

Gregorian reform. Popular sentiment supported this exemption because the secular courts were so severe. On a single gallows one might see twenty men hanging for trivial offenses. The bishop could not impose the death penalty. He might adjudge the accused guilty and turn him over for punishment to the civil power. Commonly, however, he exacted only purgation. He might condemn the culprit to an ecclesiastical prison, but still, there would be no taking of life.[19]

Again the clergy should be free from all lay interference both in the inception and conduct of their office. The Church should determine appointments and the new incumbents should swear fealty only to the pope. Such demands might have been readily conceded if the Church had not owned one-half of the land on which all political institutions were based. Church lands, moreover, were not consolidated but dispersed in strips and patches which if withdrawn from the emperor's control would leave him with an inchoate and unmanageable domain. The Church might easily have been accorded independence had she been willing to renounce her endowments but she argued that so many donations had been given in trust and were not to be alienated to the sons of perdition.

But if the bishops were not to be appointed by lay patrons nor to swear allegiance to lay rulers, by whom then were they to be inducted and invested? A special machinery was developed by the Church to meet this need, namely, the College of the Cardinals. The suggestion had been made long since in the spurious Decretals of the ninth century which significantly emanated from the lower church clergy of France who desired the centralization of Church government and the enhancement of the papacy as a defense against the highhandedness of overlords, alike lay and clerical. The proposal was made that the pope be fortified by a college of assistants; thereby the central administration would be strengthened and the local metropolitans set down a notch

[19] Leona C. Gabel, "Benefit of Clergy in England in the Later Middle Ages," *Smith College Studies in History*, XIV, Nos. 1–4 (October 1928–July1929).

in the hierarchy.[20] Not until the eleventh century was the idea implemented and the Cardinals established with the function of choosing popes quite independently of any lay directives.

By this move the hierarchy was further elaborated and the gradations within the clergy still more accentuated. In one respect, however, the cleavage within the ranks was diminished. When the altar was moved to the rear of the apse the bishop no longer stood behind the communion table but took his place with the other clergy in the choir stall. Though he had there a throne, he was still but one in a row.[21]

While the clerical body was being welded, the line between the clergy and the laity was heightened. There were two postures at communion. The priest stood; the people kneeled. And there came to be two positions. The priest at the altar; the people before the altar rail. Only the priest partook of both elements. From the laity the wine came to be withheld.

But nothing did so much to set the clergy apart from the body of the faithful as did the imposition of celibacy. In the earlier period it had not been demanded. The Bishop of Mans, for example, had been openly married and called his wife *Episcopissa*. In 966 Rutherius declared that all of the clergy in his area were married and some of them more than once. If the decree prohibiting repeated marriages were enforced only boys would be left in the Church. He endeavored to institute a reform but was driven to seek the sanctuary of an abbey. At the same time, for centuries an incompatibility had been sensed between sexual relations and ministry at the altar and the married priest was enjoined to abstain during the period of his ministration.[22] The Gregorian reform, partly for practical reasons to break up the system of hereditary bishoprics and partly for ascetic reasons because

[20] Ernest Harold Davenport, *The False Decretals* (Oxford, 1916).
[21] Edwin Hatch, *The Growth of Church Institutions* (New York, 1887), chap. 12.
[22] Henry C. Lea, *An Historical Sketch of Sacerdotal Celibacy* (Boston, 1884), 152.

virginity was rated higher than marriage, undertook to make the reform universal. Opposition was intense but the rule became canon law.

Coincidently a device was introduced to demark the clergy as a special class by imposing upon them a distinctive dress which would serve both to enhance their prestige and to guard their morals by setting them apart. Complaint was made of those clad in scarlet, wearing rings, "with short tunics, ornamentally trimmed, with knives and basilards hanging at their girdles." The rules prescribed that the head must be tonsured, the beard closely trimmed, sleeves must be short, coats long, and colors somber. There was as yet no specific uniform for the clergy as to street attire save for the distinguishing mark of the tonsure.[23]

These reforms occasioned much stout resistance particularly from the civil government. There was no serious objection to having the clergy dress differently nor did civil rulers too much care if the priests were unmarried, save that celibacy terminated a system by which the noble and royal houses had profited. Vastly more serious from the point of view of the state was the abolition of lay investiture. For how could a king be sovereign in his own domain if he could not count on unqualified obedience from subordinates who controlled one-half of the land? Plainly France, Germany, England, and Spain would be ruled from Rome. Again, exemption from the civil courts constituted a serious threat to the administration of even-handed justice throughout the realm, particularly in a society where the ratio of the clergy to the laity was estimated as somewhere between 1 to 50 and 1 to 25.[24]

This opposition, though serious, was cowed. Henry II of England, who in resisting clerical immunities occasioned the murder of an archbishop, had to do penance at his tomb. Henry IV in Germany hurled defiance at Gregory VII when the pope categorically insisted on the imposition of clerical

[23] Edward L. Cutts, *Parish Priests and Their People in the Middle Ages in England* (London, 1898), pp. 164, 166–167, 183.

[24] H. Maynard Smith, *Pre-Reformation England* (London, 1938), p. 138.

celibacy and the abolition of lay investiture. The emperor for his truculence was placed under excommunication and his subjects released from their oaths of obedience. The emperor thereupon found himself devoid of subjects; in order to recover his scepter he had to stand a suppliant in the snow at Canossa.

The line, though tortuous, runs from this dramatic papal triumph to the dazzling pontificate of Innocent III in the thirteenth century when the objectives of the Gregorian reform were accomplished to an astounding degree.

A culture had emerged properly designated as Christendom. The Christian faith, save for a remnant of the Jews and occasional heretics, was dominant from Caledonia to Calabria. And the lord pope was more effectively the head of the society than was any civil ruler. St. Peter's vicar exalted the lowly and abased the proud. Never did he claim to rule as a temporal sovereign, save of course in the papal states and in those areas which became fiefs of the papacy, namely Sicily, Portugal, and England. Elsewhere he claimed jurisdiction only over sin, but inasmuch as most human endeavor is tainted with sin, the pope's area of possible jurisdiction was large.

This authority was exercised without direct force of arms. The pope might indeed call upon one prince to discipline another. The popes had not been above leading armies to repel the Normans. But Innocent III did not undertake to police the world. He ruled by admonition and the spiritual weapon of excommunication carrying with it the exclusion from blessedness in the life eternal.

When this point in a church history course is reached, the class gasps and inquires how the pope ever came to exercise such authority that at his word an emperor excluded from the altar should be deemed by his subjects unfit to govern Christian folk. Truly one cannot but be amazed that excommunication should have been so seriously regarded as to have become a political weapon. This never could have taken place if the Church for centuries had not been training the populace on remote farms and in distant hamlets. A host of unrecorded emissaries must have instilled this faith.

The first stage in the fashioning of Christendom was the conversion of the northern peoples. Seculars and regulars alike contributed. The task of these missionaries differed little from that of the first Apostles, save that the audience was different. The gospel now was addressed not to the cultivated philosopher or the ecstatic initiate of the mystery cults but to cruder folk: Druids scarcely beyond human sacrifice, Teutons worshiping Thor within the sacred Oak. From fragmentary remains of that time one would judge that Christ was presented as the Redeemer on the rood, by death conquering death and insuring for man blessedness in the world to come. One recalls the sermon of Paulinus when he pointed to the swallow flitting through the Saxon banqueting hall from darkness to darkness as a parable of the life of man, were it not that Christ has shed light and hope on the darkness beyond.[25] Again King Oswy at Whitby is claimed to have decided for the Roman representative because he was the agent of St. Peter, holder of the keys to the gates of heaven.[26] At the other extremity of the empire Cyril and Methodius impressed the Bulgar king by a picture of the judgment to come. The power of the death-conquering Christ was reinforced by the intercession of the saints whose relics were a part of the missionary's equipment. Among polytheistic peoples the saints readily became the successors of the gods. The pacific aspects of Christianity proved no deterrent to a warlike folk who saw in Peter the doughty knight with his broad sword cleaving clean the ear of the high priest's servant.[27] The ethical demands of the gospel were laid with emphasis upon unbridled peoples, witness the early development of the penitentials. Not only were penalties imposed on earth but punishments and rewards offered in the life to come. The Pauline doctrine of justifica-

[25] *Bede's Ecclesiastical History*, II, xiii, tr. L. Gidley (Oxford, 1870), 150.
[26] *Ibid.*, III, XXV, 254.
[27] Norman Boggs, *The Christian Saga*, 2 vols. (New York, 1931), p. 329.

tion by faith apart from works was too precarious a word to commit to these undisciplined hordes.

Conversion was by peoples rather than by individuals. The desirability of this method is much debated in our own day. Frequently the churches have demanded a personal commitment and an understanding of the faith as a prerequisite for baptism. The result has been that converts have suffered a complete social dislocation and, disowned by their own people, have had to find a home within a European or Europeanized community. This was not the course adopted in the winning of the West. Commonly kings and queens were converted and at their behest whole peoples received the waters of baptism. Such conversion was of necessity highly superficial and genuine Christianization had to come afterward.

Only then did the real work begin. Once more the regulars and the seculars shared. We have already noted how readily monasticism adapted itself to the rural economy and how the monks altered the contours of the land. They ministered likewise to the folk round about by draining their swamps and by training their children; in some cases also by serving their churches. The monk, however much he might cherish seclusion and prize contemplation, was never actually withdrawn from the social fabric. No pope of the twelfth century, for example, was so influential as the monk St. Bernard. So frequently was he called upon to leave the cloister that he referred to himself as a bird out of his nest. His critics called him a frog out of his pond. Whether he was rebuking the Count of Champagne or the King of France, settling the papal schism or fomenting the Second Crusade, this indefatigable, inexorable, and irresistible abbot so swayed his fellows that mothers are said to have hidden their sons at his approach.

But the monks were not dedicated primarily to the service of the community and the ministry of the abbot was first of all to his own sons in the cloister. The letters and the sermons of St. Bernard rebuke the foibles of monks with an itch for singularity, who enjoy better the singing of one psalm alone in the choir when the brothers are asleep than an entire psalter in the company of the brethren. Again the monk is rebuked who seeks to distinguish himself by spectacular austerity, and lacking a mirror, is continually scrutinizing the visibility of his ribs.[28] Bernard is again the lyrical preacher as he discourses on Christ the bridegroom in the Canticles or as he dwells with rapture on the vision of the ineffable.

When society became more stabilized, increasingly the needs of the people were met by churches whether in cities, towns, or hamlets. In the urban centers there were cathedral churches staffed by a considerable corps of the clergy responsible for the cure of souls in the area and sometimes, as in the case of Chantry priests, committed to saying masses for designated persons living or dead. The cathedral churches were manned sometimes by seculars, sometimes by regulars. In England the great secular cathedrals were St. Paul's, York, Lincoln, Salisbury, Exeter, Hereford, and Litchfield. These were governed by a dean and a chapter. The regular cathedrals were at the same time Benedictine abbeys, namely, Canterbury, Durham, Winchester, Norwich, Ely, and Worcester. The monks in theory elected the abbot, and he was also the bishop.[29]

The bulk of the population lived in the villages, and in ecclesiastical parlance belonged to vicarages. The term arose because the incumbent was commonly a substitute. Many changes brought the system to pass. In the early Middle Ages a landlord frequently built a chapel and appointed to it a rector, assigning certain lands for his support. Out of this arrangement grew the tithe system, but inasmuch as the private chaplain to the landlord was frequently expected to be his boon companion in hunting and hawking and sometimes did not reside at all but delegated his functions to a vicar, the bishops struggled to emancipate the rural churches

---

[28] *De Gradibus Humilitatis,* XIV, G. B. Burch, ed. and tr. (Cambridge, Mass., 1940).
[29] R. S. Arrowsmith, *The Prelude to the Reformation* (London, 1923), pp. 14–15.

from lay control. One expedient was to assign them to monasteries, which became themselves the rectors and the recipients of the revenues.[30] Sometimes they undertook to provide for the cure of souls from their own ranks, but of this arrangement there was grievous complaint inasmuch as the only baptismal font was located at the monastery, and the villages might be a dozen miles away. In case of extremity an infant might die on the road. Therefore a substitute for the rector, a vicar, was assigned to the parish.[31] His living was precarious since the monastery continued to appropriate approximately two-thirds of the income.[32] Such exactions were not wholly without warrant, at any rate in medieval eyes, because the monasteries were engaged in prayers for the living and the dead and also in extensive hospitality. Yet the bishops generally fought the monasteries on behalf of the vicars and themselves, and if there were no monastery in the picture, the bishop made his own levy. On the Continent the bishop often took one-fourth or one-third of the income, and when such imposts were replaced by free gifts these in turn became involuntary. An effort was made on one occasion to restrict a bishop to not more than a bushel of barley, a keg of wine, and a pig worth sixpence.[33] The bishop also could plead necessity, for his obligations, too, were heavy. One bishop reported that he had to entertain three hundred guests on a single day, not to mention sixty or eighty beggars.[34] Then, too, there were scholars whose educational expenses could be defrayed only through a church living, and when the average vicarage comprised, as in England, four thousand acres,[35] why should it not support more than the vicar? All of this was plausible enough, yet the net result was that the vicar had in part at

[30] Cutts, *op. cit.*, p. 97.

[31] R. A. R. Hartridge, *A History of Vicarages in the Middle Ages* (Cambridge, England, 1930), pp. 163, 196.

[32] *Ibid.*, p. 14.

[33] Hatch, *op. cit.*, p. 55.

[34] Arrowsmith, *op. cit.*, p. 9.

[35] John R. H. Moorman, *Church Life in England in the Thirteenth Century* (Cambridge, England, 1945), p. 12.

least to support himself by the cultivation of his own glebe, which was expected to yield one-half of his income.[36] There are references to vicars so poor as to be driven to steal. One need not greatly marvel that they were on the lookout for more lucrative benefices and did not too long remain in a particular cure.[37]

Neither should one be altogether amazed if vicars who lived so precariously were not distinguished for erudition. The story is told of a dean who conducted an examination of his subordinates. He called on one to parse the opening sentence of the canon of the Mass, *Te igitur clementissime Pater.* "What governs *Te?*" he was asked. *"Pater,"* was his reply, "because the Father governs everything." The dean marked him down as *sufficienter illiteratus.* Yet when the laity were interrogated as to the sufficiency of their parson in the role of preacher and teacher, they gave him a favorable report, and one may well conceive that he who could not parse the Latin Mass might be able to instruct his flock in the rudiments of faith and conduct.[38]

The parish priest at any rate was the most instructed person in the community. To him men turned as counselor, teacher, lawyer, doctor, and friend. His foremost function was the performance of the Sacraments. Baptism was deemed essential for salvation. If a priest were not present, a midwife might administer the rite using Latin, good or bad, or even English provided there were the intent to baptize.

For adults the great sacrament was the Mass. It was conducted in Latin, and the people did not understand the lines. In any case much of the liturgy was inaudible. The congregation was encouraged to occupy itself with private devotions so that two parallel services were taking place coincidently. At the same time the dramatic acts of the liturgy, such as the elevation of the host, were readily intelligible and besides the Church was richly endowed with

[36] Smith, *op. cit.*, p. 60.
[37] Arrowsmith, *op. cit.*, p. 46.
[38] Moorman, *op. cit.*, pp. 92–93.

symbolism that it might be "a book to the lewd [ignorant] people that they may read in the imagery and painture that clerks read in the book." [39]

The ignorance of the people is not, however, to be exaggerated. They understood much. They knew that the Mass arose from the Supper which the Lord shared with his disciples before he suffered. They knew that it re-enacted the suffering of the Lord. On the altar the cross of Calvary was again set up. If he who there suffered was God then the incarnation also had to be repeated. The very bread and wine were changed not to the sight of the eye, the touch of the hand, or the taste of the mouth but in substance into the very flesh and blood of God. The faithful in eating partook of His very life. The gospel was reduced to one central event—the Passion. And the Passion meant the forgiveness of sins, communion with the ever-dying and ever-risen Lord. The Mass was celebrated not simply on behalf of those attending but also for the souls departed whose bodies lay beneath the stones in the cathedral floor. Here the Church Militant met with the Church Triumphant and earthly pilgrims were rapt into the company of the saints in heaven.

Quite as influential as the Mass in the Middle Ages was the sacrament of penance involving contrition, confession, and satisfaction. In the confessional the priest came into direct contact with the parishioner and subjected him to a thoroughgoing spiritual examination in faith and in morals:

The clergy were taught to probe into the most secret places of a man's life so that his confession might be full and nothing kept back from God. Some of the questions which he was told to put to the penitent were very searching. "Have you ever borrowed things and not returned them?" "Have you taught your children the Creed and the Lord's Prayer?" "Have you without devotion heard any predication?" "If your children are 'shrewes' have you tried to teach them good manners?" "Have you ever ridden over growing corn?" "Have you left the churchyard open so that beasts got in?" "Have you eaten with such main that you have

[39] Bernard Lord Manning, *The People's Faith in the Time of Wyclif* (Cambridge, England, 1919), p. 13.

cast it up again?" This was indeed a searching cross-examination, from which no one could hope to emerge faultless.[40]

Yet the outcome was not despair. Confession expunged sins so that the devil was compelled to erase them from his record.[41] Alongside of the sacraments were the sacred ceremonies, often immemorial usages reaching back into a remote pagan antiquity, invested now with Christian symbolism, teaching men the sacred meaning of the seasonal round. At Christmas

children stole into church to see the crib. . . . At Candlemas the congregation marched around the church with their lighted candles. All received ashes on Ash Wednesday that they might understand the defilement of sin. On Maunday Thursday, great men washed the feet of the poor. On Good Friday men crept to the Cross in humble adoration of Him who had died for them. On Easter Eve the new fire was hallowed from which the Paschal candle was lighted. At Rogationtide the fields were blessed and religion consecrated the daily toil. At Whitsuntide the dove descended from the roof of the church, while clouds of incense perfumed the air. At Corpus Christi time were the glad processions of those rejoicing in Emmanuel, God with us. At Lammas the loaf . . . was presented as an act of thanksgiving. On All Hallows five boys in surplices chanted "*Venite omnes virgines sapientissimae*" in honour of those who had gone in to the marriage supper of the Lamb. On St. Nicholas Day or Holy Innocents a boy pontificated, reminding all of the command to turn and become as little children![42]

Such customs at their best served to hallow the terrestrial pilgrimage.

Of all the means at the disposal of the Church for the instruction and edification of the flock none was more efficacious at its best than preaching. The Church expected it of the parish priest and strove to give him aid and counsel in the task. One of the great manuals of the art of preaching

---

[40] Moorman, *op. cit.*, p. 87. Quotations modernized.

[41] Lecoy de la Marche, *Anecdotes historiques—Etienne de Bourbon* (Paris, 1877), p. 155.

[42] Smith, *op. cit.*, pp. 133–134.

was *The Pastoral Rule* of Gregory the Great. The pope there instructs the pastor first as to how he shall demean himself:

He is to be discreet in keeping silence, profitable in speech, a near neighbor to everyone in sympathy, exalted above all in contemplation; a familiar friend of good livers through humility, unbending against vice of evil doers through zeal for righteousness; not relaxing in his care for what is inward from being occupied in outward things, not neglecting to provide for outward things in his solicitude for what is inward.

The pastor is then counseled to adapt the Word to the hearer, and the manual proceeds by setting up series of contrasting pairs. Those who are well should be enjoined to employ the health of the body to the health of the soul. The sick are to be admonished to consider themselves the sons of God subject to the scourge of discipline. The meek must not be suffered to grow torpid in laziness nor the passionate to be deceived by zeal for uprightness. Let the humble hear how eternal are the things they long for, how transitory the things they despise; let the haughty hear how transitory are the things they court, how eternal the things they lose. These and many other injunctions deal with eternal types and *The Pastoral Rule* was therefore of use in any culture, but it certainly was not addressed specifically to the condition of the parson in the Middle Ages.[43]

Jacob of Voragine, who flourished in thirteenth-century Italy, pointed out that times had changed, and whereas preachers in the early days of the Church were like fishermen, who in one cast of the net drew in a multitude, today the preacher is more like a hunter, who with great labor and outcry catches but a single animal. If in fishing the catch is not large, the reason may lie with the fish. There are those who adroitly avoid the net of preaching. In other words, the problem is how to get at them at all. The fault may lie also with the fisherman:

They fish at the wrong time, they fish too deep, they fish with poor tackle or broken nets, or they fish in the wrong place. Those

[43] *PNF*, Ser. 2, XII, 40–41 *passim*.

who fish among riches, pleasures, and honor, are fishing in the wrong place. Those who look for death-bed repentances, or try to instruct others when they themselves are ignorant are fishing at the wrong time. Those who look for money or honor throw their hooks too low, and those who preach in word while their lives do not correspond, fish with broken nets.[44]

A booklet entitled *Instructions for Parish Priests* by John Myrc (Mirk), written in English somewhat earlier than 1450, is rather remarkable for enjoining preaching and then saying so little about it. The opening section is a reminder to the priest that his preaching will be in vain if his life is evil.

> For little of worth is the preaching
>   If thou be of evil living.

He must be chaste, eschew oaths and drunkenness.

> Taverns also thou must forsake
>   And merchandise thou shalt not make.
> Wrestling and shooting and such manner game
>   Thou must not use without blame.
> Hawking, hunting and dancing
>   Thou must forgo for anything
> Cutted clothes and peaked schoon [shoes]
>   Thy good fame they will for-done.
> Markets and fairs I thee forbid
>   But it be for the more need.
> In honest clothes thou must gone [go]
>   Basilard and baudrick wear thou none.
> Beard and crown thou must be shave
>   If thou would thy order save.
> Of meat and drink thou must be free
>   To poor and rich by thy degree.
> Gladly thou must thy psalter read
>   And of the day of doom have dread.
> And ever do good against evil
>   Or else thou might not live well.

[44] *Materials from the Life of Jacopo da Varagine,* ed. Ernest Cushing Richardson (New York, 1935), pp. 102–103.

> Women's service thou must forsake
>   Of evil fame lest they thee make.
> ... Thus this world thou must despise
>   And holy virtues have in vise [view]
> If thou do thus, thou shallt be dear
>   To all men that seen and hear.
> Thus thou must also preach
>   And thy parish gladly teach
> When one hath done a sin
>   Look he lie not long therein
> But anone that he him shrive
>   Be it husband, be it wife
> Lest he forget by Lenten's day
>   And out of mind it go away.[45]

The poem then goes on to discuss excommunication, baptism, the Mass, behavior in church, payment of tithes, articles of belief, and above all how to conduct confession. One might indeed infer from these instructions that although preaching was enjoined, it was either not too highly regarded or else considered too simple to require elaboration. All of which raises the question how much preaching there was in the Middle Ages. Owst, who has written two superb volumes on the subject as it bears on England, points out that Gasquet considered the office of preaching to have been adequately fulfilled, whereas Coulton held that it was shamefully neglected. Owst concludes that there could scarcely have been so much contemporary complaint of neglect if Coulton were not more nearly right. But then again H. Maynard Smith warns that we are in danger today of passing from a sentimental view of the Middle Ages seen from a sanctuary where the sun irradiates the stained-glass windows, to a realistic view of the Middle Ages as seen from a gutter on a gloomy day. At any rate the literature of complaint and denunciation demonstrates that some people were fully alive to the need of preaching in the parishes and did their best to remedy the deficiencies. On the other hand, the activity of the friars in invading the parishes in order to supplement

---

[45] John Myrc, "Instructions for Parish Priests," *Early English Text Society* (1868), pp. 1–3 (modernized).

the work of the priests, particularly at the point of preaching, is itself the proof that they were indeed remiss.

Or if not remiss, they were incompetent or impeded. Opportunities for anything beyond a grammar-school education were scant. The printing press was not available to supply cheap and plentiful tools, and congregations were inattentive and disorderly. Inasmuch as the church was the only large covered building in the community, it was used for buying and selling. Even during the services gallants ogled the ladies, women gossiped, pickpockets stole and prostitutes solicited.[46] The preacher was driven to meretricious devices for attracting attention such as suspending the eggs of ostriches in the churches.[47] When the congregation dozed, a preacher cried, "There was a king named Arthur," and as ears pricked up, he castigated the hearers for listening only when titillated by tales.[48]

A favorite device was that of playing one portion of the audience against another, all the more readily because men and women were seated separately, and the various professions were distinguishable by their costumes. Gibes at the women were especially relished. In the sermon manuals one finds several examples. For instance, there is the tale of a man who, desiring to be relieved of his wife without culpability, departed on a journey leaving with her two boxes of candy, one poisoned, the other harmless. He instructed her under no circumstances to touch the box which he and not she knew to be fatal. On his return, as he expected, she was dead. But this sort of raillery could not be overdone because the women predominated in the audience, and if the laugh were on them, their feelings must then be relieved by castigation of the men for gluttony, drunkenness, swearing, and the like.[49]

Most of the illustrations in the extant handbooks are

[46] Moorman, *op. cit.*, p. 79.

[47] Smith, *op. cit.*, p. 106.

[48] G. R. Owst, *Preaching in Medieval England* (Cambridge, England, 1926), p. 175.

[49] G. R. Owst, *Literature and Pulpit in Medieval England* (Cambridge, England, 1933), pp. 389–390.

fantastic allegorizations of the characteristics of animals applied to humankind or stories of preposterous miracles by the saints or the Virgin Mary. The moral pointed by the tales was, however, perfectly sound, and sometimes the examples were taken from real life, as in the case of a judge who received from one of two litigants an ox while his wife received from the other a cow. The verdict was in favor of the latter, and when the former complained, he was told that the cow would not suffer the ox to speak.[50] Just what this illustrates is another matter. A further example is devoid of ambiguity. In this instance a homily tells of a lady

that had two "little doggis," loved them so that she took great pleasunce in the sight and feeding of them: and she made every day dress and made for them dishes with sops of milk, and often gave them flesh. But there was once a friar that said to her, that it was not well done that the dogs were fed and made so fat, and the poor people so lean and famished for hunger. And so the lady for his saying was wroth with him, but she would not amend it. So the lady came to a bad end, as she deserved.[51]

Preaching at its worst must have been banal, at its best superb. The note of prophetic denunciation against extortion is not lacking in the sermons of those who stood face to face with the extortioners. Take this excerpt from a sermon in *The Handbook of Bromyard.* The despoiled, he says,

With boldness at the last judgment will they be able to put their plaint before God and seek justice, speaking with Christ the judge, and reciting each in turn the injury from which they specially suffered. Some of them were able to say, as the subjects of evil lords—"We have hungered. But those our lords standing over there were the cause of this, because they took us from our labours and our goods." Others—"We have hungered and died of famine, and those yonder did detain our goods that were owing to us." Others—"We have thirsted and been naked, because those standing opposite, each in his own way, so impoverished us that we were unable to buy drink and clothing." Others—"We were made infirm. Those yonder did it, who beat us and afflicted us

[50] *Ibid.*, p. 342.
[51] Margaret Deanesley, *A History of the Medieval Church* (London, 1934), p. 203.

with blows." Others—"We were without shelter. But those men were the cause of it, by driving us from our home and from our land; . . . or because they did not receive us into their own guest-houses." Others—"We were in prison. But those yonder were the cause, indicting us on false charges, and setting us in the stocks." Others—"Our bodies have not been buried in consecrated ground. Those yonder are responsible for this, by slaying us in numerous and in various places. Avenge, O Lord, our blood that has been shed."

Bromyard adds:

Without a doubt the just Judge will do justice to those clamouring thus. Terrible as is the indictment of the wronged, terrible likewise will be the fate of the oppressors. Many who were here on earth are called nobles shall blush in deepest shame at that Judgment-seat, when around their necks they shall carry, before all the world, all the sheep and oxen and the beasts of the field that they confiscated or seized and did not pay for.[52]

Raoul Ardent celebrates in his sermon the foolishness of the Cross. God, he says,

hid His divine power in human weakness, and His wisdom in foolishness. For to men it has seemed foolishness that God became man, that the Impassible suffered, that the Immortal died. Therefore, the wisdom of God, by foolishness, conquered the craft of the Devil. . . . Let us, therefore, brethren, learn from the example of our Redeemer to conquer the evil of this world, not by pride, but by humility, by patience, and gentleness. Let us learn to conquer the wisdom of this age, not by craftiness, but by the foolishness of God. For indeed, to this age it seems foolish and futile to despise the world, to reject the age, to forsake all things, to love poverty and inferior station, to desire things invisible. And yet, this foolishness conquers the wisdom of both the devil and man.

Bernard of Clairvaux declares contemplation to be vain if it produces not the fruits of holiness. He inquires:

Does it appear to you that two persons have equal and similar love towards Christ of whom the one sympathizes indeed piously with His sufferings, is moved to a lively sorrow by them, and easily

[52] Owst, *Literature and Pulpit*, pp. 300–301.

softened by the memory of all that He endured; who feeds upon the sweetness of that devotion, and is strengthened thereby to all salutary, honourable, and pious actions; while the other, being always fired by a zeal for righteousness, having everywhere an ardent passion for truth, and earnestly desiring wisdom prefers above all things sanctity of life, and a perfectly disciplined character; who is ashamed of ostentation, abhors detraction, knows not what it is to be envious, detests pride, and not only avoids, but dislikes and despises every kind of worldly glory; who vehemently hates and perseveres in destroying in himself every impurity of the heart and of the flesh; and lastly, who rejects, as if it were naturally, all that is evil, and embraces all that is good? If you compare these two types of affection, does it not appear to you that the second is plainly the superior?

Bede the Venerable chanted the ineffable joys of the celestial city:

O truly blessed Mother Church! So illuminated by the honour of Divine condescension, so adorned by the glorious blood of triumphant martyrs, so decked with the inviolate confession of snow-white virginity! Among its flowers, neither roses nor lilies are wanting. Endeavor now, beloved, each for yourselves, in each kind of honour, to obtain your own dignity—crowns, snow-white for chastity, or purple for passion.

With how joyous a breast the heavenly city receives those that return from fight! How happily she meets them that bear the trophies of the conquered enemy! With triumphant men, women also come, who rose superior both to this world and to their sex, doubling the glory of their warfare; virgins with youths, who surpassed their tender years by their virtues. Yet not they alone, but the rest of the multitude of the faithful shall also enter the palace of that eternal court, who in peaceful union have observed the heavenly commandments, and have maintained the purity of the faith.[53]

Whether the preaching of the friars was basically different from that of the parish priest is not easy to determine. Perhaps because the former were itinerants, they could be freer in denunciation, since on the morrow they

[53] Ray C. Petry, *No Uncertain Sound* (Philadelphia, 1948), pp. 132, 156–157, 108–109.

would be up and off. Because they had been impelled to
come in the first place to the parishes out of missionary zeal,
their sermons were more fervent. They were renowned for
their ability to allay feuds at home and to promote crusades
abroad. The Franciscan Salimbene gives a vivid account of
the revival called the Great Alleluia in northern Italy in
the early thirteenth century.

> Brother Benedict of Parma . . . called the Brother of the
> Horn . . . was like another John the Baptist to behold. . . . His
> beard was long and black and he had a little horn of brass, where-
> with he trumpeted; terribly did his horn bray at times, and at
> other times it would make dulcet melody. He was girt with a
> girdle of skin, his robe was black as sack-cloth of hair, and falling
> even to his feet. His rough mantle was made like a soldier's cloak,
> adorned both before and behind with a red cross, broad and long,
> from the collar to the foot, even as the cross of a priest's chasuble.
> Thus clad he went about with his horn, preaching and praising
> God in the churches and open places; and a great multitude of
> children followed him, oft-times with branches of trees and lighted
> tapers. . . . [He would cry] "Alleluia, alleluia, alleluia!" Then he
> would sound his trumpet; and afterwards he preached, adding a
> few good words in praise of God.

Brother John of Vicenza, another of the preachers in the
revival, had the reputation of being able to raise the dead.
When then the Florentines heard he was coming to their
city, they exclaimed, "For God's sake let him not come
hither for we have heard how he raiseth the dead, and we
are already so many that there is no room for us in the
city." [54]

How much such preaching accomplished is difficult to
assess. A modern author, writing about Franciscan preaching in Italy, describes the popularity of the evangelists whose
engagements had to be regulated by the popes. He tells of
the great audiences of eighty thousand assembled at one
time, of the feuds reconciled and crusades launched.[55] All of

[54] G. G. Coulton, *From Saint Francis to Dante* (London, 1906), pp. 21, 29.
[55] Karl Hefele, *Der hl. Bernhardin von Siena und die franziskanishe Wander-
predigt in Italien während des 15, Jahrhunderts* (Freiburg im Breisgau, 1912).

this failed to inaugurate the millennium but one may surmise from the very survival of the Church that preaching
did much to sting the callous, hearten the discouraged,
fortify the faint, and enrapture the questing. Witness
Chaucer's gentle picture of the faithful parish priest and
the testimony of an anonymous English poet who to his
bishop rendered this testimony:

> He preached on so fair manner
> That it was joy for to hear
> And when his sermon ended was
> The folk with mikel joy up rose
> And thanked Jesus in that place
> That gave their bishop so much grace.[56]

In a remarkable way the Church succeeded also in en-
listing the laity in her service. One recalls the dramatic
account of how the nobles assisted in the building of the
cathedral at Chartres by harnessing themselves to carts
that like beasts they might pull loads of wine, oil, grain,
stone, and timber, both for the building and the builders.
One reads how they pulled in silence save for the confession
of sins and suppliant prayer.[57] Another chronicle relates how
the villagers constructed their own parish church:

Inasmuch as the Castle Church of Clitheroe, being their parish
church, was distant twelve miles, and the ways very foul, painful,
and perilous, and the country in the winter season so extremely
and vehemently cold, that infants borne to the church are in
great peril of their lives, and the aged and impotent people and
women great with child not able to travel so far to hear the Word
of God, and the dead corpses like to remain unburied till such time
as great annoyance to grow thereby, the inhabitants about 1512,
at their proper costs, made a chapel-of-ease in the said forest.[58]

Nor should one forget the guilds which contributed this
stained-glass window or that. Nor the architects of the
cathedrals, laymen largely, who dreamed in stone and compelled the medium both to conform to its nature in carrying

---

[56] Owst, *Preaching*, p. 169 (modernized).
[57] Thompson, *op. cit.*, p. 672.
[58] Cutts, *op. cit.*, pp. 120–121.

weight and to defy its nature by seeming to soar after the illimitable. The strolling players, the jongleurs, even the troubadours, sang not only of amours but related the legends of the saints. By a tale thus told, Peter Waldo was converted.

Nor are the rulers, who so often quarreled with churchmen, to be regarded as the sons of Belial. They represented themselves as reformers, often genuinely. At any rate, they functioned as equal partners in a Christian society endowed with the two swords, temporal and spiritual, each responsible to and for the other. Henry IV in the investiture controversy complained of Gregory VII as one who had stepped out of his proper role by fomenting war. This emperor was a traditional, early medieval Christian who objected to the new trend whereby the clergy were embracing weapons or stirring up warriors to battle under the banners of the Church. Moreover, Henry's father had displaced and replaced bishops, not primarily in order to advance political interests but because the unworthy were desecrating the see of St. Peter. Lay princes and town governments felt a very real responsibility for the morals of the churchmen in the areas under their jurisdiction. The great conflict of the Middle Ages was not between Christ and Lucifer but between St. Peter and Caesar, a Christian Caesar like Constantine and Theodosius with a genuine concern for the Church. In fact one can talk about a priesthood of all believers even in the Middle Ages, in this sense that each according to his station had a share in, and a responsibility for, a Christian world order.

At the same time there was much to disappoint in so magnificent an achievement; success itself bred corruption. The very process of Christianizing Europe entailed the paganizing of the Church. Legend has it that the missionary Boniface was about to strike with his ax the sacred Oak of Thor as the pagans stood by expecting the god of thunder to smite the blasphemer with his bolt. Instead lightning struck the tree splitting it into four equal parts whereby it was the more readily cut up into planks for the construction of a church.[59] Here is a symbol of the way in which paganism was incorporated into Christianity. Sacred oaks became churches, and the gods, if they did not survive as fairies, were transmuted into saints. In the field of morals bellicosity was not subdued but only enlisted for crusades.

Even reforms recoiled. The whole history of monasticism is the story of trying to keep poor. The Benedictines at first lived by their labor but when serfs came with the soil the monks became, as we noted, administrators or scholars or contemplatives, and perchance even simply drones. The Cistercians tried to revive the original pattern insisting on manual labor and undertaking to break in wastelands. They were so successful that their produce exceeded their needs and they entered into commerce and waxed fat. Francis and Dominic tried a new way. They would labor; they would beg, but the wages and the alms should not exceed the daily needs. The orders grew. Supplying five hundred brethren by daily begging proved to be a very precarious assignment. Begging therefore was allocated to experts. And then the Church offered to take the onus of owning property and of allowing the Franciscans to enjoy the use. The Conventual Franciscans accepted this subterfuge. The Spirituals refused and the order was rent. In the end and almost of necessity the moderates came to predominate.[60]

The great Gregorian reforms achieved an astounding success and yet only at the price of dilution. The peace campaign ended in crusades and crusades fell into disrepute when the very dregs of Europe were enlisted for the Holy Land, when Christian princes were willing to sell Christian slaves to the Turks, when the financing of crusades became a racket, and when disasters made men doubt whether after all *Dieu le Veult*.[61]

The imposition of clerical celibacy in the Middle Ages met with only restricted success. Many of the clergy refused

[59] Willibald, *The Life of Saint Boniface*, G. W. Robinson, tr. (Harvard translations, 1916).
[60] Ernst Benz, *Ecclesia Spiritualis* (Stuttgart, 1934).
[61] Palmer Throop, *Criticism of the Crusade* (Amsterdam, 1940).

to abandon their wives but this gallant gesture degenerated into a system of clerical concubinage condoned and even taxed by the Church. A medieval prince-bishop frivolously remarked that as a bishop he was celibate but as a prince he was the father of a large family.[62] The very papacy was invaded by laxity, witness the license of Renaissance popes. The prevalence of irregularities is revealed in the story that word reached a concubinous vicar of an impending visit from the bishop to terminate the relationship. The vicar's lady, carrying a basket, intercepted the bishop on the way, who inquired where she was going. She replied that she was taking a present to the bishop's lady at her lying in.[63] The bishop paid his call without raising the question. On another occasion when after a revival in Wales the clergy resolved to put away their concubines, the bishop actually forbade them because he would lose the revenue derived from the tax on such infractions of the canon law.[64] The abolition of clerical concubinage was a major item on the docket alike of the Protestant and the Catholic reformers of the sixteenth century.

When so many reforms proved abortive, the very zeal by which they had been engendered kindled a new effort for the correction of abuses. Curiously the thirteenth century is not only the high period of the papal theocracy but also of sectarian movements. There were other factors to be sure than Christian reformatory zeal. The heresy which most disturbed Innocent III was a revival of ancient Gnosticism with its sharp disparagement of life in the flesh. The Cathari owed their origin to contacts with another Gnostic group, the Bogomili of Bulgaria with whom the Crusades had brought them in contact. These folk, however, thought of themselves as Christian, employed the Gospels, and outdid the most monkish of monks in their austerities.

The critique of the Cathari cannot be brushed off by branding them as heretics, when there were other sectaries

[62] J. P. Whitney, *Hildebrandine Essays* (Cambridge, England, 1932), p. 16.

[63] Moorman, *op. cit.*, p. 64.

[64] Smith, *op. cit.*, p. 46.

who made the same complaints and who very definitely were not heretics but only schismatics, and schismatics only because cast out against their will. Such was the case of Peter Waldo, a product of the rising mercantile class in southern France in the twelfth century. He sold his goods, gave to the poor, and dedicated himself to a life of poverty. All this was perfectly regular and would have received the approbation of the Church without the least cavil, but he felt an urge to acquaint himself with the Scriptures and then to inform others. He began to preach. Since he was an unauthorized layman, he was subjected to a theological examination. A contemporary records that he was asked, "Do you believe in God the Father Almighty?" "Yes," he replied. "Do you believe in Jesus Christ, His only Son, our Lord?" "Yes," was the answer. "Do you believe in the Virgin Mary, the Mother of Christ?" "Yes," he responded. There was a roar of consternation, for he should have called Mary the Mother of God. The expression "Mother of Christ" indicated that he was a Nestorian heretic. He was refused permission to preach but he defied the order and thus became the originator of a schismatic group.[65]

A generation later St. Francis was in a similar position, but this time Pope Innocent III, perhaps mindful of the blunder of his predecessor, granted a quasi permission, and the saint became the father of a great preaching order. The line between the sectaries and the new monastic preaching orders was always tenuous. St. Francis believed his Rule to have been given by the Holy Spirit and many of his followers preferred on that account the Rule to the Church. The Fraticelli became schismatics. Among the Dominicans Savonarola was a prophetic proclaimer of diluvial doom on a generation scornful of the way of salvation. In general the sermons of the sectaries were marked by a strong ethical emphasis and a recurrent note of denunciation of those churchmen whose lives identified them as anti-Christs and

---

[65] Walter Map, "De Nugis Curialium," Dist. 1, cap. xxxi, in *Anecdota Oxoniensa* (Oxford, 1914), 61.

limbs of Lucifer—so Wycliff, so Hus and their respective followers.

Against the heretics and the schismatics the Church invoked the Inquisition. Churchmen should inquire and pass sentence. Civil rulers should implement their decisions at the stake. The Inquisition was deemed a department of the cure of souls. Its object was not to burn heretics in the body but to save them by the fear of a brief temporal fire from the unquenchable flames. The whole technique of the Inquisition was designed to break down the suspect that he might confess, adjure, be reconciled, and saved. Of course, it was also important that he should supply the names of others that they too might be subject to the pressures needful for the saving of their souls.

Such methods intimidated some but served only to stimulate in others a more passionate rebellion. We are frequently disposed to accept unqualified their strictures on that Church which occasioned their criticism and which sought by such means to stifle their complaints. We must remember, however, that the Church cannot have been devoid of vitality when she was able to bear such sons. They might be her undoing. They were at the same time the witness to her residual integrity.

A veritable symbol of the late Middle Ages is Dante Alighieri who even better than the great Aquinas conveyed the mood of a life lived *sub specie aeternitatis*. Dante was a layman. Likewise he was an imperialist and not a papalist, exiled from Florence because he favored the emperor rather than the pope. In his political theory he desired to restrict the Church severely to the spiritual sphere. Highly versed in the universal language of the Church, the Latin tongue, nevertheless he composed the great poem of medieval faith in the language of the common folk. The *Divina Commedia* is written in the Italian vernacular. He desired the continuance of the great Christian society under the two luminaries, the Church and State, yet he was as critical of particular popes as were the prophetic reformers. In the tradition of the Spiritual Franciscans he portrayed Christ upon the cross, deserted by all save *La Donna Poverta*.

II. Continuities and Changes from
Medieval to Renaissance Christianity

5 Christian Views of Human Destiny

Christians commonly have speculated less on the fate of mankind than on the future of the Church, whether on earth or in heaven. Nevertheless the Church is catholic and does have a concern for the destiny of mankind.

Christian thinking on the subject is commonly divided by historians into three periods: the first from Christ to Augustine, the second from Augustine to Joachim of Fiore, and the third from Joachim until now. The first might be characterized as the period of the Second Coming; the next as that of the New Jerusalem; and the third as that of the Holy Ghost. During the first, we are told, the expectation of the speedy return of Christ remained vivid; during the second, this hope having waned, attention was centered in part on the realization of the Kingdom through the Church on earth and even more on the New Jerusalem beyond this vale of tears. The Church, however, failed so miserably that the expectation of a divine incursion was revived by Joachim of Fiore, who looked to see the institutional church superseded by the Church of the Spirit. This hope, though constantly disappointed, was constantly renewed, and the outcome was that the organized church was continually plagued by a succession of millenarian sects.

This periodization of Christian eschatological thinking may be regarded as sufficiently valid to provide a scheme for

First published in *Religion in Life* (Winter 1941–1942); copyright 1941 by Whitmore & Stone.

our discussion. Nevertheless quite varied types have been
present side by side in all times, nor do the three epochs
exhaust the periods. A fourth might be added to cover in
modern times the idea of progress which is in a measure a
secularization of the Christian hope.

The first period from Christ to Augustine exhibits five
varieties which may be designated by the captions: (1) the
Kingdom of God; (2) the dated Second Coming; (3) eternal
life; (4) progress of the Word; (5) the peace of heaven.

Of these the first is the ideal of Jesus and of Paul. The
Master and the apostle may be grouped together because for
essential purposes the differences in their eschatological
thinking are slight. Both talked of the Kingdom of God and
Paul in addition of the return of Christ. The basic features
were the same. In neither was the time element crucial. The
primary point was that God reigns and holds in check the
spiritual adversaries in the heavenly places, the demons and
world rulers of this darkness. The power of God had already
been made manifest for Jesus by the expulsion of demons and
for Paul through the resurrection of Christ from the dead
with consequent triumph over darkness, death and the
devil. As a result a new order had already begun. The dispensation of Adam was at an end. His fall had corrupted
the image of God in man, had introduced sin and death, and
according to Jesus had necessitated the introduction of the
law of Moses because of the hardness of men's hearts. But
now in the Pauline scheme the law of Moses was abrogated
because the law of the members warring against the law of
the spirit was broken. In consequence perfection became, if
not a reality, at least a definite goal of the Christian community, which should "become blameless and harmless,
children of God without blemish in the midst of a crooked
and perverse generation." [1]

While the time element was not crucial, it was not
obliterated. Paul periodized the drama of redemption in
three stages: the first, from Adam or from Moses to Christ;
the second, beginning with the incarnation, and the third,

[1] Phil. 2:15.

to be ushered in by the second advent. The last phase would differ from the preceding chiefly in extent and completeness. Then the last enemy would be subjugated and God would be all in all.[2] Mankind as a whole would be included as well as all those who had previously fallen asleep.[3]

The effect of this expectation of a second and more comprehensive coming of Christ was not to declare a moratorium on the ethic of the Kingdom until the entire framework should be changed and all social relationships altered. "The night is far spent, the day is at hand." The day, be it observed, has not yet dawned. What then? Shall we wait for the day? Not so, but let us even now "walk becomingly *as in the day*." [4] The total effect of the eschatology of the Kingdom was thus to heighten effort and to stir the Christian community to unparalleled endeavor, because the victory was already won and remained only to be more fully manifested.

With regard to human institutions, however, this eschatology did work in a conservative direction. Because the time was short, no drastic change should be made in social relations. The slave should not seek to be free, the married to be unmarried, nor the unmarried to be married. Government was accepted or at least tolerated. It should be obeyed and supported. All of this means that the higher ethic of the Christian society was to be practiced within the existing social scheme. There should be no withdrawals from society and no cessation of ordinary daily occupations. Utilization in a spirit of detachment was the attitude applicable to property, the State and the family, and that was largely so because the hour of the last act in the drama of redemption was unknown and in any case not quite imminent, since first must come the great tribulation.

The second type of eschatology, that of the dated Second Coming, shifts the center and breaks down the restraints by the apparently trivial difference that the time of the end is

[2] I Cor. 15:26.
[3] I Thess. 4.
[4] Rom. 13:12-13.

supposed to be immediate and known. In consequence
marriages may be dissolved and property given away, the
State repudiated and the organized church dissolved. Bands
of enthusiasts gather together at an appointed time and
commonly also at a designated place, whether it be Pepuza
for the Montanists, Strasbourg for the Melchiorites, or
Muenster for the Anabaptists.

The third type, that of eternal life, eschews all setting
of dates, and for that matter all historical chronology. The
only chronology that matters is that of the stages of the
interior life. These are not infrequently described as three,
namely, purgation, illumination and unification. The end of
the road is to be at one with God; deification for the believer
and entrance into life eternal. The idea "eternal" is conceived not so much in temporal as in qualitative terms.
Eternal life is possible both now as well as hereafter. Here
we have the familiar line of thought of the fourth Gospel,
Irenaeus, Athanasius, John of Damascus, and in fact of all
the eastern and many of the western mystics. The social
consequences of this type of eschatology are difficult to
predict. A measure of withdrawal from the hurly-burly and
ascetic discipline are to be expected, but union with God is
not incompatible with the performance of daily tasks, and
the inner harmony of the human and divine may be more
readily manifested by the glow of the countenance than by
the visibility of the ribs.

The fourth type, that of the progress of the Word,
shows a process taking place within the framework of society
comparable to the inner development of the one who travels
the mystic way. In Jewish language mankind is envisaged
as gradually accepting the yoke of the Kingdom. In Stoic
language the *logos* subdues the world. Origen is the representative of this view in Christianized form. "Our belief,"
he declares, "is that the Word shall prevail over the entire
rational creation, and change every soul into His own perfection; in which state every one, by the mere exercise of his
power, will choose what he desires, and obtain what he
chooses. For although, in the diseases and wounds of the

body, there are some which no medical skill can cure, we hold that in the mind there is no evil so strong that it may not be overcome by the Supreme Word and God. For stronger than all the evils in the soul is the Word, and the healing power that dwells in Him; and this healing He applies, according to the will of God, to every man. The consummation of all things is the destruction of evil, although as to the question whether it shall be so destroyed that it can never anywhere arise again, it is beyond our present purpose to say." [5]

This optimism with regard to the power of the Word conditions Origen's whole view of society. Remember, however, that if he is using Stoic terminology the Word in question is not simply the Stoic *logos*, but the spirit of that Jesus who had already by His winsomeness achieved unparalleled victories. [6] Here is the key to the pacifism of Origen. Not that he expected mere nonresistance of itself to overcome enemies. Rather he looked to the power of Christ, already the greatest cohesive force in the Roman Empire, to subdue also the rude souls of the barbarians, so that the picture drawn by Celsus of a Christian nonresistant Rome overrun by hordes of non-Christian barbarians would no longer have any point. [7]

The fifth type is characteristic of those who despair of the Kingdom on earth and entertain hope only for heaven. Of such was Augustine. His career is marked by waning confidence in man and society. Once he believed that the precepts of the Sermon on the Mount could be fulfilled perfectly as they had been by the apostles. [8] In the *Retractions* the statement is qualified to mean that "the precepts can be fulfilled, as we believe them to have been fulfilled by the apostles, only in the sense of human perfection, that perfection which is possible in this life. The words, 'as we believe them to have been fulfilled by the apostles,' must be

[5] c. Cels. VIII, 72.
[6] c. Cels. I, 29.
[7] c. Cels. VIII, 72.
[8] *PL*, XXXIV, 1235.

understood as that measure of perfection of which this life
is capable, not of that perfection which will be realized we
hope in that most perfect peace of which it is said, 'O death,
where is thy sting?' " [9]

With the vanishing of the ideal of individual perfection
passed also the dream of peace on earth. "Such security is
never given to a nation that it should not dread invasions
hostile to this life." [10] There will ever be conflict with the
pagan, the heretic, the bad Catholic, and even with the
brother in the same household. "Often a man grown weary
says to himself: 'Why should I endure so many who return
evil for good? I want to help them. They are bent on destruction. Why should I eat out my life in contention? I
have no peace. I make enemies of those who should be
friends if they would listen to counsel. Why go on forever?
I will return to myself. I will be with myself. I will call upon
God.' Return, then, to thyself and thou shalt find strife.
'What strife shall I find?' you inquire. 'That the flesh lusteth
against the spirit and the spirit against the flesh.' " [11]

These words of Augustine mark the end of an era. The
hope of the early Christian community is gone. Coincidently
the picture of the whole historical drama is altered into one
eternal conflict on earth and rest only in heaven. The way
for this development already had been prepared in part by
the postponement of the eschatological hope. Lactantius advanced the date 200 years; Hippolytus 300. Still more significant was the interpretation of history of the Donatist
Tychonius, who regarded the whole of history as a poised
conflict between the *civitas diaboli* and the *civitas Dei*. He
was himself a dated eschatologist and expected the sudden
overturning of the kingdom of the devil 300 years after the
death of Christ—that is, in the year 381. Augustine had out-
lived this date and would set no other. He did, indeed, expect an ultimate denouement, but it should come at the
end of a thousand years, and a thousand years is merely a

[9] I, 19, I.
[10] *Civ. Dei*, XVII, 13.
[11] *PL*, XXXV, 1656.

round number to denominate the length, whatever it be, of life on earth. The course of that life will be marked in the future as in the past by the conflict of the two powers.

Yet this view does not leave one utterly without hope for earth or fear for heaven. On earth something can be achieved, a relative peace and a relative justice. Even the State can clear itself of the charge of *magnum latrocinium* through justice, and justice is possible in and only in a Christian society which, practically speaking, means under the guidance of the Church. In consequence she becomes the embodiment of the Kingdom insofar as any kingdom can be realized on earth. Perfect achievement is granted only in heaven, and even there only to the elect. The reprobate will be tormented in hell, and hell is nothing other than the perpetuation of unresolved conflict. Eschatology, then, by Augustine is shifted in part to the Church on earth, in larger part to Zion, city of our God.

The other two great periods of Christian eschatology call for less discussion because the types recur in varying degrees and with but slight modifications.

The early Middle Ages took over the elements of the Augustinian scheme but in a very different spirit. The northern barbarians suffered from no paralysis of the *senescens saeculum,* no qualms arising from the Sermon on the Mount, and no distaste for society driving them to monasticism. What they took from Augustine was the picture of the Church as the Kingdom of Christ, useful not merely for salvation in heaven, but for the achievement of a cultural unity on earth. Monasticism itself, when eventually adopted by the invaders, became not so much a retreat as an outpost for the winning and holding of new territory. Those who were thus absorbed in the discharge of a colossal task on earth desired no interventions from heaven and were altogether too busy to indulge in much speculation with regard to the end of history. The tendency was rather to portray the institutionalized Church as the earthly counterpart of the Trinity or as the terrestrial image of the celestial hierarchies.

At the same time heaven, hell and the judgment played a conspicuous part in popular imagination. The motive was not so much despair of earthly achievement as fear of what would happen when the mortal span was ended. The lustiest of warriors might well recoil from the prospect of revolving over a brisk fire on a spit in perpetual motion. More sensitive spirits would voice the *contemptus mundi*, without, however, relaxing their mundane efforts and without predicting a speedy terminus to Christian society on earth. Here Saint Bernard may be regarded as a type. He loved the retirement of Clairvaux and dreamed, if he did not sing, of Jerusalem the Golden. Yet no one was more active in the affairs of his day.

All of this is not to say that Chiliasm was defunct. Although the theologians discouraged precise calculations, whether around the year 1000 or otherwise, the "tenacity of popular superstition" was unbroken in its appeal to the mob mind, and one of the reasons for the Crusade of 1065 was the belief that the judgment day would fall on Easter of that year because the date would be March 27, to which medieval calendars assigned the historical resurrection.

The revival of dated eschatology comes in the twelfth century with Joachim of Fiore and is a part of a much larger phenomenon of the coincident solidification and disruption of medieval Christendom. Curiously enough, the late twelfth and the early thirteenth centuries were marked by the highest development of papal power, the swarming of heretical sects and the revival of dated eschatology. The mutual relations of a dominant papacy, divisive sectarianism and revolutionary eschatology are not easy to disentangle. The ferment apparently began through the reformatory efforts of a militant pope, Gregory VII, who in his zeal to eradicate the marriage of the clergy, verged on the Donatist moralistic theory of the Church. The pope came perilously close to undercutting the sacramental view of the Church when he called upon the laity to refuse to take the sacrament at the hands of the married clergy. He did not declare distinctly that the sacrament would be invalid in the hands of a married priest. That would have been Donatism unabashed. What he demanded was a strike of the laity comparable to the interdict which is a strike of the clergy. Both weapons were dangerous. The strike of the clergy induced a mysticism independent of external rites. The strike of the laity easily suggested to the less discriminating the moralistic theory of the Church, and very soon a host of unquenchable spirits set about reform without tarrying for or regarding any.

When the Church did tarry, the eschatological hope was revived and Joachim was its great proclaimer. History for him was divided into three periods, each of which was subdivided into seven. His own day was assigned to the last phase of the second period. The third therefore was about to dawn. From the numbers of Revelation the date was set in the year 1260, which was still sixty years in advance of the prediction. In the interim a great leader should emerge to usher in the new age of the Spirit. By such predictions Joachim created a powerful ferment. He made himself few identifications save to hint that the Rome which is Babylon is the Roman Church. She would, however, give way gracefully to her successor without schism or revolution. The ideas of Joachim were made much more concrete and subversive when adopted by the Spiritual Franciscans, who identified not only the papacy with Babylon, but Francis of Assisi with the new leader and Frederick II with Anti-Christ. Similar ideas accompanied the Hussite movement.

The Protestant Reformation in a fashion repeated the pattern of the late Middle Ages, for the religious revolution did not disintegrate the Christian society of the Middle Ages, but divided it rather into a number of replicas from which the sects split off. The essential features of the medieval church were carried over into the established Protestant groups, such as the Lutheran, Anglican and even the Calvinist. From these broke away the sects like the Anabaptists and the later Independents. The Reformation as a whole was more eschatologically minded than had been the Church of the Middle Ages, but there was a difference between the Protestantism of the right and of the left. The line of demarcation was at the point of setting dates. This Luther, Zwingli and Calvin refused to do, whereas the Melchiorites and Muensterites chose the hour and selected the place for the New Jerusalem. In consequence the nondated eschatologists settled down to tasks on earth. Particularly the Reformed churches were hopeful and active in this endeavor. But the greater their zeal the keener their impatience at delay and the greater their readiness then to steady their faith by the hope of a speedy divine intervention. When the majority of the group discountenanced such "extravagances" a minority would secede. Protestantism has thus exhibited a succession of millenarian sects from the Anabaptists on the continent in the sixteenth century to the later Fifth Monarchy Men and Irvingites in England, the Labadists in France, the Ellerites in Germany, and the Millerites and Russelites in America.

In the meantime alongside of various religious eschatologies came to be ranged a somewhat secularized version, the idea of Progress. Its roots were complex and not entirely secular. Basic was the ancient ideal of Origen of the progress of the Word. The Origenistic concept was revived by the Neoplatonists of the Florentine Academy in the Renaissance, who pinned their faith to enlightenment. Erasmus was their disciple and the line runs from him to the eighteenth century. Here is one of the most important ingredients of the idea of progress, later to be re-enforced in the secular area by the literary comparison between the ancients and the moderns, by a special twist given to the doctrine of organic evolution and by the spectacle of technological advance. Faith in progress supplanted for liberal Protestantism the chiliastic hope. The notion of progress itself developed varieties, some more humanist, some more theistic.

A distinctly more secular form of eschatology has persisted alongside of the religious varieties from pre-Christian times until now. This is an eschatology which focuses hope upon the return of some political figure: in Judaism on the

Davidic Messiah, in ancient paganism on the deified Alexander. The theme was applied to the Roman imperial house in the fourth Eclogue of Virgil. The late Middle Ages revived the concept as applied to Frederick Barbarossa or Kaiser Sigismund. Re-enforcement was often found in astrology. Modern Fascism is shot through with this imperial mysticism. The only difference is that the Dux is already here, rather than on the way, but the realization of the leader's mission lies in the future so that this, too, is an eschatology.

A new and very important turn was given to all hopes for the possibilities of history by the discovery of America. The first form of the new hope was primitivistic, inspired by the discovery of a race of men unpolluted through the corruption of a depraved culture. Mexico was hailed as the God-given land for the erection of More's Utopia. The Indian, however, soon came to be regarded not as a *bon sauvage*, but as a "dirty dog." But America still offered a thrilling opportunity for selected communities from the Old World to set up in an unhampered environment holy commonwealths amid the roses of Sharon.

The plight of those of us today who were reared in Protestant Modernism is that we find ourselves thrown back into very much the situation of Augustine. The course of events has shattered the more external hopes. There is no virgin soil. There are no new and unpolluted men. The enlightenment of the Divine Word has not yet exorcised the demons of political realism. At the same time we are still too sophisticated to turn back to the crude device of a dated second coming, and the hope of immortality is not sufficiently concrete to offer any perfect consolation. In this respect we are in an even worse state than Augustine. Yet chastened and sober as we are we must nonetheless set about gathering up the valid elements from the ancient hopes. What will happen no one can predict. For the moment we can only testify to our faith in the Church as the new Eden of God, in the Word as the enlightener of man, and in God who in the convulsions of history abases the mighty and exalts them of low estate.

Selected Bibliography

BENZ, ERNST, *Ecclesia spiritualis Kirchenidee und Geschichtsphilisophie der Fran-ziskanischen Reformation*, Stuttgart, 1934.

CASE, SHIRLEY J., *The Millenial Hope*, Chicago, 1918.

Chiliasmus, Article in *Realencyclopedie*.

DEIJLL, WILLEM S. C., *Het Chiliasme ter Tijde der Hervorming*, Amsterdam, 1872.

DEMPF, ALOIS, *Sacrum Imperium*, Munich 1929.

FRICK, ROBERT, "Die Geschichte des Reich-Gottes-Gedankens in der alten Kirche bis zu Origenes und Augustin," *Beihefte z. Zt. f. d. neutestamentliche Wissenschaft* VI (1928).

FROMME, LEROY E., *The Prophetic Faith of Our Fathers*, 4 vols., Washington, D. C., 1946–1954.

GARIN, EUGENIE, "La 'dignitas hominis' e la letterature Patristica," *La Rinascita* I, 4 (1938).

JORANSON, EINAR, "The German Pilgrimage of 1064–1065" in *The Crusades . . . essays presented to Dana C. Munro*, New York, 1928.

KAMLAH, WILHELM, *Apocalypse und Geschichtstheologie*, Berlin, 1935.

KAMPERS, F., *Vom Werdegange der abendländischen Kaisermystik*, Leipzig, 1924. *Alexander der Grosse und die Idee des Weltimperiums* in *Prophetie und Saga,* Frieburg i. B., 1901.

KÖSTLIN, J., "Ein Beitrag zur Eschatologie der Reformateren." *Theol. Stud. u. Krit.* LI (1878).

VAN SCHELVEN, A. A., *Die Idee van den Vooruitgang*, Kampen, 1927.

WADSTEIN, ERNST, *Die eschatologische Ideengruppe: Antichrist—Weltsabbat—Welt-ende und Weltgericht*, Leipzig, 1896.

6 Religious Liberty and the
Parable of the Tares

The parable of the tares is the proof passage for religious liberty. *Sinite utraque crescere*[1] is the counterpart of *compelle intrare*.[2] The apostles of liberty repeat the text with monotonous iteration, although there is an occasional variety in the emphasis. Some stress the rationalistic argument: we do not know enough to separate the tares from the wheat. Others emphasize the eschatological approach: we can afford to be patient because God will burn the tares at the harvest. Others again make a legalistic appeal: Christ has commanded us to leave the tares alone. More interesting are the expedients employed by the persecutors to evade the liberal implications of the parable. The simplest device is to identify the tares not with the heretics, but with the moral offenders within the church. Another subterfuge is to identify the overly zealous servants with the ministers, not with the magistrates, who are not to be hampered by the parable.

We begin with the use of the passage in the early centuries. At once we discover that the interpretation varies in accord with the conception of the church. Those who compare

First published under the title of "The Parable of the Tares as the Proof Text for Religious Liberty to the End of the Sixteenth Century," in *Church History*, I, 2 (1932).

[1] Matt. 13:30.
[2] Luke 14:23.

the church to the ark of Noah, outside of which there is no salvation, are loath to expel the moral offender—were there not unclean beasts in the ark?—but eager to force in the heretic, who is surely lost if he remain without. On the other hand those who regard the church as a community of the saints naturally expel the moral offender, who sullies the sanctity of the New Jerusalem, whereas the heretic is by no means to be forced in, lest an unworthy element be introduced. The one identifies the tares with the delinquent within, the other with the heretic without.

In the age of persecution, almost of necessity, the parable was applied to the moral offender. The church was not yet in a position to coerce the heretic. Ecclesiastical discipline was the only available weapon. Under these circumstances the parable became the favorite resort of those who would err on the side of mercy. The first to appeal to the passage with this intent was Callistus, the bishop of Rome from 217 to 222 A.D. Before his time those guilty of adultery and fornication could never be reconciled with the church on earth. He it was who first let down the bars and ventured to remit these offenses to those who had done suitable penance. In defense of his action he appealed to three Biblical passages. The first was the commission to Peter, "And I will give unto thee the keys of the kingdom of heaven, and whatsoever thou shalt bind on earth shall be bound in heaven, and whatsoever thou shalt loose on earth shall be loosed in heaven." [3] The second was Noah's ark which "was a symbol of the church, for in it were dogs, wolves, ravens and everything clean and unclean; and so he declared it must also be in the church." And the third was our passage, "Let the tares grow together with the wheat." [4]

---

[3] Matt. 16:19.

[4] Tertullian, who does not mention Callistus by name, is our authority for the appeal to Mt. 16, 19. De Pudicitia 21, *CSEL* XX¹, 269, *ANF* IV, 99. Hippolytus is the authority for the use of Noah's ark and the parable of the tares. *Refutatio Omnium Haeresium* IX, 12, *PG* XVI, pt. 3, 3386. *Die griechischen christlichen Schriftsteller*. Hippolytus, Bd. 3 Elenchos IX, 12, 20–23, pp. 249–250.

λέγων πᾶσιν ὑπ᾽ αὐτοῦ ἀφίεσθαι ἁμαρτίας. . . . ᾽Αλλὰ καὶ παραβολὴν τῶν ζιζανίων πρὸς τοῦτο ἔφη λέγεσθαι. ῎Αφετε τὰ ζιζάνια συναύξειν τῷ σίτῳ, τουτέστιν ἐν τῇ ἐκκλησίᾳ τοὺς ἁμαρτάνοντας. ᾽Αλλὰ Καὶ τὴν κιβωτὸν τοῦ Νῶε

In all of the succeeding controversies over ecclesiastical discipline, and particularly as to the treatment of those who had lapsed in persecution, the liberal party invariably made appeal to the parable of the tares. A new corollary was drawn from the command to leave them alone, namely that because of their presence in the church the wheat ought not to separate itself and form a schismatic communion. This is the point of Cyprian, who rejoiced that the Roman confessors had returned to the unity of the church, "for even though tares appear in the church our faith and charity ought not thereby to be impeded, so that on account of the presence of the tares we withdraw from the church. Our business is to see to it that we are wheat." [5] This use of the passage is, of course, precisely what we should expect from one who said that he who is without the church has no greater hope of escape than did he who was without the ark of Noah.[6]

Jerome took exactly the same position against the purist, Lucifer of Cagliari, who would not admit to ecclesiastical office those who had ever been tainted with the Arian heresy. Jerome told him that Noah's ark is a type of the church containing doves, lions, stags, worms, and serpents. "While the householder slept an enemy sowed tares and when the servants proposed to root them out the Lord forbade them, reserving to himself the separation of the chaff from the grain. . . . No one can take to himself the prerogative of Christ and judge men before the day of judgment. If the church is purified now what will be left for the Lord?" [7] Note the eschatological emphasis.

εἰς ὁμοίωμα ἐκκλησίας ἔφη γεγονέναι, ἐν ᾗ καὶ κύνες Καὶ λύχοι καὶ Κόρακες καί, πάντα τὰ Καθαρὰ Καὶ ἀκάθαρτα, οὕτω φάσκων δεῖν εἶναι ἐν ἐκκλησίᾳ ὁμοίως. These passages are collected and discussed by James T. Shotwell and Louise Ropes Loomis, *The See of Peter* (New York, 1927) and by Oscar D. Watkins, *A History of Penance* (London and New York, 1920), who gives also the Greek text.

[5] *Ep.* 51 in *PL*, 4, 352; *Ep.* 50 in *ANF* V, 327. *Ep.* 54, 3 in *CSEL* III², 622. Nam, etsi videntur in Ecclesia esse zizania, non tamen impediri debet aut fides aut charitas nostra, ut quoniam zizania esse in Ecclesia cernimus ipsi, de Ecclesia recedamus. Nobis tantum modo laborandum est ut frumentum esse possimus.

[6] *De Unitate Eccl.* VI, *CSEL* III¹, 214. *PL* 4, 519; *ANF* V, 423.

[7] *Dialogus Adversus Luciferianos* 22, *PL* 23, 177, *PNF*, Ser. 2, VI, 331–332.

Augustine faced the same problem again with the Donatists who would have no fellowship with those who had betrayed the Scriptures in the persecution of Diocletian, nor with their descendants to the third and fourth generation. The Donatists took the position that they were the wheat and could have nothing to do with the church in Africa which was composed wholly of tares. Augustine would admit neither assertion. He is very scornful of the Donatist claim to be wheat. "Just look at the hordes of Circumcellions, look at the convivial drunkards, look at the lewd lechers. Do you call these wheat?" [8] "You are nothing but tares, for if you were wheat you would tolerate the tares among you." [9] On the other hand the Catholic church in Africa is not wholly composed of tares. The wheat has been unfairly blamed for offenses of which it is innocent.[10] And granted that the church of Africa be so corrupt, Africa is not the field, which is rather the world. The Donatists, in separating themselves from the tares in Africa, have cut themselves off from the wheat elsewhere, which was both innocent and ignorant of what had taken place in Africa. In any case the harvest is not now and the Circumcellions are not the reapers.[11] The moral of course is that there should be no secession because of the tares. "The good fish should not leave the net through the holes made by the bad, the sheep should not forsake the pasture of unity because of the goats, the wheat should not abandon the threshing floor because of the chaff, which is either now being dispersed . . . or will be separated at the final winnowing." [12] Here we have again the eschatological emphasis. Patience is to be the more readily practiced because of the hope of an ultimate

---

[8] *Contra Ep. Parmeniani* III, 3, 18, *CSEL* 51, 122.

[9] *Ep.* 76, *CSEL* 34, 326. 12–13, *PNF*[1] I, 343. Fingitis vos ante tempus messis fugere permixta zizania, quia vos estis sola zizania. Nam si frumentum essetis, permixta zizania toleraretis.

[10] *Ep.* 43, *CSEL* 34, 103. 14–15. *PNF*[1] 1, 283.

[11] *Ep.* 53, III, 6, *CSEL* 34, 156, 21. *PNF*[1] 1, 299; *Ep.* 76, 2 and 3, *CSEL* 34, 326–327. *PNF*[1] 1, 343–344; *Ep.* 93, 15 and 32, *CSEL* 34, 459 and 477. 18. *PNF*[1] 387 and 394. *Contra litteras Petiliani* II, LXXVIII, 174, *CSEL* 52, 108. *PNF*[1] IV, 570.

[12] *Contra litteras Petiliani* III, II, 3, *CSEL* 52, 164, *PNF*[1] IV, 597.

separation. "You are with the tares in the field. You will not be in the barn." [13]

Augustine would not leave the impression, however, that he is entirely averse to ecclesiastical discipline provided the necessary conditions are present. These may be discovered from a close reading of the parable of the tares. "When the Lord said, . . . 'Let both grow until the harvest,' he gave the reason saying, 'lest when you gather up the tares you root out the wheat at the same time,' by which he shows sufficiently that where there is no fear of this and the wheat is firmly established, that is when the offense is public and universally condemned, bereft of defenders or at least of any who would secede, then the severity of discipline must not sleep." [14] This severity must by no means be suffered to reach the point of causing a schism. We should correct with mercy what we can, and bear with patience what we cannot. What we are unable to remove from our midst let us remove from our hearts. [15]

Augustine throughout moves entirely along conservative lines. By his time the coercion of heretics had become an acute issue with which no one was more concerned than he. Yet in his tolerant period he never, to my knowledge, appealed to the parable of the tares as against the coercion of heretics, nor in his later period did he feel the necessity of explaining away the liberal implications. In letter 93 in which he justifies coercion and introduces the ominous, *compelle intrare*, even here he does not feel that *sinite utraque crescere* is an embarrassment. In this very epistle he continues to use the passage as did Callistus against the Mon-

[13] *PL* 38 (Aug. 5, 1) Serm. LXXIII, pp. 470–471; Serm. XXIII, *PNF*[1] VI, 334.

[14] *Contra Ep. Parmeniani*, III, 2, 13, *CSEL* 51, 115. 4–13. nam et ipse dominus, cum seruis uolentibus zizania colligere dixit: sinite utraque crescere usque ad messem, praemisit causam dicens: ne forte, cum uultis colligere zizania eradicetis simul et triticum, ubi satis ostendit [ut], cum metus iste non subest, sed omnino de frumentorum stabilitate certa securitas manet, id est quando ita cuiusquam crimen notum est et omnibus execrabile apparet, ut uel nullos prorsus uel non tales habeat defensores. per quos possit schisma contingere, non dormiat seueritas disciplinae. . . .

[15] *Ibid.* III, 2, 14–15, *CSEL* 51, 116–118.

tanists, Cyprian against the Novationists, and Jerome against the Luciferians.[16]

In the meantime the way was being paved for another interpretation. Tertullian called Praxeas a tare.[17] The point is not that he should be let alone, but that he will be rooted up sooner or later. Yet it is significant that the parable should be applied to a heretic by a man who thought of the church as a community of the saints, and who violently opposed the lenient policy of Callistus toward the moral delinquent. If Tertullian here draws no inferences for religious liberty he could state the case clearly enough elsewhere, as when he said, "It is not in the nature of religion to coerce religion which must be adopted freely and not by force." [18]

Origen similarly identified the tares with "corrupt doctrines adhering to the soul." [19] He too draws no liberal inferences here, but elsewhere in reply to the jibe of Celsus that the Christians hate one another with a perfect hatred, Origen answers that those who hold different opinions and will not be convinced, after a first and second admonition, are indeed to be rejected,[20] but the corrupters of Christianity are not to be regarded with hatred.[21]

We have already noticed that Jerome, in combatting the Luciferians, applied the parable to the moral delinquent, but in another passage he extended the application to all offenses, including heresy. We thus see that these interpretations are not mutually exclusive. It is quite possible to be lenient toward the sinner and toward the heretic, or to be severe toward both, or again to discriminate. Jerome, in spite of his scurrilous polemic, pleaded for patience toward

[16] Ep. 93, IX, 33 and X, 36, CSEL 34, 479 and 481, PNF¹ I, 394 and 395. Cf. De Moribus eccl. Cath. XXXIV, 76, PL 32 (Aug. 1) 1342, PNF¹ IV, 62. Contra Faustum Manichaeum XIII, 16, CSEL 35, 397, PNF¹ IV, 205.

[17] Adversus Praxean 1, CSEL 47, 228, ANF III, 598.

[18] Ad Scapulam 2, PL 1, 699, ANF III, 105. Sed nec religionis est cogere religionem, quae sponte suscipi debeat, non vi.

[19] Τὰ προσπεφυκότα τῇ ψυχῇ φαῦλα δόγματα. PG 13, Comment. in Mt. X, 840.

[20] Tit. 3:10.

[21] c. Cels. V, LXIII, Die griechischen christlichen Schriftsteller Origenes, Bd. 2, p. 67, ANF IV, 571.

the heretic, "since he who is to-day depraved by noxious doctrine tomorrow may turn and begin to defend the truth." A loophole is left open however. We are enjoined to reserve judgment "where the case is dubious." What if we think it clear? In any case we are consoled that some heretics and hypocrites are sure of hell in the end.[22]

Chrysostom squarely identified the tares with the heretics. The Master commanded that they be let alone lest the wheat be rooted out as well:

> This he said forbidding wars and bloodshed and slaughter to arise. We ought not to put a heretic to death because thereby we should let loose a truceless war upon the world. Our Lord restrains the servants by these two reasons, first, lest the wheat be hurt and secondly that the tares will be punished eventually if incurable. If then you wish to punish them without hurt to the wheat wait until the proper time. And what is the meaning of this, "Lest you root out the wheat with them?" Either he means that if you resort to arms and slay the heretics many of the saints also will necessarily be slain with them, or else he means that in all probability many of the tares may change and become wheat. . . . He does not therefore forbid us to restrain heretics, to stop their mouths, to take away their freedom of speech, to break up their assemblies and societies, he forbids us merely to kill and slay.[23]

[22] Comment. in Evang. Matth. II, XIII, *PL* 26, 93–94.
   Omnia scandala referuntur ad zizania. . . . inimicus homo superseminet zizania, hoc est, haereticorum dogmata. Quod autem dicitur; Ne forte colligentes zizania, eradicetis simul et frumentum, datur locus poenitentiae, et monemur ne cito amputemus fratrem: quia fieri potest, ut ille qui hodie noxio depravatus est dogmate, cras resipiscat et defendere incipiat veritatem. . . . Praemonet ergo Dominus, ne ubi quid ambiguum est, cito sententiam proferamus; . . . manifestum est haereticos quosque et hypocritas fidei gehennae ignibus concremandos.

[23] In Matthaeum Homil. *PG* 58, 477–478, *PNF*[1] (Chrysostom) X, 288–289.
   Τοῦτο δὲ ἔλεγε, κωλύων τοὺς πολέμους γίνεσθαι καὶ αἵματα καὶ σφαγάς. Οὐ γὰρ δεῖ ἀναιρεῖν αἱρετικόν· ἐπεὶ πόλεμος ἄσπονδος ἔμελλεν εἰς τὴν οἰκουμένην εἰσάγεσθαι. Δύο τοίνυν τούτους αὐτοὺς κατέχει τοῖς λογισμοῖς· ἑνὶ μέν, τῷ μὴ τὸν σῖτον βλαβῆναι· ἑτέρῳ δέ, τῷ καταλήψεσθαι τὴν κόλασιν πάντως αὐτοὺς ανιάτως νοσοῦντας. Ὥστε εἰ βούλει καὶ κολασθῆναι αὐτοὺς, καὶ χωρὶς τῆς τοῦ σίτου βλάβης, ἀνάμεινον τὸν προσήκοντα καιρόν. Τί δέ ἐστι, Μὴ ἐκριζώσητε ἅμα αὐτοῖς τὸν σῖτον; Ἢ τοῦτό φησιν, ὅτι Εἰ μέλλοιτε κινεῖν ὅπλα καὶ κατασφάττειν τοὺς αἱρετικούς, ἀνάγκη πολλοὺς καὶ τῶν ἁγίων συγκαταβάλλεσθαι. ἢ ὅτι ἀπ᾽ αὐτῶν τῶν ζιζανίων πολλοὺς εἰκὸς μεταβαλέσθαι καὶ γενέσθαι σῖτον . . . Οὐ τοίνυν κατέχειν αἱρετικοὺς καὶ ἐπιστομίζειν, καὶ ἐκκόπτειν αὐτῶν τὴν παρρησίαν, καὶ τὰς συνόδους καὶ τὰς σπονδὰς διαλύειν κωλύει, ἀλλ᾽ ἀναιρεῖν καὶ κατασφάττειν.

Entirely in line with Chrysostom is Pseudo-Augustine, who distinctly raised the question as to whether the parable is to be applied to the moral offender within or to the heretic without. He answered that the tares are the heretics. The delinquents are rather the chaff, but both are to be left, the one until the harvest, the other until the winnowing.[24]

In the Middle Ages both in the East and in the West there are isolated echoes of Jerome and Chrysostom. In the East Theodore Studita (born 759 A.D.) observed that Chrysostom's prediction of war as the fruit of repression had been only too well fulfilled in the Iconoclastic controversy. "The Lord," declared Theodore, "has forbidden such violence by the command, 'No, lest in gathering up the tares you root out the wheat at the same time. Let both grow until the harvest.' That the tares signify the heretics both present and to come is pointed out by Chrysostom." Then follows the quotation given above ending with the prediction of wars.

These have come to pass in our day, for the whole world about us is full of bloodshed and slaughter, in which many of the saints have passed away.... What then shall we say, that it is not lawful to kill heretics? It is not lawful even to curse them.... Rather should we pray for them as the Lord himself showed at the time of his passion saying, "Father forgive them, for they know not what they do." ... The ignorant should be taught, not punished. To be sure the magistrate bears not the sword in vain, but not against those in whose case the Lord has forbidden it. The rulers of bodies may punish those who are convicted in the body, but not those who have offended in the soul, for this belongs to the rulers of souls, and the penalties which they inflict are excommunication and the like.[25]

[24] Quaestionum Septemdecim in Evangelium Secundum Matth. 1, Quaest. XI, XII, *PL* 35, 1367–1369.

Sed recte quaeritur utrum haeretici sint, an male viventes Catholici ... verumtamen quoniam Dominus agrum ipsum, non Ecclesiam, sed hunc mundum interpretatus est, bene intelliguntur haeretici (XI, 1). Toleranda sunt autem non solum zizania usque ad messem ... sed etiam paleam usque ad ventilationem (XI, 5).

[25] *Ep.* Lib. II, CLV, *PG* 99, 1482–1486. ὁ Κύριος ἀπηγόρευσεν ἐν τοῖς Εὐαγγελίοις τοῦτο, εἰπών· Οὔ· μήποτε συλλέγοντες τὰ ζιζάνια, ἐκριζώσητε ἅμα

A like protest was uttered by Theophylactus, bishop of Achrida in Bulgaria in the eleventh century. "The tares," said he, "are the heresies or evil thoughts . . . the servants are the angels, who were distressed at the presence of heresies and evil in the soul and desired to pull up and kill the heretics and evil minded. But God did not suffer the destruction of the heretics by wars lest the righteous also suffer and be destroyed. Likewise God does not desire that a man be cut off because of evil thoughts lest the wheat also perish. If, for example, Matthew had been killed while he was a tare, the wheat of the Word which was later to sprout from him would have been destroyed together with him. So also in the case of Paul and the thief." [26]

In the West, Bede repeated Jerome.[27] Remigius of Auxerre said that the Lord desired "all heretics and whatever doctors to be left for His own judgment because only

αὐτοῖς τὸν σῖτον. Ἄφετε συναυξάνεσθε μέχρι τοῦ θερισμοῦ . . . καὶ ὅτι τὰ ζιζάνια τοὺς αἱρετικοὺς εἴρηκε, τούς τε τηνικαῦτα δηλονότι, καὶ τοὺς ὑφ' ἑτέρων ἤγουν ἅπαντας, ἀκουσώμεθα τοῦ Χρυσοστόμου αὐτὸ τοῦτο ἑρμηνεύοντος· ἐφ' ᾧ τάδε . . . (citation from Chrysostom) Ὅπερ καὶ γέγονεν ἐν τοῖς καθ' ἡμᾶς χρόνοις. Καὶ γὰρ αἵματα καὶ σφαγαὶ ἐπλήρωσαν τὴν καθ' ἡμᾶς οἰκουμένην· καὶ πολλοὶ τῶν ἁγίων συναπῆλθον . . . καὶ τί λέγομεν περὶ τοῦ μὴ ἐπιτρέπειν κτένεσθαι τοὺς αἱρετικούς; οὐδέ γε κατεύχεσθαι αὐτῶν συγκεχώρηται ἡμῖν . . . Οὔτε οὖν . . . κατεύχεσθαι δεῖ ὅλως· μᾶλλον μὲν οὖν ὑπερεύχεσθαι· ὡς αὐτὸς ὁ Κύριος ὑπέδειξεν ἐν τῷ τοῦ πάθους καιρῷ, λέγων πρὸς τὸν ἑαυτοῦ Πατέρα· Πάτερ, ἄφες αὐτοῖς τὴν ἁμαρτίαν· οὐ γὰρ οἴδασι τί ποιοῦσι . . . Διδάσκεσθαι γάρ, οὐ τιμωρεῖσθαι χρὴ τοὺς ἀγνοοῦντας . . . Οὐ γὰρ εἰκῆ, φησί, τὴν μάχαιραν φοροῦσιν . . . οὐ μὴν ἐφ' οὓς ὁ Κύριος ἐκώλυσεν, ἐπιτρέπειν χρή. Σωμάτων γὰρ ἄρχοντες, τοὺς ἐν τοῖς σωματικοῖς ἁλόντας ἐξὸν αὐτοῖς κολάζειν· οὐχὶ τοὺς ἐν τοῖς κατὰ ψυχήν· τῶν γὰρ ψυχῶν ἀρχόντων τοῦτο· ὧν τὰ κολαστήρια, ἀφορισμοί, καὶ αἱ λοιπαὶ ἐπιτιμίαι. This passage is summarized by Luigi Luzzati, *God in Freedom* (New York, 1930), pp. 100–105.

[26] *Enarratio in Ev. Matthaei* XIII, *PG* 123, 283–286. Ζιζάνια, αἱ αἱρέσεις, ἢ οἱ πονηροὶ λογισμοί . . . Δοῦλοι δέ, οἱ ἄγγελοι οἱ ἀγανακτοῦσιν ἐπὶ τῷ εἶναι αἱρέσεις, ἢ πονηρίας ἐν τῇ ψυχῇ, καὶ βούλονται ἀνασπᾶν καὶ ἐκκόπτειν ἐκ τοῦ βίου τούς τε αἱρετικοὺς καὶ τοὺς τὰ πονηρὰ λογιζομένους. Ὁ Θεὸς οὐ συγχωρεῖ τοὺς αἱρετικοὺς διὰ πολέμων ἀναλίσκεσθαι, ἵνα μὴ συμπάσχωσι καὶ συναλίσκωνται καὶ οἱ δίκαιοι. Ὁμοίως οὐδὲ διὰ τοὺς πονηροὺς λογισμοὺς θέλει ὁ Θεὸς ἐκκόπτειν τὸν ἄνθρωπον, ἵνα μὴ καὶ ὁ σῖτος συνδιαφθαρῇ. Οἷον ἐὰν ὁ Ματθαῖος ζιζάνιον ὢν ἐκόπη ἐκ τῆς ζωῆς, συνεξεκόπη αὐτῷ καὶ ὁ ὕστερον μέλλων ἐξ αὐτοῦ βλαστῆσαι τοῦ λόγου σῖτος· ὁμοίως καὶ ὁ Παῦλος, καὶ ὁ λῃστής.

[27] *PL* 92, 68–69.

with difficulty can they be brought to a knowledge of the truth." [28]

A striking plea for liberty was based upon the parable in 1048 by Wazo, the prince bishop of Luik, writing to the bishop of Chalons, who had taken council with him as to how to treat the heretics in his district. Wazo replied:

"Let both grow together until the harvest." What does our Lord indicate by these words if not the patience which he desires preachers to show to their erring neighbors, especially since those who are tares to-day may be wheat tomorrow. . . . Let us have no more of the judgment of men, who are but dust. Let us hear rather the judgment of the creator lest we seek by the sword of the secular power to remove from this life those whom the creator and redeemer God so spares that they may return to his will from the snares of the devil by which they have been held. Thus, thus indeed ought we to reserve them for the final harvest of the Father . . . because those whom the field of this world regards as tares, the harvest may discover to be wheat and those whom we now hold as adversaries in the way of the Lord, possibly the omnipotent God will place above us in the heavenly country. . . . In the meantime we ought to remember that we who are called bishops did not in our ordination receive the sword of the secular power, so that we are bound to God, our maker, not to kill and to make alive. There is another way to treat schismatics of which you are not ignorant, namely that they be deprived of Catholic communion. . . ." [29]

---

[28] *PL* 131, 930. ut omnes haeretici et quilibet doctores proprio arbitrio relinquantur, quoniam difficulter possunt trahi ad scientiam veritatis.

Aquinas in the *Catena Aurea* quotes from Remigius' Commentary on Matthew. The English translators (Oxford, 1841) say that in their day the commentary of Remigius was not in print. In the portions printed by Migne I cannot discover the passages cited by St. Thomas.

[29] Paul Fredericq, *Corpus Documentorum Inquisitionis haereticae pravitatis Neerlandicae* (Ghent and The Hague, 1889) 1, 6–7. Sinite utraque crescere usque ad messem. . . . Quid his verbis nisi patientiam suam Dominus ostendit, quam praedicatores suos erga errantes proximos exibere desiderat, maxime cum hi qui hodie zizania sunt, possibile sit cras converti et esse triticum? . . . Cesset ergo iudicium pulveris, audita sentencia conditoris, nec eos queramus per secularis potentiae gladium huic vitae subtrahere, quibus vult idem creator et redemptor Deus sicut novit parcere, ut resipiscant a diaboli laqueis quibus capti tenentur, ad ipsius voluntatem. Sic, sic nimirum tales ultimae illius patris familias messi a nobis convenit reservari, quidque messores suos de his facere iubeat, sicut et de nobismet ipsis cum timore et tremore oportet expectari, quia horum quoslibet,

We now come to Thomas Aquinas, who here as else-where, synthesized previous thought and practice. He had before him the commentaries on the parable by Jerome, Chrysostom, Augustine, and Pseudo-Augustine, which he regarded as genuine, of Remigius, Bede and others.[30] To harmonize these with one another and with the practice of the church, which in his day allowed the execution of heretics, was a problem calling for a signal ingenuity. Well might Saint Thomas have said with Julian the Apostate, when set to drill troops, "O Plato, Plato, what a task for a philosopher!" St. Thomas was equal to it. He did not lighten the task by identifying the tares with the moral offenders only, but boldly applied the passage with Jerome, Chrysostom, and Pseudo-Augustine to the heretic. How now avoid their conclusion that the tares should not be rooted out? Here Augustine's change of front was a great mercy. Aquinas skillfully placed Chrysostom and Augustine side by side without comment. Chrysostom declares that "the Lord does not forbid all restraint upon heretics . . . but only that they should be put to death." Then Augustine takes up the theme. "This indeed was at first my opinion, that no one should be driven by force into the unity of Christ." [31] Does not this juxtaposition leave the impression that Augustine has reversed Chrysostom's objection to the death penalty? Whether or no, the parable was still to be explained. Here Aquinas availed himself of the observation made by Augustine in a very different connection, namely, that the Lord is concerned only for the wheat and not for the tares which may be rooted out provided they are easy to distinguish and the wheat is well established. Augustine was

quos mundi huius ager zizania habet, messis illa forsitan triticum inveniet, et quos in via Domini adversarios nunc habemus, possibile omnipotenti Deo est in illa coelesti patria nobis facere etiam superiores. . . . Interim nichilominus meminisse debemus, quod nos, qui episcopi dicimur, gladium in ordinatione quod est secularis potentiae non accipimus, ideoque non ad mortificandum sed pocius ad vivificandum auctore Deo inungimur. Est tamen aliud quod sollicite de praedictis agendum est scismaticis, quot et vos nequaquam ignoratis, ut ipsi eisque communicantes catholica communione priventur. . . .

[30] *Catena Aurea*, English Translation (Oxford, 1841), Matthew II, 495–502.
[31] *Catena Aurea*, *loc. cit.* from Augustine *Ep.* 93, V. 17, *CSEL* 34, 461.

talking about the discipline of the delinquent. Aquinas
applies this comforting reflection to the coercion of the
heretic. The theory of the Middle Ages was complete.[32]

The inquisitors of the sixteenth century found the
exegesis of Aquinas highly useful. In 1556 Claes de Praet
asked his examiner whether he regarded him as tares or
wheat. The reply, of course, was that Claes corresponded
to the tares. "Then why do you not let me grow until the
harvest?"

"Because the master of the field gave this command to
his servants lest they hurt the wheat and pull it out along
with the tares, but I can skirt along the edge and pluck out
one or two here and there sometimes six or eight or even ten
or twelve, yes, and sometimes a hundred without hurting
the wheat." [33]

When now we turn to the Protestant Reformation we
find the outstanding reformers taking practically the same
ground as the inquisitors. Some of the old devices for
emasculating the parable reappear, but there are new ones
too, and the most common is to relegate the parable to
ministerial rather than magisterial ethics. The minister is to
use no constraint against the heretic, nor indeed against
any one else. That is not his business. The magistrate, however, must not be hampered by the command to "let both
grow," which if extended to the civil sphere would prevent
the punishment of the malefactor quite as much as of the

---

[32] *Sancti Thomae Aquinatis Doctoris Angelici Opera Omnia* (Rome, 1895)
VIII, Secunda secundae Summae Theologiae Quaest. X, art. VIII, pp. 88–89.
Utrum infideles compellendi sint ad fidem. Here St. Thomas quotes Chrysostom
on Mt. XIII, Augustine *Epp.* 93 and 185 in favor of the coercion of heretics and
Contra Epist. Parmen. III, II, where Augustine points out that the tares may be
rooted out if there is no danger to the wheat. Quaest. XI art. III Utrum haeretici
sint tolerandi, p. 100. Si tamen totaliter eradicentur per mortem haeretici, non est
etiam contra mandatum Domini, quod est in eo casu intelligendum quando non
possunt extirpari zizania sine extirpatione tritici, ut supra dictum est, cum de
infidelibus in communi ageretur.

[33] Van Braght, *Het bloedig Tooneel* (Amsterdam, 1685) II, 170. Dat de Heere
des ackers sijn dienaers beval/ dat was daerom/ dat sy dat goed kruyd niet bederven
souden met dat quaet uyt te trecken: Maer ik kan wel gaen langs de kanten/ en
plucken hier en daer een plucxken of twee/ ja somtijts ses of acht/ ja tien of twaelf/
ja somtijds een hondert of twee/ sonder het goede te bederven.

heretic. Melanchthon expressed this opinion most un-
equivocally in a memorandum with regard to the Anabaptists addressed to Philip of Hesse in 1536. The passage
reads, "The words in the parable of the tares, 'Let both
grow,' which may be cited against (our position) do not
apply to the civil magistracy, but only to the ministerial
office, which exercises no corporal coercion. From this it is
clear that the magistrate is bound to punish corporally
blasphemy, false teaching, heresies and their partisans." [34]
Likewise Justus Menius asserted that the magistrate is not
affected by the texts "Let both grow until the harvest," and
"Go in peace and sin no more." For him the texts are, "He
beareth not the sword in vain," etc. [35]

Calvin and Zwingli in combatting the Anabaptists applied the parable, as the early Fathers had done against
similar purists, not to the heretics, but to the evildoers on
whose account there should be no secession. "Christ told
us," wrote Zwingli, "to let the tares grow with the wheat
until the harvest. We entertain the bold hope that some
may return to a sound mind who now are opposed. And if
they do not, the good may always live among the bad. I fear
that a secession in the present state of affairs would cause
confusion." [36]

Calvin appeared in the role of Portia pleading with the
heartless Anabaptists to exercise greater leniency toward

[34] *Corpus Reformatorum* III, 199. Das aber dagegen angezogen werden diese
Worte vom Unkraut; lasset beides wachsen, das ist nicht zu weltlicher Obrigkeit
geredt, sondern zum Predigtamt, dass sie unterm Schein ihres Amts keinen leib-
lichen Gewalt üben sollen. Aus diesem ist nun klar, dass weltlich Obrigkeit schuldig
ist, Gotteslästerung, falsch Lehre, Ketzereien und die Anhänger um Leib zu strafen.

[35] Paul Wappler, *Die Stellung Kursachsens u. des Landgrafen Philipp v.
Hessen zur Täuferbewegung, Reformationsgeschichtliche Studien und Texte.* Heft 13 u.
14. (Münster i. W. 1910) pp. 87, 110, cf. 61. A similar passage from Georg Major
(1563) is cited by Nikolaus Paulus, *Protestantismus u. Toleranz im 16. Jahrhundert*
(Freiburg i. Brei., 1911) pp. 58–59.

[36] In Catabaptistarum Strophas Elenchus Huldrici Zuinglii *Huldrici Zuinglii
Opera.* Schuler and Schulthess. III, 363. Quemadmodum Christus ipse docuit in
talibus rerum primordiis, qualia tum nostra erant. Praecepisse eundem quoque, ut
et zizania crescere cum tritico pateremur usque in diem messis; spem autem nos
audacem habere in diem plures esse ad bonam mentam redituros, qui nunc ab-
horrerent. Quod si minus fieret, piissimis tamen semper vivere licere inter im-
piissimos. Secessionem in eo rerum statu quid turbae daturam me vereri.

the fallen. These inexorable saints, according to Calvin, excommunicate even on account of involuntary sins and declare that the voluntary are irremissible. "I say that this opinion is an execrable blasphemy against the grace of God." [37] But "let us adhere to the words of our Lord that to the end of the world we must endure many tares for fear that if we pull them out we destroy also the good grain." [38] "We ought not to withdraw from the church because of every trivial difference in doctrine and our indulgence should go much further in tolerating imperfection of life." [39] "Let them (the Anabaptists and the like) remember that the church is like a field sown with good grain in which an enemy by guile introduced tares which are not to be purged until the harvest." [40]

So long as the parable was restricted in this fashion to the evil liver within the church the question of heresy could be avoided, but Calvin was not the man to evade difficulties, and in his justification of the execution of Servetus, he came to grips with the problem. A rigid application of the parable, he pointed out, would eliminate both the sword of the magistrate and all ecclesiastical discipline. "Christ then did not command that all rigor should cease, but merely that those evils should be endured which cannot be corrected without danger." Is not this the position of Aquinas and the inquisitors? "Christ would also remind us that no matter how zealously each may strive according to his office to eradicate vice, nevertheless severity will never succeed to the point that no vestiges of evil will remain." [41]

[37] "Briève Instruction Contre Les Anabaptistes." *Corpus Reformatorum, Calvini Opera*, VII, 74. Je dy que ceste opinion est un blaspheme execrable contre la grace de Dieu.

[38] *Ibid.*, p. 67. Tenons donc en somme ce que dit nostre Seigneur, que jusque à la fin du monde il nous faut endurer beaucoup de mauvaises herbes, de peur que si nous voulions tout arracher, nous ne perdions le bon grain quant et quant.

[39] *Institutio* VIII, 13 and 14, *Calvini Opera* 1 (the editions of 1539–1554), p. 545. sed dico non temere ob quaslibet dissensiunculas deserendam nobis ecclesiam. . . . In vitae autem imperfectione toleranda multo longius procedere indulgentia nostra debet.

[40] *Ibid.*, p. 546.

[41] Refutatio Errorum Michaelis Serveti, *Calvini Opera* VIII, 472. Si praecise nobiscum agunt ex verborum formula, non tantum prohibentur magistratus ab usu

Theodore Beza, also justifying the execution of Servetus, was more explicit than Calvin. All of the older interpretations, said Beza, are forced. Chrysostom and Augustine said that the tares should be left because they might turn into wheat, that is, the heretics into the orthodox. But this interpretation will not do. "The Master called those tares who were sown by the devil, that is the reprobate, who are and always will be tares. If any of the heretics return to a sound mind, they must from the beginning have been the elect although for a time they appeared as tares."[42] Chrysostom and Theophylactus do violence to the parable when they say that the mouths of the heretics are to be stopped although their lives are to be spared. So also does Augustine when he says that severity should not sleep provided there is no danger of schism.[43] As a matter of fact the parable has "nothing to do either with civil or ecclesiastical discipline." [44] To press the details of parables always leads to absurdities. We must consider the main point, which in this case is a word of consolation. "We can never hope for the complete purification of the church in this world, but this world will not last forever." [45] By the best piece of exegesis which we have thus far met, Beza cleared the ground for the burning of heretics. "The servants," he tells us, "did not ask, 'Do you wish us to kill a vile blasphemer and contender against thy sacred majesty and a disturber of the authority of the church?' To this question, if by the servants you mean the civil magistrates, the Master would have replied exactly what Moses decreed against blasphemers and contentious false prophets." [46]

---

gladii, sed omnem disciplinam e medio tolli oportet.... Non igitur quemlibet rigorem cessare Christus iubet, sed toleranda esse mala admonet quae sine pernicie corrigi nequeunt. Et certe quamlibet sedulo et animose quisque pro suo officio eradicandis vitiis incumbat, numquam eousque proficiet severitas quin multae vitiorum reliquiae maneant.

[42] *De Haereticis a Ciuili Magistratu puniendis Libellus, aduersus Martini Bellii farraginem, et nouorum Academicorum sectam.* (1554), pp. 145–146.

[43] *Ibid.*, pp. 146–147.

[44] *Ibid.*, p. 153.

[45] *Ibid.*, pp. 152–153.

[46] *Ibid.*, p. 154. Quare vt libere dicam quod sentio, neque de Ciuili, neque de

I have saved Luther until now because his interpretations of the parable are both diverse and dubious. One can almost trace the development of his attitude to religious liberty by merely observing what he makes of the tares. In 1518 he wrote, "Let the Apostle indeed be deemed worthy of credence when he says, 'There must be heresies,' [47] but we say, 'By no means, but we should burn heretics and destroy the root with the fruit, the tares with the wheat.' " [48]

Again in 1525 Luther introduced, as a commentary upon this passage, one of his noblest pleas for religious liberty. His words are:

Secondly as to how we should treat heretics and false teachers, we ought not to eradicate and exterminate them. Christ says openly here that they should be left to grow together. God's Word is our only recourse, for in such matters he who is wrong to-day may be right tomorrow. Who knows whether the Word of God may touch his heart? But if he is burned or otherwise destroyed his conversion is rendered impossible. He is cut off from the Word of God and he who might otherwise have been saved is of necessity lost. That is why the Lord said that the wheat might be rooted out with the tares. This is atrocious in God's eyes and absolutely indefensible.

See then what mad folk we have so long been who have wished to force the Turks to the faith with the sword, the heretic with fire

---

Ecclesiastica iurisdictione hic agi puto.... (153) Quam obrem in hac quoque parabola singulas eius partes ad eius finem & scopum puto applicandas.... Consolatur autem nos Paterfamilias noster a quo sati sumus, & nobis praedicit perpetuam quidem fore hanc Ecclesiae in hoc mundo conditionem, & nunquam hic defutura zizania: itaque non esse quod integram Ecclesiae repurgationem in hoc mundo speremus, sed hunc mundum perpetuum non fore.... (152–153). Neque item quaerunt, Num vis vt scelestum et blasphemum atque adeo factiosum hunc maiestatis tuae & Ecclesiasticae auctoritatis perturbatorem e vita deturbemus? Respondisset enim profecto Paterfamilias si per seruos, ciuiles Magistratus accipias, hoc ipsum quod per Mosen edixit in blasphemos & factiosos pseudoprophetas (154).

[47] I Cor. 11:19.

[48] *WA* 1, 625. 5. Luther goes on to say that we are not to leave the church on account of the tares. "If Christ and his saints had done this who would have been saved?" I was chagrined to discover how grievously I had blundered in translating this last sentence in the *Harvard Theological Review*, XXII, no. 2, April 1929, p. 122. The following excerpts from Luther and Erasmus are so extensive that I have thought it better to omit the originals, especially since they are not difficult of access.

and the Jews with death, to root out the tares with our own power as if we were the people who could rule over hearts and spirits and make them religious and good, which God's Word alone must do. But by death we cut them off from the Word, so that it cannot operate and we do our best to bring upon our heads the responsibility for two deaths, in that we destroy at once the body temporally and the spirit eternally and we say afterwards that we have rendered God a service and have earned some credit in heaven. Wherefore the inquisitors and murderers, if their brows be not iron, might well be terrified by this parable, if they had genuine heretics before them. As it is they burn true saints and are themselves heretics. What does this come to, if not that like imbeciles they are rooting out the wheat and calling it the tares?[49]

Luther here introduces some of the considerations which constantly reappear in the literature of religious liberty, namely that the spiritual alone may judge of the spiritual and that the whole attempt to repress heresy by force has resulted rather in the martyrdom of the saints.

By 1528 Luther was rapidly shifting ground though he had not yet come to approve of the death penalty for the sectaries. "Here at Wittenberg," he wrote, "we have now a little sheaf of pure wheat, although we have not quite eliminated the tares, but round about us almost everything is full of tares in every place with scarcely an exception." [50]

But where I know that there is one Christian, I would tolerate an entire land of Unchristians rather than destroy one Christian with the Unchristians. What did the Lord mean when he said, "Let both grow together?" Are we by no means to root out the tares? This is very needful teaching for us preachers, for I would gladly be one of the servants to help root out the tares, but it cannot and should not be. But is one then to do nothing and let the tares grow entirely unhindered? Here our Papists are grown canny and throw this text up to us and say that we here at Wittenberg have done wrong to suppress the private masses. We should have left masses and cloisters alone. But they do not rightly regard the text, for the Lord does not say that we should not ward off the tares, but merely that we should not root them out. Then they

[49] *Fastenpostille* 1525 *WA* 17^{II}, 125.
[50] *WA* 52, 831. 12–15.

carry the text further and say that since many cloisters were destroyed through God's anger in the Peasants' War, they should now be rebuilt . . . but Christ was talking about growing, not about sowing.[51]

The Lord Christ wished to show that his kingdom is and should be distinct from the civil kingdom. Christ's kingdom does nothing with fist and sword. God has commanded the civil kingdom to bear the sword and root out the bad. . . . [52]

Here Luther is relegating the parable to ministerial rather than to magisterial ethics, but he does not yet draw the full consequences.

A prince or a town must see to it and not suffer more than one kind of preaching in the territory in order to avoid disunity and commotion. . . . The authorities should hear both sides and judge the matter according to the certain rule of Scripture and God's Word. The side which teaches correctly according to Scripture and God's Word should be allowed to remain. The other . . . should be dismissed, but there should be no extermination. . . . The tares are already condemned and adjudged to the fire. . . . Why then attack a thief who is already condemned to the gallows?[53]

The next sermon on this parable is to be dated somewhere between 1531 and 1535.[54] In the meantime Luther had come to approve of the death penalty for blasphemy. This sermon significantly begins with a reference to Augustine's change of mind.[55] Luther then avails himself of two devices which we have already met for evading the liberalism of the parable. The first is to apply the story to the moral offender rather than to the heretic. "The meaning," writes Luther, "is that Christ is not talking especially of the heretics, but he is giving a comparison to the kingdom of heaven, that is of the whole Christian church." [56] We are

---

[51] *Ibid.*, p. 835.

[52] *Ibid.*, p. 836.

[53] *Ibid.*, p. 838.

[54] It is given without date in Dietrich's *Hauspostille* published in 1544. The other sermons in the collection range from 1531 to 1535. See *WA* 52, 130–135 and the introduction.

[55] *Ibid.*, p. 130, cf. p. 135.

[56] *Ibid.*, p. 130, 21 f.

to expect impurity in the church. "Many take offense because among us too the tares are found in heaps and there is more greed, usury, unchastity, debauchery, lying and cheating than under the papacy. On this account the Gospel and the preachers are taunted by nearly every one, with the reproach, 'If the teaching were right the people would be better.' The Gospel, however, is not to blame, but the devil who sowed the tares." [57] Luther had reason to be grateful to these unworthy folk for providing a means of diverting the parable of the tares from the heretics. At the same time he employed the other device of restricting the parable to the ministerial sphere. The magistrate is not restrained.

"Each should give a hand to the other. The spiritual government uses the Word and the ban, the civil uses the sword and force that the people may be godly and all offense may be avoided. . . . The magistrate bears the sword with the command to cut off offense. . . . Now the most dangerous and atrocious offense is false teaching and an incorrect church service." [58]

A sermon by Luther in 1546 has been interpreted by some as applying to magistrates, by others as directed only to ministers. Luther is reported to have said that the "tares are to be rooted out but not killed. Keep them from the altar and the pulpit. In no other way can they be restrained. . . . For with human power and force one cannot root them out or make them different." [59] One would think that this would have to apply to the magistrate because Luther never would have conceded that killing lay within the province of the minister.

Now we turn to the liberals of the sixteenth century, whether in the Catholic or the Protestant camp. The first is Erasmus. In the *Paraphrase on Matthew* he wrote, "The servants who wish to root up the tares before the time are those who think that false prophets and heresiarchs are to be removed by sword and death, whereas the Master

[57] *Ibid.*, p. 132 condensed.
[58] *Ibid.*, pp. 135. 26–29 and 134.40–135.3.
[59] *WA* 51, 173–187.

wished not to destroy but to tolerate them if perchance
they might turn and from tares become wheat. If they do
not turn they are reserved for the judgment of Him who will
punish them some day." [60]

Bedda took exception to this interpretation and Erasmus defended himself in a disconcerting combination of
slashing and hedging.[61]

"Augustine," wrote Erasmus, "did not disapprove if God
stirred up the princes to coerce those who disturb the tranquillity
of the church, but who ever heard that the orthodox bishops ex-
cited kings to butcher heretics who were nothing more than
heretics? . . . The bishop's task is, as far as he may, to teach, correct and cure. What sort of a bishop is he who can do nothing
more than constrain, torture and commit to the flames? . . . In a
case where the theologian accuses, imprisons, prosecutes and turns
over the victim to the secular judge and where the judge commits
to the flames not on his own motion, but in accord with the sentence of the theologian, where the theologian acts as the author
and executor of the penalty, how much I ask you does this differ
from the shedding of blood?" [62]

Then Erasmus retrenches, or does he merely hit harder
under the semblance of retrenchment? In the *Paraphrase*, we
are told, he was speaking not for himself, but in the person
of Christ, nor was he applying the parable to the present
time, but to the days of the martyrs. Then he bursts out
again. "Did Augustine who would spare the Donatist
assassins, Augustine who thought that the honor of the
servants of God was stained by the blood of their enemies,
did he think that a simple heretic, even though obstinate,
should be burned in the flames? However I neither urge nor

---

[60] Paraphrasis in Evang. Matthae Cap. XIII. *Opera Omnia* VII, 80 E. Servi
qui volunt ante tempus colligere zizania, sunt ii, qui Pseudoapostolos & Haeresi-
archas gladiis ac mortibus existimant e medio tollendos, cum paterfamilias nolit eos
exstingui, sed tolerari, si forte resipiscant, & e zizaniis vertantur in triticum. Quod
si non resipiscant, serventur suo Judici, cui poenas dabunt aliquando.

[61] *Supputatio Errorum in Censuris Beddae*, Prop. xxxii, *Opera Omnia* IX,
580–583.

[62] *Ibid.*, p. 581.

discourage princes from butchering heretics. I am explaining the office of an ecclesiastic." [63]

Erasmus reverted to the theme in his reply to the Spanish monks. Here again he blazed up. "When I con-consider," he says, "with what mercy Christ planted, nourished, advanced and established his church throughout the centuries I scarcely see how I can approve of the example of some of those who to-day on account of scholastic opinions drag men to prison and the stake, as now we see priests burned because they would rather call a girl, with whom they live, a wife than a concubine." [64] Then again Erasmus hedged, saying that he was applying the parable neither to his own depraved time nor to the sword of the magistrate.[65] But once more he flashed out. "We must consider whether princes, on account of any error should commit a man to the flames who seems to be a heretic. It is very harsh to burn men on account of articles which are not only dubious and controversial, but even trivial, and most harsh to do so because of propositions which the theologians have just made up out of their own heads." [66]

The Faculty of the University of Paris was not satisfied with these explanations and complained of the scandal to be drained from the cup of his honeyed words. Erasmus replied that he dared not mingle human comments with the majesty of the Gospels.

That is the sort of interpreter I should have been if, in the name of Christ or the evangelist, I had explained that the tares should be left four hundred years, until the church was well established, and then killed, if I had done that when Christ said that the tares should be left until the harvest, and himself explained that this meant to the end of the world. . . . I hear some twisting the words of Christ as if he meant that heretics should be spared only when there is no danger that the true doctrine be eradicated along with the error, the good killed with the bad. If

[63] *Ibid.*, pp. 581–582.
[64] Adversus Monachos Quosdam Hispanos, *Titulus* IV, Contra Sanctam Haereticorum Inquisitionem. *Opera Omnia*, IX, 1054 D.
[65] *Ibid.*, p. 1056.
[66] *Ibid.*, p. 1056 E–F.

this condition is not present they are by no means to be spared. Since this interpretation does not sufficiently agree either with the parable or with the ancient interpreters, I did not dare to introduce it in the name of the evangelist or of Christ. . . . If there is so much danger from my *Paraphrases*, intended for private reading, because I did not expressly commend the killing of heretics, how much more is to be feared from Jerome, Chrysostom, and Augustine, whose works are read by all as having authority and that in the churches? Or why did St. Thomas renew the offense in his *Catena*, citing those passages which the theologians now condemn? But how could any one infer from this passage that I do not approve of killing heretics when I oppose the partisans of this position in published works?[67]

Name one.

The Protestant liberals drew heavily from Erasmus. Sebastian Franck borrowed both his ideas and his citations, but Franck adds his own characteristic version of the Augustinian conflict of the *civitas Dei* and the *civitas terrena*. For Franck the *civitas Dei* is always small and always persecuted. "Some think," said Franck (and he might have counted himself among the number), "that Christ, when he so vigorously forbade the rooting out of the tares before the harvest, perceived that the world is blind and has no judgment or knowledge of the truth, especially the scribes and the blind leaders of the blind, who had they been given authority to root out the tares, inasmuch as they are themselves the tares, would have rooted out the wheat as the tares, so that they alone would remain in the field, as they have always done not only against the prophets, Christ and the apostles, but also, as many examples show, in our own day." [68]

---

[67] Ad Censuras Facultatis Theologiae Parisiensis Declaratio Erasmi LXXIV, *Opera Omnia*, IX, 905–906.

[68] *Chronica Zeÿtbuch und Geschÿchtbibel* (1531) ccccliiij. Etlich meinen Christus in dem das er das unkraut vor dem schnid ausszureüffen so fleissig verpeüt/ dahin gesehen hab/ das die welt plindt ist/ und kein urteil noch erkantnüs der warheit hat/sunderlich yr schrifftgelerten und plindenfürer/ solt yr nun gestat/ der gwalt gegeben/ und der zaum glassen worden sein dz unkraut ausreüffen/ so hette si nun dieweil sie selbs ein unkraut ist/ dz treidt für unkraut aussgeräuffet/ dz sie den acker allein in hette/ wie sie alwegen gepflegt hat/ und nit allein in proheten/ Christo/ Apostelen/ sunder auch heüt vil exempel erscheinen.

Sebastian Castellio made *Sinite utraque crescere* almost the motto of his tract *On the Coercion of Heretics*, directed against the execution of Servetus. Here we find collected the opinions of Chrysostom, Augustine, and Pseudo-Augustine, Erasmus, Luther, and Franck. The excerpts from Erasmus and Franck in turn cover much of the earlier literature. Another excerpt from Conrad Pellikan incorporates Erasmus. But Castellio has also his own emphasis. By sharp exegesis he endeavors to demonstrate that the parable must apply not to the moral offender, but to the heretic. "The tares cannot be robbers, adulterers and similar malefactors, for the devil did not sow them after the Gospel, since they were already here, but the tares must be the false doctrine which the devil sowed after the Gospel, that is the heretics and hypocrites." [69] They are to be let alone because we do not know enough to sort them out. Castellio's normal plea in this connection is rationalistic.

What if we say that we cannot err? Those who killed the godly have always said the same. . . . Who ever thought he held a false religion? The Jews erred who persecuted Christ and the apostles; the Gentiles erred who persecuted the Christians. The pope erred in persecuting Lutherans and Zwinglians. Henry VIII of England erred when he killed Papists, Lutherans, Zwinglians, and Anabaptists. Luther erred when he called the Zwinglians devils and consigned them to hell. Will the Zwinglians and Calvinists alone escape error?[70]

[69] *Contra Libellum Calvini* Fv verso, p. 102, Cal. 96. non videtur zyzania appellare latrones et adulteros, caeterosque eius generis maleficos. Non enim sevit Diabolus post Evangelium, cum essent jam ante Evangelium. Sed videtur zyzania appellare eos, quos Diabolus sevit falsa doctrina post Evangelium cuiusmodi sunt Haeretici et hypocritae.

[70] *Ibid.* Fvj and verso. pp. 103–104. Cal. 96. Quod si dicemus nos non errare, idem semper dixerunt qui pios occiderunt. . . . Quis unquam putavit se tenere falsam religionem? Errarunt Iudaei qui Christum et Apostolos persecuti sunt. Errarunt gentiles, qui Christianos persecuti sunt. Erravit Papa, qui Lutheranos et Zuinglianos persecutus est. Erravit Henricus Angliae Rex, qui Papistas et Lutheranos, et Zuinglianos, et Anabaptistas interfecit. Erravit Lutherus, qui Zuinglianos, Diabolos appellavit et in Gehennam damnavit. An soli Zuingliani et Calviniani non errabunt?

Compare the Preface to the French Bible and see my article "Sebastian Castellio and the Toleration Controversy of the Sixteenth Century," in *Persecution and Liberty, Essays in Honor of George Lincoln Burr* (New York, 1931), p. 197.

Elsewhere Castellio made an almost legalistic appeal to the command of Christ. "By zeal for Christ we root out the tares though he commanded that they be left to the harvest lest the wheat be destroyed. By zeal for Christ we persecute others. He commanded us to turn the other cheek. By zeal for Christ we do evil to others. He commanded us to render good for evil." [71]

Castellio was not in the least halted by the fears of Beza that a too extensive application of the parable would make the magistrate unduly merciful to criminals. "The king prefers that all the robbers in his kingdom should live rather than that one of his sons should be killed along with them." [72]

Acontius like Castellio was a sharp exegete, pointing out the error of those who supposed that the tares were to be left only in case there was danger to the wheat. "The Master did not say, 'Go, but be extremely careful that you do not destroy the wheat with the tares.' But he absolutely forbade them to go, and he desired that the tares as well as the wheat should grow until the harvest. [73]

Among Protestant princes Philip of Hesse in 1545, fifteen years after Luther had gone the way of Augustine, reverted to this passage among others, in favor of mercy. "These passages," [74] he said, "stand in the way so that we cannot feel easy of conscience that a man who errs in faith should be so sharply dealt with, since over night a man may be instructed and turn from his error. If we should condemn

---

[71] *Traité des Hérétiques*, ed. by A. Olivet (Geneva, 1913) pp. 136–137. Par zèle de Christ, nous arracherons l'ivraie, lequel afin que le blé ne fut arraché, a commandé l'ivraie etre laissée jusques à la moisson....

[72] *Contra Libellum Calvini* Fv verso, p. 102–103, Cal. 96. Quemadmodum rex malet ut omnes in suo regno Latrones, viverent, quam si unus regis filius cum omnibus latronibus occideretur.

[73] *Jacobii Acontii Satanae Stratagematum libri octo.* Curavit Gualtherus Koehler. (Monaci, 1927) pp. 77–78. Non enim dicit: "age, ite, sed videte etiam atque etiam, ne una cum zizaniis etiam triticum evellatis," sed omnino vetat ire vultque tam zizania quam triticum crescere usque ad messem.

The arguments of Castellio and Acontius were summed up by Minus Celsus *De Haereticis capitali supplicio non afficiendis.* 1584. pp. 27b–40.

[74] Matt. 13:30; Luke 9:55; Rom. 14.

such a one so summarily to death we fear greatly that we should not be innocent of his blood." [75]

We should expect the Anabaptists to appeal to this parable in the interests of liberty. Bullinger writes as if the party as a whole understood the tares to be false teachers who should be let alone.[76] Certainly this was the view of Menno Simons. His appeal is usually legalistic. "If," he asks, "our persecutors are Christians, as they claim, if they regard the Word of the Lord as true, why then do they not hear and follow Christ's word and command? Why do they start weeding before the time? Why do they not fear that they will pluck the wheat and not the tares? Why do they assume the office of the angels?[77]

David Joris introduces the characteristic teaching of the mystic and spiritual reformers that the spiritual man is alone competent to judge of spiritual things.

Because God is a spirit and his operation is inward, he does not desire in these last days that any one, even though he be his servant, should judge in matters of belief and pass sentence and weed out before the harvest.... Better to die a thousand deaths than to destroy one faithful Christian or righteous soul. If any one objects that Christian and righteous hearts are not killed, but heretics, false leaders, etc., then I say in the end it will be manifest whether the Scripture has not been strikingly fulfilled here as

[75] Paul Wappler, *Die Stellung Kursachsens und des Landgrafen Philipp von Hessen zur Täuferbewegung.* pp. 233–234. Diese spruch liegen vns dermassen jm wege, das wir jn vnsern Gewiessen nit wol fienden mogen, wie gegen einem menschen, so jm glauben etwas jrrig ist, so scharpf solt gefaren werden, dann es mocht sich ein mensch vber nacht vnderrichten vnd weysen lassen vnd wieder von seinem jrthumb abtretten. Solt nhun derselbig so gestracks von vns zum dodt verurteilt werden, sorgen wir warlich, wir mochten seins bluts nicht vnschultdig sein.

[76] *Der Widertöufferen ursprung/ fürgang/ Secten/ wäsen/ fürneme und gemeine jrer leer Artickel/* (Zürich, 1560) p. 184b. The Anabaptists say das unkrut bedütet die kinder des bösen/ oder falsche lerer/ und der Herr heiter gebotten hat/ lassends beyde mit einanderen wachsen/ so sol ye die Oberkeit das unkrut mit straaffen oder töden nit ussritten. Cf. 233–234b.

[77] Van't Kruys Christ. *Opera Omnia Theologica* (Amsterdam, 1681), pp. 149–150. Zijn nu onse vervolgers Christenen gelijk sy meenen/ ende des Heeren Woordt voor recht houden/ waerom en hooren en volgen sy dan Christus Woordt ende Gebodt niet? waerom plucken sy dat uyt voor den tijdt Waerom en vreesen sy niet dat sy de Terwe plucken sullen/ ende niet dat onkruyt? waerom treden sy in der Engelen dienst? cf. p. 304b.

elsewhere, in that upright hearts, like Christ in the world, have
been put to death as heretics and perverters, even as knaves and
evil doers. . . . But God wishes that the tares be left. . . . God alone
judges in the spirit over the soul and life. Men judge of the body
only.[78]

Some of the chiliasts of the Reformation completed the
cycle and discovered in the parable not merely permission
but direct warrant for the extermination of the ungodly on
the ground that the time of the harvest is now at hand. So
Thomas Müntzer cried that the evil-doers should be suffered
to live no longer. "The tares must be rooted out of the vine-
yard of the Lord in the time of the harvest. Then the fair
red wheat will take firm root." [79] Münzer's wheat seems to
be turning into wine. On one point, however, he is still clear,
that the time of the harvest is come.[80] Likewise Bernhard
Rothmann reminded his readers that in the time of the
Restitution, which is at hand, the Son of Man will send his

[78] *T'Wonder-boeck* (1551) pt. 2, chap. XCJJJ, fol. 121a–122a. Want Godt dan
een Gheest is/ sijn werckinge nv inwendich heeft/ heeft hy in desen laetsten Daghen
niet ghewilt/ dat yemandt (of sy schoon syne Dienaers sijn) in dese sijns Gheloofs
saken richten/ veroordelen/ verderuen/ oft yet wtroeden solden/ voor den tijt des
Oogstes . . . lieuer duysent dooden daerom te steruen unde alles te verliesen datmen
gehebben mocht/ dan een gheloouich Christen oder gerechtighe Ziel om te brenghen.
Secht yemant: men brengt geen Christen oder Gherechtighe herten om/ maer
ketters unde valsche Verleyders/ Schelmen unde Booswichten. So antwoord' Ic:
Dat wert sich aent eynde wel bevinden/ of die Schrift in desen/ als in alle t'andere
niet mercklijck vervult/ alle Oprechte van herten mit Christo in die Werlt ghelijck
Ketters unde Verleyders/ Ja als die meeste Schelmen unde Oeueldaders niet om-
bracht werden/ . . . . Alsoo oordeeldt alleen Godt inden Gheest ouer Ziel unde
Lijf/ maer die mensche alleen ouer t'Lijf.

Cf. tract 20 (according to the notation of Van der Linde, *David Joris*
(The Hague, 1867) Van de gerechte ware Zion. cap. III, translated in Gottfrid
Arnold's *Kirchen und Ketzer-Historie.* (Frankfurt a. M., 1715) II, 649a.

Tract 194, Een suuerlycke bewyssreden. Aiij verso.

Tract 139, Een droeuich Suchten p. 55.

Cf. also the testimony of one of the Anabaptist martyrs in *Bibliotheca
Reformatoria Neerlandica* (The Hague, 1904) II, p. 304.

[79] Cited by Joachim Zimmermann, *Thomas Münzer* (Berlin, 1925), pp. 107–
108. Man muss das Unkraut ausraufen aus dem Weingarten Gottes in der Zeit der
Ernte, dann wird der schöne rote Weisen beständig Wurzeln gewinnen und recht
aufgehn.

[80] *Ibid.*, p. 130.

angels to bind up all that is offensive in his kingdom.[81] Again Matthys at Münster is represented as crying to the "ungodly," "Begone, you impious one and never return, flee, you enemy of the Father. . . . The field of the Father is to be purged, the tare to be eradicated root and branch lest it oppress the good seed." [82]

If one may venture another interpretation, perhaps the tares might be identified with overly ingenious exegetes.

[81] Restitution rechter und gesunder christlicher Lehre. *Neudrucke deutscher Literaturwerke des XVI, und XVII. Jahrhunderts.* No. 77 u. 78. *Flugschriften aus der Reformationszeit.* VII. p. 99. Also salt ock sin in der vullenbrenginge dusser werldt, des menschen sone werdt senden sine baden unde se werden sammelenn uth sinen rike alle ergernisse, und alle de dar unrecht doen, und werden se werpen in einen vürauen.

[82] *Hermanni a Kerssenbroch Anabaptistici Furoris . . . Narratio.* hrsg. von H. Detmer. *Die Geschichtsquellen des Bisthums Münster* sechster Bd. zweite Hälfte. (Münster, 1889). p. 536. "Apage te hinc, impie, nunquam rediture, effuge, inimice et, hostis Patris, Recede, omnis boni perturbator! Secerne te a bonis! Purganda est Patris area, lolium stirpitus eradicandum est, ne segetem bonam opprimat.

7 Interpretations of the Immoralities of the Patriarchs

The Old Testament has always been something of an embarrassment to the Christian church. The book was Scripture and its heroes were to be taken as examples. Nevertheless there was much in their conduct which ran counter to the prevailing Christian ethics. A problem thus arose both in exegesis and in ethics. Were the patriarchs to be justified? Should they be imitated? Marcion evaded the difficulty by simply rejecting the Old Testament, pointing out the complete antithesis, for example, between the precept, "Let not the sun go down upon your wrath," and the conduct of Joshua, who kept the sun up till his wrath went down.[1] In the main the fathers resolved such difficulties by allegory, but even this key did not suffice. There was no denying that Moses really slew the Egyptian, that the Israelites robbed them, that Abraham lied, that Jacob was polygamous, and that Samson committed suicide, not to mention the deeds which made it appropriate to attribute to David the penitential psalms. Origen, the prince of allegorists, admitted that the incest of Lot and the polygamy of Abraham and Jacob were "mysteries not understood by us."[2]

First published under the title, "The Immoralities of the Patriarchs according to the Exegesis of the Late Middle Ages and of the Reformation," in *The Harvard Theological Review*, XXIII, 1 (1930).

[1] Harnack, *Marcion, T. u. U.*, 45, p. 105.
[2] *De Principiis*, iv. 9; *PG* XI, 360.

The Middle Ages and the Reformation had four solutions for the problem. (1) The first was that the heroes of the old covenant had a special command, or revelation, from God, which is not repeated in our day. (2) Some thought, however, that these revelations might recur. (3) Others, who could not pretend to revelations but were interested in the revival of some features of the Old Testament morality, justified both the patriarchs and themselves on the basis of natural law, of the law of necessity, and of Aristotelian *epieikeia*. (4) The fourth solution was to seek an escape by way of definition. The patriarchs did not really lie, nor kill, nor steal.

The first position was the most common, that the patriarchs had a special command, or revelation, from God granting a dispensation from the commandments. Bernard of Clairvaux said:

> That which is promulgated from on high can by no means be changed save by God who gave it. The commands, Thou shalt not kill, Thou shalt not commit adultery, Thou shalt not steal, and the rest, admit of no human dispensation. . . . But God can relax what he will and when he will, as when he permitted the Israelites to despoil the Egyptians or the prophet to join himself to a harlot, etc.[3]

It will be observed that the dispensation which Bernard allowed was only for the second table of the decalogue. This restriction was definitely stated by Bonaventura, who distinguished that which is only relatively evil, *malum in se*, from that which is intrinsically evil, *malum secundum se*. Offences against the first table are intrinsically evil, those against the second table are only relatively so.[4]

Scotus provided the theoretical basis for the distinction, when he said that although God is absolute, and right is right because he wills it, nevertheless he can do nothing illogical and self-contradictory, as would be the case were he to permit himself to be hated by man. For that reason

---

[3] *PL*, 182, cf. note 95 in Migne, 864.
[4] E. Pluzanski, *Essai sur la Philosophie de Duns Scot* (1888), p. 272.

there can be no dispensation from the first table, which en-
joins duties to God, but only from the second, which has
reference to man. This God did relax; for example, in neglect
of the fifth commandment he ordered Abraham to kill his
innocent son Isaac, of the sixth he commanded Hosea to
unite himself with other women, of the seventh God permitted the Israelites in Egypt to take to themselves gold
and silver vessels and clothes, and this was also an offence
against the eighth commandment, because the goods were
taken on the pretext of a loan.[5]

Occam abandoned the Scotist restrictions and declared
that God could grant a dispensation not merely for theft
and adultery, but even for hate against himself.[6]

For the second position, that special commands may
recur, one would naturally look in the Middle Ages to the
Spiritual Franciscans, for whom the rule of Saint Francis
was itself a divine revelation, and who had revelations of
their own;[7] but that they appealed to these divine com-
munications to rehabilitate patriarchal morality does not
seem likely in spite of the vile stories circulated by their
opponents.[8] Dolcino, to be sure, taught that one might lie
and break an oath to the Inquisition, but whether he
grounded this liberty on a special inspiration I do not know.
In the Middle Ages I have not been able to discover a single
clear illustration of this second position.

The third view, that the conduct of the patriarchs was
in accord with the law of nature, the law of necessity,
Aristotle's *epieikeia*, is adumbrated by John of Salisbury,
who justified tyrannicide by an appeal to the examples of
Ehud, Jael, and Judith. Not a word was said about a special
revelation.[9] Occam stated the position more clearly when he
said that by reason of utility and necessity one may act
counter to the words and deeds of Christ, provided one does

[5] J. Klein, *Der Gottesbegriff des Johannes Duns Skotus* (1913), pp. 161 ff.

[6] Pluzanski, *op. cit.*, p. 268, note 3

[7] H. C. Lea, *A History of the Inquisition in the Middle Ages*, III, pp. 30, 79,
87, and 110.

[8] *Ibid.*, pp. 83, 97, 113.

[9] Polycraticus viii, xx; *PL* 199, 794.

not do violence to his intent. If one does not know Christ's intent a revelation is necessary. (This is the first solution which we mentioned above.) But there are many cases in which Christians may judge of the intent of Christ without a revelation. Christ told the disciples to resist not evil, but Paul called the high priest a whited sepulchre. Christ told the disciples not to take two cloaks, nor shoes, yet in manifest necessity they might do otherwise, fulfilling the mind though not the words of Christ.[10] Lying is legitimate if one has the proper intent. Jehu was justified in deceiving the priests of Baal, and David in misleading Abimelech.[11] As ground for the transgression of the code Occam appealed to natural law and to Aristotle's *epieikeia*.[12] This same doctrine was employed by the conciliarists, who, in order to end the schism, desired, in defiance of canon law, to give to a general council authority to depose and to make popes on the principle that necessity knows no law. Did not the Maccabees, when they fought on the sabbath, transgress the divine law?[13]

The fourth solution was by way of definition. The Lombard said that just as killing is homicide only when practised by the private citizen and not in the case of the magistrate, who executes the law, so the despoiling of the Egyptians was not theft for those who acted in accord with the divine command, but only for those who were moved by cupidity.[14] Thomas Aquinas, armed with this exegetical device, declared that there had been no dispensation from either table of the law. The sacrifice of Isaac was not homicide and the despoiling of the Egyptians was not theft, because these acts were in accord with the divine command.

[10] *Dialogus*, ed. 1494, pars 3, lib. ii, tract. i, cap xxii–xxiv, fol. cci and verso.

[11] *Ibid.*, pars 1, lib. vii, cap. iv, fol. cxv.

[12] *Ibid.*, lib. vi, cap. c, fol. cx verso.

[13] So Heinrich of Langenstein, cited by Friedrich Kropatscheck, *Das Schriftprinzip der lutherischen Kirche*, vol. I, *Die Vorgeschichte, Das Erbe des Mittelalters* (Leipzig, 1904), p. 386 note 3. See also Karl Wenck, "Konrad v. Gelnhausen und die Quellen der konziliaren Theorie," *Historische Zeitschrift*, 76, 1896, pp. 44 f. He contends that the conciliarists took the doctrine of the *epieikeia* not from Occam but from Thomas. Cf. J. B. Schwab, *Johannes Gerson*, 1858, index under Epikie.

[14] *PL* 192, 832.

Judith did not really lie to Holofernes; her words were true according to a certain mystical sense.[15] This solution is to all intents and purposes the same as the first if the character of the act is regarded as altered solely by reason of the divine command. What is that but a dispensation based on a special command? If, however, appeal is made to extenuating circumstances, we have practically the solution by way of the law of nature and necessity.

In the period of the Reformation all these positions recur. The most common is the first.

Luther took in the main the view that the patriarchs had a special inspiration which is not repeated in our day. The following passages illustrate the point.

If any one wishes to imitate Noah [wrote Luther] and get drunk, he deserves to go to hell. So Paul swore, but it is not permitted to me.[16]

Samson was called upon by God to plague the Philistines so as to save the children of Israel. . . . But no one will follow this example, be he a true Christian and full of the Spirit. . . . First you must be like Samson; then you may do as Samson.[17]

The Spirit can and does produce works which seem to be contrary to all of God's commands, but they are only against the commands of the second table, which have reference to one's neighbor, and are in accord with the first three commands in the first table, which refer to God. You must first be a Peter, Paul, Jacob, David, and Elias. Then in God's name you may well curse with highest merit before God.[18]

As for the fact that the Jews smashed altars and idols, they had in that time a special command of God for that work, which we in this time do not have. As for Abraham sacrificing his son, he had a special command of God for it.[19]

From the following passage it would appear that Luther recognized also the force of the law of necessity. He wrote:

Although the patriarchs had many wives, Christians never-

---

[15] Pluzanski, p. 276; cf. Klein, pp. 161–162.
[16] *WA*, XI, 205, 8.
[17] *Ibid.*, XI, 261, 16 f.
[18] *EA*, VIII, 42.
[19] *Ibid.*, LIII, 267.

less should not follow such an example, because *there is no necessity*, nor improvement, nor special word of God which commands the like, and great offense and disturbance might come of it.[20]

Still again it would seem that Luther did not definitely exclude the possibility of contemporary revelations for the rehabilitation of patriarchal morality. With reference to the bigamy of the Landgrave Philip of Hesse, Luther wrote:

> Ehud and Samson had a special calling and promise of divine help. If the Landgrave had had such a calling and had believed the word of God, then God might have accomplished his purpose through him, even though he were a sinner.[21]

Luther looked to the Holy Spirit for genuine direction in matters of conduct.[22] Nevertheless even the earlier Luther was not prepared to dissociate the divine guidance from the written Word, and in the conflict with the radicals he took the position that no special word of God could be acknowledged unless corroborated by a miracle. To the peasants he wrote:

> If you persist in your undertaking in the teeth of the law of God and of Christ in the Old Testament and in the New, and of the law of nature, then you must produce a new special command from God, corroborated by signs and wonders which give you authority to do this.[23]

But when the Anabaptists claimed to produce miracles, Luther raised the requirements. "I won't suffer," he declared, "a preacher in office, *even though he works miracles*, unless he is sure that he has the right teaching and Word and a certain office." [24]

In the main, then, one finds in Luther the Scotist solution.[25]

[20] *Ibid.*, LIII, 390.

[21] *WA*, Tischreden I, p. 368, Nr. 768. Melanchthon, in Enders and Kawerau, IV, 79: Tunc venient nobis inspirata consilia a Deo, quae nunquam cogitavimus.

[22] Karl Holl, *Gesammelte Aufsätze, Luther*, p. 234.

[23] *WA*, XVIII, p. 304; cf. 96–97 and *EA*, LIII, 255.

[24] *EA*, XLVIII, 139–140.

[25] On Luther's whole position see Karl Müller, "Luthers Äusserungen über das Recht des bewaffneten Widerstandes gegen den Kaiser," Sitzungsberichte, Munich Academy, Philos., philol. und hist. Kl., 1915, Abh. 8, p. 8, and Karl Holl, *Gesammelte Aufsätze, Luther*, p. 227.

Calvin pursued the same method, and repudiated tyrannicide, explaining the examples of Moses and Othniel as due to a "legitimate calling of God," with which they were "armed from heaven." [26] Sometimes, however, Calvin adduced extenuating circumstances. For the practice of polygamy Abraham had a special reason which is not valid to-day, in that it was needful for him to raise up seed for the fulfilment of the promise. Similarly, Jacob was justified in using the handmaids at the instance of his wives, but the taking of Rachel is inexcusable, for this was an indulgence of the flesh.[27]

The second position, that the patriarchal morality may be revived by virtue of special revelations here and now, came very clearly to light among the Anabaptists at Münster. Their leader, Bernhard Rothmann, relates that "we laid off our arms and weapons and prepared us for the slaughter," until God "through a spiritual revelation" showed us that "now is the time of the restitution of all things," and that "we and all true Christians in this time may not only ward off the force of the godless with the sword, but also because he has placed the sword in the hands of his people to avenge all unrighteousness." [28]

Whether Bernadino Ochino should be classed with this group is open to question. He was banished from Zurich, in the seventy-sixth year of his age, chiefly because of a dialogue on polygamy which concluded with the statement: "But if you do that to which God impels you, provided you are thoroughly convinced that it is a divine prompting, you will not sin." [29]

Usually Ochino took the Scotist view, and justified

[26] Corpus Reformatorum, *Calvini opera*, II, Instit. iv, xx, pp. 1115–1116, legitima Dei vocatio.

[27] *Opera*, X, pp. 258–259.

[28] Restitution rechter und gesunder christlichen Lehre (*Neudruck deutscher Literaturwerke*, Nos. 77 and 78), pp. 107 and 110. Rothmann says that they were taught "durch geistlike apenbaringe."

[29] *Dialogi*, xxx, ii, p. 227: Tum si id feceris ad quid te Deus impellet, dummodo diuinum esse instinctum exploratum habeas, non peccabis. I give citations from Ochino and from some of the following authors in the original, because their works are comparatively inaccessible.

Moses' killing of the Egyptian, Samson's suicide, and Rahab's lie on the basis of a divine inspiration.[30] Jesus blamed his disciples, not because they desired to call down fire from heaven, but because they asked him whether they might do so, thus betraying their uncertainty and the lack of a special inspiration.[31] There is a slight divergence from the Scotist view in that Ochino regarded as incapable of dispensation not so much the love of God as the love of one's neighbor. One might indeed steal and kill if it could be done in love.[32]

One finds also in Ochino a recognition of the law of necessity.

If [he wrote] one is in extreme need, and has exhausted all other just means, and cannot live without stealing, provided he take only that which is necessary for his urgent and imminent necessity, in that case he would not sin, he would not be a robber, he would not deserve punishment, and he would not be obliged to restore, even though later he became rich, and that, because he would not have taken the goods of another, since necessity would have made his own that which he took, provided that he from whom he took was not in a like necessity.[33]

Again Ochino sometimes verged on the Marcionite

[30] *Il Catechismo* (Basileae, 1561), pp. 89, 91, and 123.

[31] The saying is placed in the mouth of Paul IV; *Dialogi*, xxx, ii, p. 395: Si vobis exploratum fuisset, vos, dum ignem de coelo deuocare vultis, Dei spiritu impelli, nihil opus fuisset, vt a me consilium peteretis: sed quia de eo dubitabatis, ideo me interrogastis.

[32] *Prediche di Bernardino da Siena* (Basileae, 1563), III, LXXVIII, IIi7–KKk, Bisogna adonque dire che se ben li precetti della seconda tauola quanto al non robbare, amazare, & altre opere estrinseche sieno dispensabili, nientedimeno quanto all' atto interno d' amare spiritualmente, et per gloria di Dio li prossimi nostri, il precetto e indispensabile. Tal che se ben possiamo per volonta di Dio tor la robba ai prossimi et anco la vita, non pero possiamo in modo alcuno non amarlo, & non desiderare & procurargli tutte quelle cose che piu gli seruano acio che illustri la gloria di Dio, etc.

[33] *Il Catechismo*, p. 107: Perche se un fusse in estrema necessità, & hauendo tentati gl' altri giusti modi possibili, non potesse uiuere senza robbare, in tal caso, all' hora tollendo solamente quello che per la urgente & imminente necessità, gli fusse necessario, & non piu non peccarebbe, non sarebbe ladro, non douerebbe esser punito, ne sarebbe obligato a restituire, se ben di poi diuentasse ricco: & questo, perche non hauerebbe tolto quel d'altri, poi che la necessità haurebbe fatto, che quel che prese fusse suo: se gia quello dal qual prese non fusse prima di lui uenuto in necessità della medesima cosa.

solution which repudiated the Old Testament ethic as contrary to the law of Christ.[34]

But what rendered Ochino's position particularly
dubious was the fact that he was himself no stranger to the
leadings of the Spirit. His flight from Italy was due to "the
counsel of God and the direction of the Holy Spirit." [35]
Just as Moses slew the Egyptian and fled in accord with the
will of God, so Ochino would not have chosen so many
mortifications if God had not moved and governed him.[36]
Such statements, had they come to the ears of the Zürich
authorities, might well have confirmed their misgivings as
to the soundness of Ochino's views on polygamy. Nevertheless, in view of his irreproachable conduct it seems to me
highly doubtful whether he meant to do more than conserve the common exegetical device for saving the rectitude
of the patriarchs.

Among those who laid claim to contemporary revelations one might perhaps include Calvin's "spiritual libertines," though their position was not precisely that. Instead
of a special revelation those who have crucified the flesh
enjoy a perfect and continuous direction of the Spirit. God
dwells in them and they become his instruments.[37] The

[34] *Dialogi*, xxx, ii, pp. 393–394; *Prediche*, III, LXXXVIII, KKk verso.

[35] *Responsio Bernardini Ochini Senensis ad Marcum Brixiensem*, 1543, p. 88:
Quod Dei consilio & spiritus sancti directioni tribuerim discessum meum, ve-
hementer irascitur.... Quod autem Dei spiritus mihi consultor fuerit & dux
itineris, conscientia mea fidelis testis est: neque ad eius rei certitudinem novum
socratis demonium excitare opus est.

[36] P. Piccolomini, "Due Lettere inedite di Bernardino Ochino," *Arch. d. Soc.
Rom. di Stor. Pat.*, vol. 28. pp. 201–207, Letter II: Moise, a tempo nutrito sotto
l'ombra della figliola di Pharaone in amazare l'egytio monstro che in verita non li
era figlio ... fugi di poi ... fu per volunta di Dio.... Diro similmente di me che
non harrei possuto scientemente e voluntariamente eleger tante calumnie con
tante mie mortificationi appresso il mondo se Dio non mi havessi mosso et gover-
nato lui. Piccolimini doubted whether this letter was really addressed to the Vene-
tian senate. The question is settled by this statement in the Responsio ad Marcum
Brixiensem B7: Quod Moisi exemplum spectat: scripsi in hunc modum clarissimi
Senatui Veneto.

[37] Karl Müller, "Calvin und die Libertiner," *Zeitschrift für Kirchengeschichte*,
XL, N. F. III, 1922, pp. 83–129. On p. 112 he gives passages bearing on this point
taken from the replies of Calvin and Farel. I have not had access to Farel's work.
The following passage is taken from C. Schmidt, "Les Libertins Spirituels," *Traités
Mystiques écrits dans les Années 1547 à 1549* (Basel, 1876), pp. 30–31: Il n'y ha

homicides of the Old Testament heroes receive justification on the ground that they acted as instruments of God. Sometimes the apologetic takes a slightly different form, namely, that those who are spiritual are bound to tell the truth only among themselves and not to the carnal. Micaiah, even without a direct command, rightly declined to cast the pearls of truth before a swine like Ahab, but told the truth in the presence of the believing Jehoshaphat.[38] Samson deceived the Philistines because they were flesh and he was spirit.[39] This reminds one of Dolcino's justification of lying and oath-breaking before the Inquisition. Farel was probably not mistaken in regarding this type of exegesis as a covert apology for the evasiveness of the Nicodemites, who, having repudiated the Roman Catholic Church, nevertheless attended mass to avoid persecution.[40]

The third position, the appeal to the law of nature and necessity, reappeared most markedly in the tracts of the Huguenot pamphleteers, who badly needed a justification for armed revolution and tyrannicide. To them Calvin's restriction of the right of tyrannicide to those who had a special revelation was a source of grave embarrassment, because they wished neither to flout the memory of Calvin, nor to cultivate revelations after the manner of the despised Anabaptists. Beza found a very ingenious way of escape

---

plus ne loy ny Euangile qui ayt pouoir sur luy. . . . Il scait prendre le feu sans se brusler et scait entrer en l'eaue sans se noyer. . . . Il ne craint deffence ne commandement, sinon ce qui est conforme a celuy de son Dieu. Car il est le filz de Dieu mesme, ayant son Pere habitant et demourant en luy, lequel le rendt fort, puissant et immuable, ne pouant produire ne donner de son coeur et thresor, que ce qui est de Dieu, car Dieu mesme parle par luy.

[38] Müller, p. 113 note 1.

[39] Schmidt, p. 41: Mais lisez le text, qui dict qu'il ne le faisoit sinon pour les decepuoir, car il estoit esprit et elle chair.

[40] Müller, p. 113 note 2. It is highly significant that Müller classes together the groups represented in Schmidt and Jaujard and the Libertins Spirituels of Calvin, and that he finds in all a quietistic mysticism of the type of the Theologia Germania. Müller, pp. 119 and 106. This judgment is of the greater interest because Müller did not know that the tracts used by Jaujard in his "Essai sur les Libertins spirituels de Genève d'après de nouveaux documents (thèse)," 1890, are in fact translations from the Dutch of David Joris. Using the notation of Van der Linde's bibliography of David Joris, Jaujard 1 is Joris 21; Jaujard 2, Joris 194; Jaujard 3, Joris 207; Jaujard 4, Joris 216.

when he explained that the Jews were given a special
revelation because they were too stupid to see that they
might have resisted tyranny without it.[41] In the "Dialogue
of Archon and Politie" appeal was made to biblical examples
such as that of Judith. Archon objected that these were due
to a special revelation, to which Politie replied, "Instead of
revelations to-day we have extreme necessity." [42] The
author of the *Discours Politique* asserted that the justification from natural law for what Ehud and Jehu did is valid
to-day. "I ask," said he, "whether for the lack of a special
revelation an act would be deemed unjust which was formerly executed by the commandment of God and thereby
shown to be just and equitable? I do not think so." [43] These
writers restricted the right of revolution, however, to the
lower magistrates. The private individual was still in
need of a special revelation,[44] though the author of the
Discours thought that in case of urgent need the private
citizen assumed a public character.[45]

Of the fourth position, the escape by way of definition,
there is an example in the statement of Oecolampadius, who
said: "I do not think it against the spirit of God and Christ,
if the brothers had killed Phinehas at a divine command, for
it is not killing which constitutes homicide or fratricide, but
it is a mind devoid of love." [46]

Finally one finds a measure of return to the Marcionite

[41] "Traité du droit des Magistrats sur leurs suiets, etc.," in *Mémoires de
l'Estat de France*, ed. by Simon Goulart, II, p. 489b: Et ce que telles delivrances ne
sont advenues que par ceux que Dieu a extraordinairement employez, ne sert de
rien contre mon opinion: ains monstre seulement la stupidité & fauts de coeur des
Israelites, non sans un iuste iugement de Dieu sur eux à cause de leurs iniquitez.

[42] *Mémoires de l'Estat de France*, III, 96b: *Archon*. Mais la pluspart de telles
executions, se faisoyent par ordonnance des revelations extraordinaires. . . . *Politie*.
Nous avons en ce temps-ci au lieu de revelations l'extreme necessité qui nous
enseigne.

[43] *Ibid.*, 294: ie demande si n'y ayant eu particuliere revelation la chose
seroit pour cela iniuste, qui a esté autresfois executee par commandement de
Dieu, & par la manifestee pour iuste et equitable? Je ne le croy pas.

[44] *Ibid.*, II, 491b; III, 105b.

[45] *Ibid.*, III, 294: Mais un tel y peut estre poussé avec cause & regards si
urgens qu'en ce cas il n'est plus privé.

[46] Cited by Nikolaus Paulus, *Protestantismus und Toleranz im 16. Jahrhundert*, 1911, p. 196 note 4.

position among the advocates of religious liberty, who wished to cut the ground from under Calvin's appeal to the Old Testament. Sebastian Castellio rejected this appeal, partly on the ground that there was a special command in those days, but

the most important reason of all is that we are subject to Christ, whose doctrine and example we ought to follow, whatever others may have said and done, because the Father has told us that this is his beloved Son, and that we ought to hear and obey him. It is this Son of God who would not permit his disciples to call down fire from heaven after the example of Elias, telling them that they did not know what spirit they were of, and that he did not come to destroy men as did Elias, but to save. It is this Son of God who has told us to come after him, and that those before him were thieves and robbers, and that is what they are who without his commandment and example, rather in fact against his commandment and example, force consciences. They cannot say that they are after Christ; rather they are before, and they show thereby that they are thieves and robbers.[47]

One cannot but note that the application of the historical method to the Old Testament has effected a very genuine relief both for religion and for morals.

---

[47] *Conseil à la France Désolée*, pp. 36–38 (the only copy in this country, to my knowledge, is at Cornell): Mais la plus grande raison de toutes, c'est que nous sommes sous Christ, la doctrine & exemple duquel nous deuons ensuiure, quoy que autres ayent dit ou fait, ueu que le pere nous a dit que c'est son cher fils, & que nous le deuons escouter & luy obeir. C'est ce fils de Dieu, qui ne permit point à ses disciples de faire descendre le feu du ciel à l'exemple d'Elie, leur disant qu'ils ne scauoint de quel esperit ilz estoint, & qu'il n'estoit point venu pour oster la uie aux hommes, comme Elie, mais pour la sauuer. C'est ce filz de Dieu qui nous a dit que nous allions apres luy; & que tous ceux qui uont deuant luy, sont larrons & brigans: ce que sont ceux qui sans son commandement & exemple, uoire contre son commandement & exemple, forcent les consciences. Car ilz ne peuent dire qu'ilz uoisent apres Christ, mais si bien deuant: en quoy ilz se monstrent larrons & brigans.

8 Michael Servetus and the Trinitarian Speculation of the Middle Ages

Michael Servetus is a very important link in the continuity of Anti-trinitarian Speculation, for by him the acids of late scholasticism were conveyed to the Anti-trinitarians of the sixteenth century. This assertion is, however, controverted. The claim was first made by Adolf Harnack who contended that the so-called *Moderni* of the school of Occam undercut the philosophical basis for the doctrine of the Trinity and left it resting solely upon the authority of the Church. When this in turn was demolished by Humanism, those who conceded the validity of the late scholastic criticism became, in many instances, Anti-trinitarian.[1] Harnack's thesis was denied by the Jesuit scholar, Father Dunin Borkowski, who insisted that the late scholastics were of no mind to disintegrate the doctrine of the Trinity and, in any case, the Anti-trinitarians of the sixteenth century were unlearned persons who can scarcely be supposed to have delved in scholastic lore.[2] Significantly, however, in his roster of these unlearned men, the learned Jesuit

First published in *Autour de Michel Servet et de Sebastien Castellion* (ed' Bruno Becker; H. D. Tjeenk Willink & Zoon, Haarlem, 1953).

[1] Adolf Harnack, *Lehrbuch der Dogmengeschichte* (2d ed. 1870) III, 659.

[2] Dunin Borkowski, "Quellenstudien zur Vorgeschichte der Unitarier des 16. Jahrhunderts," in 75 *Jahre Stella Matutina Festschrift* (1931) I, 91–138, particularly pp. 135–137.

omitted the name of Michael Servetus to whom Harnack had alluded. Yet Harnack did not adduce the evidence on which his surmise rested. This article seeks to validate and document his claim.

To do so involves something more than a mere enumeration of the citations from medieval authors in the works of Servetus. These can readily be supplied, but there is need further to understand how Servetus approached his sources and what he did with them. And there is the prior question of what the sources were trying to say and whether Servetus understood them. One may seriously doubt whether his initial impulse toward Anti-trinitarian speculation was derived from the scholastics and not rather from the New Testament. Servetus was not primarily a speculative thinker, but a man of intense personal religion and of deep practical concern. He was a Spaniard. His country was the land in which for centuries three religions had lived side-by-side: Judaism, Islam and Christianity. The spirit of the crusades had injected into Christianity an intense hostility toward the other two which issued in the program of baptism or banishment. Those who accepted baptism and subsequently fell back into any of the practices of their former religion were treated as relapsed heretics and, if convicted by the Inquisition, were delivered to the secular arm to be burned at the stake. In the early years of the sixteenth century the residue of infidelity had been largely cowed and the rigors of the Inquisition were, for the time being, relaxed, but the problem was never altogether absent from the Spanish mind.

The question was insistently posed as to why the Jews and the Moors should be so hard to convert to the one true and saving faith. The most obvious difference between Judaism and Islam on the one hand and Christianity on the other was the doctrine of the Trinity, which to the outsider appeared no better than tritheism and with some justice, for popular pictorial representations displayed the Trinity now in the guise of three identical old men, now as one body with three heads, and now even as one head with three faces. Was then this doctrine which must be accepted on pain of banish-

ment or death, actually true and essential to the Christian
faith? Troubled by this question Servetus examined the New
Testament and was perfectly amazed to discover that this
tenet so rigorously required and so obstinately refused was
actually not formulated in the Sacred Scriptures. There is,
indeed, something about the Father and something about
the Son and something about the Holy Ghost, but the traditional formula of the three persons and the one substance
is not there. The word Trinity does not occur. The key
word, *homoousios*, that is to say that the Son is consub-
stantial with the Father, is likewise absent. And although
the Son is declared to be the only begotten of the Father,
the Spirit is nowhere declared to have proceeded either from
the Father or from the Son. Much of this formulation was
the work of the Council of Nicaea which frankly admitted
that the doctrine implicit in Scripture cannot be unequivo-
cally expressed in Biblical terms. Servetus was convinced
that nothing should be deemed essential to the Christian
faith which is not in the Scriptures. For that reason he set
the fall of the Church at the Council of Nicaea. All that
came after was to his mind corruption and the scholastic
authors were subjected to the strictures of one common
condemnation.

This appears to be a plausible reconstruction of Servetus'
thinking, though whether or no this is the exact chronological
sequence is beyond our ken. Perhaps he read first the New
Testament and then turned to the scholastics only to swell
his list of nonsensical authors. Perhaps their critique drove
him to the New Testament for an answer. One thing is plain,
that alike in his earlier and in his later works he drew heavily
on the arsenal of the *Moderni*. There were five representatives of this school whom he cited, namely, Occam, Holcot,
D'Ailly, Gregory of Rimini and John Major. References to
other post-Nicene writers are comparatively scant. He men-
tions Augustine, Joachim of Fiore, Peter Lombard, Richard
of St. Victor, Henri de Gand and Scotus.[3] Odd that he passed

---

[3] Augustine's *De Trinitate, Trin. Err.* 26*b*, 40*b*, 41*b*. *R. passim.*—Peter Lombard, *Sent. Dist.* ii, 5; xiii, 3; xxxii, 6; xxxiii, 2. *Trin. Err.*, 26*b*, 27*b*, 28*b*, 37*a*, 39*a*,

over entirely the great scholastics, Albertus Magnus, Thomas Aquinas and Bonaventura!

In order to understand what Servetus did with his sources, how he interpreted them and what he learned from them one must first survey briefly the course of Trinitarian speculation from Augustine to the Reformation. The origins of the doctrine of the Trinity need not be delineated at this point. By the time of St. Augustine the concept was fully formulated and the problem had come to be not so much what is the true position but whether or no the traditional formula could be known and defended. The question was much more epistemological than metaphysical. At the same time changes in metaphysics altered the meaning of the doctrine and coincidently affected the possibility of knowledge and of demonstration.

The medieval writers on the subject fall into three classes.[4] Servetus has citations from all three, though of the differences between them he was scarcely aware. The first school, originating with St. Augustine, may be called the Illustrative, the second, commencing with Richard of St. Victor, the Demonstrative and the third, starting from Occam, the Fideist. The first claimed that the doctrine of the Trinity, though incapable of demonstration, can at least be illustrated. The second affirmed that it may not only be illustrated but also demonstrated. And the third denied

---

42a. *R.*, 26, 28, 30, 39, 41, 46, 77, 510.—Joachim of Fiore, *Trin. Err.*, 33a, 39a. *R.*, 39, 40.—Richard of St. Victor, *De Trinitate* III, ii, *PL* cxcvi, 916. *Trin. Err.* 31b.— Henri de Gand, *Quodlibet* vi, q. 2. *Trin. Err.*, 31b.—William of Occam, *Quaestiones et Distinctiones super I Librum Sententiarum, Dist.* xxvi (1485). *Trin. Err.*, 42a–b. *R.* 42, 45.—Duns Scotus, *Trin. Err.* i, *Dist.* 25–35, *R.*, 45.—Robert Holcot, *Super Quatuor Libros Sententiarum* i, q. 5. *Trin. Err.*, 32a–b. *R.*, 29.—Gregory of Rimini, *Lectura in I et II Librum Sententiarum,* i, xiii (1482). *Trin. Err.*, 39b. *R.*, 41.— Pierre D'Ailly, *Quaestiones . . . super I, III et IV Sent.*, i, q. 5 (1499). *Trin. Err.*, 32b. *R.*, 29.—John Major *In Primum Sententiarum, Dist.* iv et v, q. 6. *Trin. Err.*, 21a–22a. *R.*, 29.

⁴ The first two types were first clearly discerned by Th. de Regnon, *Études de théologie positive sur la Sainte Trinité,* 2 vols. (1892). The third type is well discerned and described by Paul Vignaux, "Luther commentateur des Sentences," *Études de Philosophie Médiévale* XXI (1935), app. "Note sur l'intelligence de la Trinité chez les théologiens Nominalistes." Many valuable suggestions in A. Stohr, "Die Hauptrichtungen der spekulativen Trinitätslehre in der Theologie des 13. Jahrhunderts," *Theologische Quartalschrift* CVI (1925), 113–135.

both, asserting that the doctrine of the Trinity can only be believed. All were talking about the same thing that God is both Three-and-One, that the Son is of the same essence as the Father, that the Spirit proceeds from the Father and the Son. The answer of St. Augustine was that the doctrine can be known only through revelation since reason unaided would never arrive at it. The doctrine is not indeed directly revealed but is deducible from the revelation in Scripture. The interpretation of Scripture formulated by the Council of Nicaea is to be accepted, though the authority of the Council cannot be adduced in dealing with unbelievers who do not accept it.[5] At long last the doctrine of the Trinity has to be received by faith since in this present life we see only in a glass darkly.[6] At the same time faith need not be blind and we should endeavor to understand insofar as we are able.[7] Some questions, to be sure, are completely beyond us, as, for example, the difference between the generation of the Son and the procession of the Holy Ghost.[8] But at other points we aspire to understand and the way lies through analogy by which the doctrine, though indemonstrable, can nevertheless be illustrated.

Augustine discovered a comparison in the constitution of man. This can be known. Man is cognizant of himself and in himself he finds a similitude of the Trinity: in the loved, the lover and love; in mind, love and the knowledge thereof; in memory, intellect and will. Here Augustine was introducing a psychological Trinity.[9] The point in the case of memory, intellect and will is that being three they are inseparable in action as are also the members of the Trinity.[10]

The Saint did not claim that this analogy constitutes proof. It is only an illustration. Yet it verges on proof because man, and not woman by the way, was made in the

[5] *PL* XLII, 772.
[6] *Ibid.*, 1067, 1069, 961.
[7] *Ep.* CXX, *CSEL* XXXIV.
[8] *PL* XLII, 770.
[9] *De Trinitate* IX and X, cf. Michael Schmaus, "Die psychologische Trinitätslehre des Hl. Augustinus," *Münsterische Beiträge zur Theologie* XI (1927).
[10] *Ep.* XLIX.

image of God and however fallen from his pristine state still retains a measure of the similitude. The term *imago Dei* applies to man's inner life and therefore to the psychological Trinity as the term *vestigium* applies to his outward structure. In both instances a measure of inference is possible from the copy to the original.[11]

Augustine's doctrine of the Trinity was by no means novel. The concept and the terminology had already been forged. But the attempt to illustrate and well nigh to demonstrate the doctrine by the psychological analogy marked a departure. The problem therefore was not so much to determine as to explain the teaching. Augustine's approach was to dominate a long line of thinkers among the theologians of the West: Boethius, The Lombard, Anselm, Albertus Magnus, Thomas Aquinas and basically Scotus.

The successors of Augustine in this line, if they diverged from him, did so in their attempts to resolve some of the residual problems which he had relegated to the category of enigmas. The Lombard was the more confident of their solution because he was brash enough to assert that the doctrine could be found on every page of Holy Writ.[12] The Council of Nicaea had never pretended so much and Augustine distinctly recognized that the doctrine of the Trinity cannot be formulated in scriptural terms.[13]

The Lombard rather blithely went to work on the problem raised by the Arians, that if the Father is ungenerated and the Son generated there must be more than one substance. Augustine had contented himself with saying that the terms generated and ungenerated are not to be understood according to substance.[14] The Lombard went further and roundly declared that the substance neither generates nor is generated.[15] At this point Joachim of Fiore bit into the problem. If The Lombard were right, that the substance

---

[11] *De Trinitate* IX and XI.
[12] *Sent.* I, *dist.* ii, cap. 5.
[13] *PL* XLII, 760.
[14] *Ibid.*, 912.
[15] *Sent.* 1, *dist.* 5.

was aloof from the process of generation, in that case Joachim feared the substance would be a fourth entity alongside of the three, a point which Augustine himself had suggested.[16] There would then be a quaternity. To obviate this conclusion Joachim reduced the one substance to such a wraith that nothing remained to hold the three persons in unity. In consequence they became three gods.[17] The followers of Joachim were even more explicit in their claim that the orthodox view entails a quaternity and the only escape is by way of tritheism.[18] The Fourth Lateran Council stepped in and declared in favor of The Lombard in 1215 by the decree *Sancta Fide de Trinitate, Damnamus*. The view of The Lombard became henceforth the authoritative position of the Catholic Church enshrined in the Canon Law.[19]

The second attitude toward the problem of the Trinity in the Middle Ages was inaugurated by Richard of St. Victor (died 1173), who held that the doctrine of the Trinity is susceptible not only of illustration but also of demonstration. To be sure, faith is always subsumed, yet:

As the beginning of all good lies in faith so the consummation and perfection of all good lies in knowledge. . . . Let us therefore press on from faith to knowledge and strive insofar as we are able to understand that which we believe. . . . It is our intent in this work to adduce in favor of that which we believe . . . not only probable but even necessary reasons and I firmly believe that necessary reasons are not lacking.[20]

Such confidence was possible only because Richard reexamined the metaphysical question and had recourse to the Platonic and Neoplatonic view of God as dynamic Being. Creation was explained in this philosophical tradition by assuming that God is diffusive, with an inner necessity of expansion or elaboration. This principle as it passed

[16] *Ep.* CXXX, *CSEL* XXXIV, 715.
[17] Carmelo Ottaviano, "Joachimi Abbatis Liber contra Lombardum," (Scuola de Gioacchino da Fiore), Reale Accademia d'Italia, *Studi e Documenti* III (1934), pp. 60 and 58.
[18] *Ibid.*, pp. 126-127, 143.
[19] *Corpus Juris Canonici*, ed. Friedberg I, ii, vol. I, p. 1.
[20] *PL* CXCXI, 887–891.

through Dionysius the Areopagite to the scholastics was formulated in the phrase *Bonum diffusivum sui*. When appropriated by Christian thinkers the principle provided a ready explanation of why God is not simple and static but dynamic and therefore diversified within His own Being.[21]

The problem for Trinitarian speculation was then to see why the process of elaboration should have stopped at three instead of continuing indefinitely after the manner of the Neoplatonic or Gnostic emanations. To explain the restriction Richard availed himself of a suggestion already available in Augustine[22] and derived from the quality of divine love. The very nature of God's love requires, argued Richard, that within Himself there should be three and only three persons. The initial assumption is that the plenitude of all goodness, and therefore love in its perfection, characterizes God. Now perfect love must have an object to love, equal to and distinct from itself because perfect love cannot be self-love, nor can the love of the Creator find perfect expression if directed to the created. If then the love of a divine person in order to be perfect must be directed toward another divine person there must plainly be at least two divine persons. The argument thus far calls only for a duality and not for a Trinity.

The next step is deduced likewise from the nature of love which, if perfect, will be without jealousy, seeking not to possess the beloved and willing that love shall be shared with a third. "Hence we see that the highest grade of goodness would not be attained in divinity if in a plurality of persons there were lacking a third." The consummation of the highest goodness calls for a completion of the Trinity.[23]

What Richard is essentially doing is to combine the Neoplatonic and the Hebraic views of God. The first posits self-expansive being, the second thinks of God as an inte-

---

[21] J. Péghaire, "L'axiome 'Bonum est diffusivum sui,' dans le Néoplatonisme et le Thomisme," *Revue de l'université d'Ottawa*, Section spéciale I (1932), 5–30.

[22] Schmaus, p. 226, *op. cit.* note 9, who points out, however, that with Augustine the triad *amans, quod amatur* and *amor* is psychological, not metaphysical.

[23] *PL* CXCVI, 922, 926–27.

grated person. Such he can be only if the process of diffusion is not indefinite. Personality imposes limitations. Thus the concepts of God as diffusive Being and of God as integrated personality are combined to provide something approaching at least a rational demonstration of the Christian doctrine of the Trinity.

The line of thought thus initiated by Richard of St. Victor runs curiously through the so-called Augustinians whereas the position of Augustine himself characterized the group who did not bear his name. The followers of Richard are William of Auvergne, William of Auxerre, Alexander of Hales and basically Bonaventura.

There is one other figure important here because mentioned by Servetus, namely Henri de Gand (died 1293) who though an eclectic properly belongs to the Victorine line of the demonstative type, even though his specific arguments are not those of Richard of St. Victor.[24] He recognized of course the priority of faith, yet sought to go even further than Richard in the discovery of demonstrative proof not only for plurality in God but also for the creation of the world. And this second demonstration served to corroborate the first and thus to confirm the Trinitarian structure of God. The creation, according to Henri, was the work of the intelligence and the will of God operating in the guise of wisdom and love. But wisdom and love in their simple and essential forms are inoperative. To act, each must take on concretion. Thus wisdom becomes active only when begotten as the word and love only after becoming concrete in the Holy Spirit. The creation of the world, in other words, required that what would otherwise have been only qualities in God should become personalized and in this way wisdom and love assumed the character of the second

---

[24] His position on the Trinity is discussed by Michael Schmaus, "Der Liber Propugnatorius des Thomas Anglicus und die Lehrunterschiede zwischen Thomas Aquin und Duns Scotus," Teil II, "Die Trinitarischen Lehrdifferenzen," *Beiträge zur Geschichte der Philosophie und Theologie des Mittelalters* XXIX, I (1930).

and the third persons in the Trinity.[25] Back of this thinking lies, of course, the ancient Stoic distinction between the λόγος ἐνδιάθετος and the λόγος προφορικός.

The argument is obviously different from that of Richard of St. Victor, but the presuppositions are the same and the solution essentially similar. Henri, too, was combining the emanationalism of the Neoplatonic tradition, as mediated through the Arabs, with the concept of God as person in the Hebrew tradition where one of the qualities of God is will. As Richard argued from the love of God, Henri did so also from the will of God. The doctrine of creation out of nothing deduced from the first chapter of Genesis conceives of God not as a perennial geyser but as a person who, by an act of will, brings being out of non-being.[26] Once again then the Neoplatonic picture of the expansive God is restricted by combination with the Hebrew view of the personal creative God.

The third school of thought on the problem of the Trinity in the Middle Ages despaired alike of demonstration and illustration and resorted, therefore, of necessity to the authority of the church in an attitude of fideism. This is the school known in its own day as Modernist, deriving from

[25] *Quodlibet Sextum*, q. II. Deus creaturas produxit non ex naturae necessitate, sed ex dispositione suae sapientiae et voluntatis electione, ut nulla necessitate sed solummodo ipsas producit libero arbitrio – –. Ad cuius intellectum sciendum quod Deus est causa productionis creaturarum per sapientiam qua ipsas cognoscit et amorem quo eas diligit.

Non tantum per sapientiam, et amorem quocunque modo se habentes, quia non per ipsos, ut sunt simplicis intelligentiae, et voluntatis, sed per sapientiam, ut est intellectus disponentis operanda, et per amorem, ut est voluntatis opus affectantis. . . . Sapientia autem disponens, et amor affectans, qui respiciunt actum, non sunt nisi sapientia et amor procedens. . . . Sapientia enim ut est essentialis non est nisi speculativa et ideae ut sunt in tali sapientia non sunt nisi rationes cognoscendi. Sapientia vero ut est personalis, sive genita in verbo, non tantum est speculativa ad cognoscenda ea, quae sunt in Deo, et extra ipsum, habendo in se rationes ideales, ut sunt solum principia cognoscendi, sed etiam est practica respectu operandorum, continens in se ideas, ut sunt principia operandi . . . quo aperte patet quod . . . intelligere et velle . . . includuntur in una et prima persona, quae innascibilis est, et Deus non de Deo, a quo ordine quodam originis in personalibus inchoatur et terminatur in persona Spiritus Sancti, in quo hierarchia supercoelestis terminatur.

[26] Jean Paulus, "Henri de Gand," *Études de Philosophie Mediévale* XXV (1938), p. 296.

William of Occam. The reason for the altered attitude toward the problem of the Trinity was a shift in philosophy to the Nominalist position, according to which universals are denied and reality is held to consist of unrelated particulars. This philosophy makes difficulty for the doctrine of the Trinity because the one substance cannot be regarded as a "universal" holding the three persons in unity. If the concept of the one substance be retained there is grave danger that it will be conceived as a fourth entity alongside of the three persons and the result will be a quaternity as Joachim of Fiore had contended. Moreover, if the three persons are not held in unity by the one substance or some comparable "universal," then they will either become three distinct entities and the outcome will be tritheism or else the three must be denied in favor of a strict Unitarianism.

Nominalism in its very beginnings had raised these questions, and alike Abelard and Anselm had pointed to such dangers in the theories of Roscellin. Their warnings were abundantly confirmed when Nominalism became the dominant philosophy. The authors cited by Servetus from this school are five, and they exhibit for us all the acids of medieval "Modernism."

The first of them is Occam himself whose Nominalism prevented him from discovering any principle of unity by which to combine in one the three persons of the Trinity. Traditionally the one substance served this purpose. But, as we have seen, Joachim made of the substance a fourth entity. To obviate this St. Thomas equated the substance with the relations between the persons. Occam inquired why in that case there should not be more than one substance or essence since there is more than one relation.[27] On the basis of his own philosophy Occam denied that even the relation had any reality because the real consists of unrelated particulars. He must recognize, of course, that the three

[27] *Sent.* 1, *Q.* XI, *Dist.* 2. Difficultas istius quae oritur identitate divinae essencie cum relacione et persona, quia si essencia et relacio et persona sint simpliciter una res numero distincta, difficile est videre quomodo sunt relaciones et plures persone et non plures essencie.

persons of the Trinity have this in common, that all are called persons. But he would not concede that the concept person is a "universal" which in any sense binds them into one.

If it be said [he declared] that person constitutes something common, and that being so there is a universal in divinity, I reply that the name person does not signify anything common but it signifies the many of which any particular may be an example just as man does not signify anything common to all men but signifies simply all men. And if it be said that at least a universal is there, I say no. . . . Person is common to three persons but it is not a universal although the concept abstractable from the divine persons is common to the three persons, yet it does not have the character of a universal. . . . The names of genera and species, such as man and animal, point to what their natures have in common, not to a common nature. They signify individuals in general. Similarly this word person does not signify an individual on the score of nature but of things subsisting in such a nature. In the case of the divine persons there is something in common. But this common element exists only in the mind and not beyond. If then it be asked what is common to the three persons I say that the community in reality is not such that any essence is common to the three persons. A community lies only in words and concepts in the same way that many may be said to constitute a whole.[28]

But if then no real bond exists to hold the three persons in unity and if the doctrine of the Trinity be retained, the

[28] *Q.* I, *Dist.* XXVL-P. Si dicatur quod si persona significat tale constitutum ergo significat unum commune et per consequens erit aliquod universale in divinis, respondeo quod hoc nomen persona non significat aliquod commune sed significat illa multa quorum quodlibet est persona sicut homo non significat aliquod commune omnibus hominibus, sed significat omnes homines. Et si dicatur saltem est ibi universale respondeo quod non . . . et ita persona est unum commune tribus personis non tamen est universale. Similiter ille conceptus abstrahibilis a divinis personis est communis tribus personis non tamen habet rationem universalis respectu illarum trium personarum. . . . Nomina enim generum vel speciorum ut homo animal imposita sunt ad significandum ipsas naturas communes, non intenciones naturarum communium sed individuum vagum . . . hoc autem nomen persona non est impositum ad significandum individuum ex parte nature sed ad significandum rem subsistentem in tali natura. Hoc autem est commune secundum rationem personis divinis sed realiter extra animas non est aliquod commune sed tamen in anima. . . . Sed quando queritur quali communitate est persona commune tribus personis dico quod non communitate rei illo modo quo essentia est communis tribus personis sed communitate vocis vel conceptus eo modo quo vel unum est commune multis.

only possible outcome is tritheism. Occam did not phrase it
quite in that way. He did say that the doctrine of the Trinity
from the philosophical point of view must mean that there
are three absolutes. He could as readily assume, he declared,
that one essence equals three absolutes as to assume that
one essence equals in reality three relations.[29] As a matter of
fact, he did say that there is no relation distinct in any way
from the absolutes. And if one concede that God is in reality
Father and Son and Spirit, then one must assume that in
God there are three absolutes in reality distinct.[30] Such a
position is obviously indistinguishable from tritheism.

Occam was fully aware of the impasse. "The proposition
that God is Three in One," said he, "is not self-evident nor
deducible from the self-evident." One can only conclude
that the articles of the faith are not amenable to demonstration. "For the syllogism: God is a Trinity, the Father is
God, therefore the Father is a Trinity, is sound according to
Aristotelian logic, but fallacious from the point of view of
faith. . . ." [31] "The diverse scientific disciplines are not able
to establish that God is Three and One. This can be proved
only in theology on the basis of faith." [32] Over against all the
conundra which arise from a consideration of the distinctions, relations and essences, one has simply to posit faith.[33]

Not only is demonstration excluded but even illustra-

---

[29] *Dist.* XXVI G. Tamen quod una essencia sit realiter ille tres relaciones ita
faciliter potest poni quam tria absoluta sunt realiter distincta et tamen quod una
essentia sit realiter tria absoluta.

[30] *Sent. Dist.* XXX, *Q.* IV F. In divinis nulla est talis relatio distincta quo-
cumque modo ab omnibus absolutis—et tamen posset concedi quod deus realiter
est pater et deus realiter est filius, sicut conceditur quod deus realiter est creans.
Sed secundum istam viam oportet ponere quod in deo essent tria absoluta realiter
distincta.

[31] *Quodlibet* II, *Q.*iij. Dico quod ista propositio deus est trinus et unus nec
est per se nota viatori nec deducibilis ex per se notis sibi sed est sibi simpliciter
neutra. . . . Primum patet quia in talibus sillogismis deus est trinitas, pater est deus,
ergo est trinitas, est fallacia secundum fidem et tamen diceret illum syllogismum
expositorium esse. Haec posset de illa fallacia per aliquam artem Aristotelis instrui
nisi crederet illum articulum fidei esse verum.

[32] *Quodlibet* V, *Q.* I. Dico quod sicut ista conclusio in qua predicatur esse
trinum et unum et quocunque conceptu Dei non potest probari in diversis scientijs
sed solum probatur in theologia praesupposita fide.

[33] *Quodlibet* VII, *Q.* xiiij. Ad oppositum est fides.

tion. Augustine supposed that a certain leap could be made from the image or the vestige of God in man. To this Occam replied that one would gain no knowledge of Hercules from an image of Hercules if one had not already known Hercules, nor could one deduce a cow from tracks in a meadow if one had not first seen a cow.[34] The doctrine of the Trinity, then, can neither be demonstrated nor illustrated but only believed. Occam verged on a doctrine, if not of double truth, at least of double logic.

The school of the *Moderni* in the wake of Occam rang the changes now on one point and now on another of his position with regard to the Trinity. Of them all Robert Holcot (died 1349) was one of the most explicit in propounding insoluble incompatibles entailed in the doctrine that three can be one. In a section of his commentary on the Sentences he enumerated sixteen contrarieties, as for example that God cannot be three persons because three persons constitute three gods and therefore one god cannot be three persons. Again the three persons are to be distinguished either finitely or infinitely. If finitely there will be finitude in God, if infinitely then the three persons will differ as much as God and the devil or man and an ass: "The divine essence generates. It must generate another god and consequently there are two gods." The fourteenth of his riddles is that the Trinity is one God, therefore the Trinity is a unity, and it is not the Father or the Son or the Spirit. Consequently there must be a fourth element in Divinity.

In dealing with all these problems Holcot comments that the Catholic faith is that which has been revealed to the Holy Fathers and set forth in the symbols. To seek to prove it by the faculty of human reason is not only presumptuous but fatuous. At the same time the Catholic may humbly seek a rational explanation. If he find it let him give

[34] *Sent. Dist.* III, *Q.* IXB. Et isto modo tam vestigium vel ymago. Per experienciam enim patet quod si aliquis nullam penitus habeat cognicionem de hercule, si videat statuam herculis non plus cogitabit de hercule quan de socrate . . . et ita est de vestigio quod si aliquis videat vestigium bovis recordabitur de bove habitualiter cognito. Sed si prius numquam habuisset aliquam noticiam de bove non plus recordetur de bove quam de asino.

God thanks. If he fail to find it he is not to brandish his
horns but to bow his head. Let him bear in mind that
natural logic is deficient in matters of faith and that the
rational logic of faith is something other than natural logic.
Aristotle himself recognized that some logic is universal and
applicable to all sciences but there is also a logic peculiar to
each discipline and, that being the case, how much more
must we assume a logic peculiar to faith? The philosophers
cannot see how one thing can be at the same time one and
three, and for that very reason they make no mention of it
in their rules.

Having said all this Holcot then does his best to answer
the problems. For example, with regard to the claim that
the persons of the Trinity must differ finitely or infinitely
and they will then be either finitely or infinitely distinguished, he replies that the quality of their distinctions does
not effect the quality of their essence.[35] Yet when the count
is in, the emphasis is upon the incomprehensibility and one
may say the irrationality of the doctrine of the Trinity.

[35] *Sent.* I, *Q*. V. Quaeritur utrum deus sit tres persone distincte videtur quod
non: quia tres persone sunt tres dij: igitur unus deus non est tres persone.

Secundum: Preterea si tres persone distinguuntur: quero aut finite aut
infinite. Si finite igitur duo finita sunt in deo: et ultra igitur aliquod finitum est in
deo. . . . Si infinite ergo non magis differunt deus et diabolus quam pater et filius: nec
homo et asinus magis different quam pater et filius.

Decimum quartum: Preterea haec est vera, trinitas est unus deus: ergo
trinitas est unitas, sed non est pater neque filius neque spiritus sanctus: ergo est
quarta res in divinis.

Ad istam opinionem dico quod sic. quia haec est fides catholica sanctis
patribus reveleta, sicut in diversis symbolis satis patet: quia hoc probare facultatem
humane rationis excedit: et ideo non solum praesumptuosum: sed et fatuum est ad
illa probanda niti . . . et ideo docet (Anselmus) infra quod catholicus debet humiliter
querere rationem quomodo sit: si potest intelligere deo gratias agat: si non potest
non immittat cornua ad ventilandum sed submittat caput ad venerandum.

Similiter non est inconveniens quod logica naturalis deficiat in his que
fidei sunt. Et ideo sicut fides est supra physicam naturalem ponens res produci per
creationem ad quam philosophia naturalis non attingit, ita moralis doctrina fidei po-
nit quaedam principia quae scientia moralis non concedit. Eodem modo rationalis
logica fidei alia debet esse a logica naturali. Dicit enim commentator . . . quaedam
logica est universalis omnibus scientiis: quaedam propria unicuique scientie et si
hoc est verum a multo fortiori oportet ponere unam logicam fidei et similiter alia
logica utitur obligatus certa specie obligationis – – – – modo philosophi non viderunt
aliquam rem esse unam et tres, ideo de ea in suis regulis mentionem non fecerunt.

Gregory of Rimini, whose Lectures on the Sentences were delivered in Paris in 1344, was not prepared quite so readily to succumb. An ultimate contradiction, of course, none of these *Moderni* would concede. But if there is a final resolution of the apparent discrepancy the theologians, said Gregory, must not readily abandon the quest. To say, because only in the case of the Trinity does three equal one, that therefore the faith is altogether irrational, is to yield too much. In that case the Catholic would not be in a position to refute the heretics. Ausustine rightly observed, noted Gregory, that if anyone opposed the authority of Scripture to manifest and certain reason he is actually reading his own ideas into the Scripture.[36] Similarly one may say that "If the sound of words appears contrary to the Catholic faith the reality itself is not actually opposed." [37]

Yet Gregory could not deny that certain aspects of Trinitarian doctrine remained to him incomprehensible. There is the question why the origin of the Son from the Father should be called generation, whereas the derivation of the Spirit from the Father and the Son should be called procession. If it be suggested that the Son comes from one and the Spirit from two, this explanation does not suffice because the origin of the fire is no different if it be kindled from two flames rather than from one. We are driven, therefore, to admit that in this life, being what we are, the solution transcends our capacities because the derivation of the Son and the Spirit is ineffable and incomprehensible.[38]

[36] *Ep.* CXLIII.

[37] *Lectura Sententiarum* (1482). *Sent.* I, *Dist.* V, fol. Nɪ. Dicitur talem modum arguendi in omnibus tenere praeter quam in divinis et causa est: quod nunquam alibi possunt tres res quarum nulla est alia esse unam rem numero. . . . Sed haec ratio est omnino irrationalis: Tum quod sic dicendo tollitur omnis via ad probandum vel reprobandum aliquid circa divina: cum enim catholici volunt aliquid probare contra hereticos prolibito dicetur discursum . . . non valere: . . . Tum quod sic dicere nichil aliud est quam fidem nostram catholicamque doctrinam contrariam esse certe rationi de plano confiteri: sicque falsam. – – – quod frivolum omnino est.

[38] *Dist.* XIII, fol. 54. Quero an processio spiritus sancti aut spiratio sit generatio? Arguitur quod sic – – – Contra spiritus sanctus non est genitus: ut dicitur in symbolo Athanasii . . . constat quod spiritus sanctus non est filius neque genitus et per consequens nec eius processio est generatio. Quamvis autem ita sit, differentiam tamen spirationis a generatione, et cur productio Filii sit generatio, non autem

Pierre D'Ailly (1350–1420?) the great Cardinal renowned alike for his share in the condemnation of Hus and
for the impetus which his ideas gave to Columbus, was even
less ready than Gregory of Rimini to surrender to the
ineffable and strove valiantly to discover a valid difference
in the production of the Son and of the Spirit. His essential
position was, however, not different. The doctrine of the
Trinity for him also was capable neither of demonstration
nor of illustration. Demonstration is impossible either from
the Old Testament or from the New. No evident reason
would have led one prior to the decree of the Lateran Council
to say with Peter Lombard that essence does not generate
essence. "But God desired that such truths be believed by
Catholics and for that reason he revealed them to the Church
and caused them to be settled by Her. Wherefore some of
the determinations of the Church do not proceed according
to evident deduction from Scripture but according to
spiritual revelation made to Catholics. If anyone inquires as
to the manner of this revelation I answer that it is difficult
to declare save to those to whom the revelation is given. It is
a special gift of God to believe correctly."

Nevertheless the procedure of D'Ailly was highly
rational in a formal sense. He was concerned to show that
the doctrine of the Trinity involves only verbal and not
real inconsistency. This assertion was supported by a series
of fine distinctions in the use of terms. Among them was the
very important distinction between *essentialiter* and *personaliter*. For example, we may say *personaliter* that there
are three gods. "But such an expression though true and
proper among experts is, nevertheless, not customary and
should be avoided for the sake of simple believers." [39]

---

productio Spiritus Sancti et cur Spiritus Sancti non sit etiam Filius ita ut ambo
producti dicantur filii et geniti, in vita ista per tales quales nos sumus explicari
reputo impossibile. Et ratio est: quoniam productio ista est ineffabilis et incom-
prehensibilis a nobis in statu praesenti.

[39] *Quaestiones super I, III et IV Sententiarum. Q.* V. De Unitate essentiae et
Trinate personarum. fol. xciii. Praedicta positio fidei non est nobis naturaliter
evidens nec potest evidenter probari. Sic nec ipsam ex scripturis novi aut veteris
testamenti potest evidenter concludi. Prima pars patet quod talis positio non est
per se nota. Nec per experientiam ita clara est. Unus qui hoc negaret indigeret

This unfortunate concession to irrationalism became
almost a slogan for the late *Moderni*. The qualifications of
D'Ailly were forgotten. The distinction between *essentialiter*
and *personaliter* was displaced by the distinction between
philosophy and theology. The statement came to be that
according to philosophy we may say there are three gods
though according to theology only one.

The sense of D'Ailly was faithfully reproduced, however, by the last of the five *Moderni* cited by Servetus,
namely the Scot, John Major (1469–1550). In his commentary on the Sentences he declared it permissible to say
that there are three gods, provided the term god be con-
strued according to the person. The saints, however, on account of the infidels had not admitted a plurality of gods
lest they give reason to believe in a plurality of essences in
deity. "Yet the case may be so understood among experts." [40]
The final and less guarded form of this statement appears in
Erasmus: "According to dialectical logic it is possible to say

---

sensum. Nec ipsa potest evidenter demonstrari in lumine naturali, quod tunc infideles possent cogi vi rationis naturalis ad assentiendum fidei articulis quod est
falsum. Si quis dicat oppositum vadat ergo ad infideles convertendum. Secunda
probatur et illam non assero sed solum pono probabiliter unde ad huius probationem
suppono tria. Prima est quod praedicta positio non continetur formaliter et expresse
in scriptura novi et veteris testamenti seu in textu biblice . . . et sancti in suis
libris non laborassent ad concludendum illam positionem ex scripturis.—Sed tales
veritates deus voluit credi a catholicis quae voluit ipsas revelare ecclesiae et per eam
determinari et sic quasqunque determinatione eccelsiae non semper procedunt per
evidentem illationem ex scripturis sed per principalem revelationem factam catholicis. Si vero quaeratur quo constat de tali revelatione etc., Dico quod difficile est
constare nisi illis quibus revelatio sit. ideo donum dei speciale est credere recte etc.

xcv verso. Secundam propositionem quam solutionem probabiliter et non
assertive pono est quod capiendum istum terminum deum secundo modo suppo-
saliter sicut iste sunt concedendae non tamen est una persona divina vel tres sunt
personae divinae quorum quaelibet est deus. sic istae sunt concedendae. Non tamen
est unus deus vel plures sunt dij. . . . Talis autem locutio licet sit vera et propria
apud doctos non tamen est consueta et propter simplices est ideo abstinendum ab ea.

[40] *In Primum Sententiarum, Dist.* 4 et 5, q. 6, fol. 39 verso. Insuper deus
capitur personaliter cum concedatur quod deus generat deum. ergo possumus con-
cedere tres sunt dij: quia sensus est tres sunt personae in divinis quarum quaelibet
est deus. . . . Ad aliud conceditur quod quaelibet persona in divinis est deus et deus
potest capi personaliter sed sancti propter infideles non admiserunt plures deos:
ne darent intelligere pluralitatem essentiarum in divinis. sed sic potest capi (dicit
aliacensis [D'Ailly] quaestione quinta) apud doctos.

there are three gods, but to announce this to the untutored would give great offense." [41]

These, then, are the medieval authors exploited by Servetus. He read them all in the light of the Modernist critique whose scepticism he far outstripped. What to the late scholastics was an unsolved conundrum was for Servetus a contradiction incapable of resolution. The doctrine of the Trinity appeared to him riddled with fallacies. What the doctors considered unfathomable was for him untenable. Their ineffable was his incredible. With devastating glee he despoiled their arsenal of riddles to demolish the ramparts of orthodoxy. The arguments of those who considered the doctrine demonstrable he simply did not understand. He interprets Henri de Gand as saying that the speculative and the practical intellect copulate together and beget.[42] Augustine's psychological Trinity was not grasped and the argument from the image and the vestige is not so much as mentioned.[43]

One wonders why Servetus found the syllogisms of the *Moderni* so cogent. Was it because he shared their Nominalism? He appears to have endorsed their empirical epistemology when he says, both in his earlier and his later works, that there is nothing in the mind that is not first in the senses.[44] On the other hand, in the *Restitutio* Servetus had drunk deeply from the wells of Neoplatonism and one would have supposed that he might thereby have been rendered hospitable to the arguments of Richard of St. Victor. The reason that he was so scornful is perhaps not philosophical at all but rather biblical. The doctrine of the Trinity was not formulated in the Bible, therefore it must be false. Any critique must in consequence be valid and any defense spurious. If this be the answer then Father Dunin Borkowski is to this extent right: that scholasticism was not responsible for Anti-trinitarianism but rather biblicism. On the other

[41] *Op. IX*, 1217c, *cf*. V, 500 D.
[42] *Trin. Err.* 32a.
[43] *R*. 27–28.
[44] *Trin. Err.* 33b, *R*. 32.

hand we cannot be certain of the sequence in Servetus' development. Conceivably scholasticism and biblicism made their impact coincidently. At any rate he drew heavily from the scholastic arsenal.

And he transmitted the scholastic difficulties to the Anti-trinitarians of the sixteenth century. This claim is validated by a document published by Delio Cantimori.[45] The author of the document, Georgio Blandrata, cited Joachim of Fiore, the decretal of Innocent III *Damnamus*, and from Holcot, Major and D'Ailly on the Sentences precisely the passages collected by Servetus.[46] Thus we see that he was the bridge from scholastic scepticism to the sectarian repudiation of the doctrine in the sixteenth century.

[45] Delio Cantimori e Elis. Feist, "Per la Storia degli Eretici Italiani del Secolo XVI in Europa," *Reale Accademia d'Italia, Studi e Documenti* VII (1937), p. 107.

[46] See my paper, *Church History* VII (June 1938), pp. 185–186.

9 Changing Ideas and Ideals
in the Sixteenth Century

The sixteenth century has been claimed by the *Journal of Modern History* as falling within its scope, and rightly so, though the line of demarcation from the previous period is seldom clear cut. The English translator of Huizinga's work on the culture of the fifteenth century has called it "The

First published in the *Journal of Modern History*, VIII, 4 (The University of Chicago Press, 1936.) Previously read at the meeting of the American Historical Association, Chattanooga, Tennessee, in December 1935.

The themes handled in this paper have received extensive treatment during the quarter of a century since the paper was written. For an appraisal of the century see Erich Hassinger, "Die weltgeschichtliche Stellung des 16. Jahrhunderts," *Geschichte in Wissenschaft und Unterricht*, XII (1951), 705–718.

The interpretation of the Renaissance has produced a considerable literature. A bibliography appeared twenty years ago, "Recent Literature of the Renaissance," *Studies in Philology*, XXXVII, 2 (April 1940), continued quarterly in *Renaissance News*. W. K. Setton gave a critical survey in "Recent Views of the Italian Renaissance," *Report of the Canadian Historical Association* (1947). By way of historiography we have Wallace K. Ferguson, *The Renaissance in Historical Thought* (Boston, 1948), and his subsequent articles: "The Church in a Changing World: a Contribution to the Interpretation of the Renaissance," *American Historical Review*, LIX, 1 (1953); "Renaissance Tendencies in the Religious Thought of Erasmus," *Journal of the History of Ideas*, XV, 4 (1954); "The Revival of Classical Antiquity or the First Century of Humanism: A Reappraisal," *Report of the Canadian Historical Association* (1957). Hans Baron has given us a new interpretation in *The Crisis of the early Italian Renaissance*, 2 vols. (Princeton, 1955), evaluated by Wallace Ferguson "The Interpretation of Italian Humanism: The Contribution of Hans Baron," *The Journal of the History of Ideas*, XIX, 1 (1958). The admirable books and articles of Paul Oskar Kristeller deal mainly with philosophy and have a distinct bearing on religion. These works and other bibliography will receive treatment in the paper on "The Religion of the Renaissance" in this volume.

waning of the middle ages." He might better have followed the original to the letter and have rendered it "The autumn of the middle ages," recalling that autumn is the time of ripe fruit containing the seeds of spring.[1]

External changes, such as discoveries and inventions, are easy to register; but their effects on the European outlook are slow and elusive. The repercussion on the old world of the finding of the new is still an unfinished story. Among the more immediate effects was the displacement of the crusading ideal. Columbus set forth purposing to dedicate the profits of the new route to India to the recovery of the Holy Land.[2] The discovery of the New Isles ended that. The invention of gunpowder in the fourteenth century did not at once extinguish knighthood, which survived until the seventeenth.[3] The sixteenth was the period of death throes. Symbolic is the figure of Ignatius Loyola brandishing his sword for the queen of Spain on the walls of Pamplona until his leg was shattered by a ball from nowhere in particular, fired by an impersonal engine of modern warfare.[4]

In the realm of ideas changes are less tangible but often more significant. If there is any area in which one may speak of the waning of the middle ages, it is in the sphere of thought. Stadelmann has well remarked that the intellectual world of the middle ages was destroyed not so much by the impact of the new astronomy from without as by the disintegration of philosophy from within.[5] The fifteenth century saw the debacle of scholasticism. There were two schools, the *Via moderna* and the *Via antiqua*, both sterile. The main

---

[1] J. Huizinga, *Herfsttij der Middeleeuwen* (Haarlem, 1928). Huizinga himself in another work, *Wege der Kulturgeschichte* (Munich, 1930), p. 138, protests against precise periodization. Compare the comment on Huizinga's "Herbst" of Konrad Burdach, "Die seelischen und geistigen Quellen der Renaissancebewegung," *Historische Zeitschrift*, CXLIX (1933–1934), 491–492.

[2] John Boyd Thacher, *Christopher Columbus*, I (New York and London, 1903), 177–180.

[3] See the article "Adel" by Georg von Below in *Handwörterbuch der Staatswissenschaften* (Jena, 1898) I, 49.

[4] René Fülöp-Miller, *The power and secret of the Jesuits* (New York, 1930), p. 37.

[5] Rudolf Stadelmann, *Vom Geist des ausgehenden Mittelalters* (Halle, 1929), p. 40.

difference between them consisted in their theory of knowledge. The *Via moderna* went back to Occam, whose epistemology made trouble for theology. He held that we can know
only the constructs which the mind sets up in response to an
external stimulus. We may be almost sure that there is an
object creating the stimulus, though even here absolute
assurance is impossible because God might cause the mind
to set up the construct even apart from the stimulus. Occam's skepticism was further increased by his nominalism,
which denied the existence of universals save in the mind.
Such a philosophy cut the ground from under many of the
traditional arguments for the existence of God and rendered
very difficult any rational defense of the doctrines of the
Lord's Supper and the Trinity. Faith and knowledge were
thus split apart, and the tendency was to emphasize authority. One might have expected Occam to be an ultra-
montane, but he was cut off in this direction by a quarrel
with the pope. In desperate need of authority, but dubious
with regard to that of the church, he fell back upon the
Bible.[6] His followers did not press the radicalism of his
conclusions. While toying with explosives, they were afraid
to set off fuses lest, if the structure were demolished, there
should be nothing with which to replace it.[7]

The *Via antiqua* sought a surer way by a return to
Thomas and Scotus. Some have seen here an affinity with
the Renaissance and its return to classical antiquity.[8] An
analogy there is, rather than a connection. But this return to
the classical scholastics did not recover their creative capacity. The *antiqui* were as sterile as the *moderni*. Neither
could do better than compile manuals of excerpts. Why

[6] Nicola Abbagnano, *Guglielmo di Ockham* (Lanciano, 1931).

[7] Gerhard Ritter, *Studien zur Spätscholastik*; Vol. I, *Marsilius von Inghen
und die okkamistische Schule in Deutschland*; Vol. II, *Via antiqua und via moderna
auf den deutschen Universitäten des XV Jahrhunderts* ("Sitzungsberichte der Heidelberger Akademie der Wissenschaften," Vols. XII and XIII [Heidelberg, 1921–
1922]).

[8] Heinrich Hermelink, *Die theologische Fakultät in Tübingen vor der Reformation* (Leipzig, 1906), and *Die religiösen Reformbestrebungen des deutschen Humanismus* (Tübingen, 1907).

these two schools should have played out is not apparent from the nature of their philosophies. The empiricism of Occam was pregnant enough in the hands of Locke and his successors. The philosophy of St. Thomas has of late experienced a vigorous revival in neo-Thomism. The rhythms of history belong to the inexplicable. The one concrete observable fact with regard to this late scholasticism in all its forms is a loss of religious vitality, a timidity in wrestling with great problems, for one school discussed concepts and another terms into the fourteenthly and the fifteenthly. Theology became a science directed toward itself rather than God and man.

Various attempts were made before the sixteenth century to attain a new grip. The Franciscan movement had been concerned since the thirteenth century for a rebirth of humanity. Francis wished to go back to the simplicity of Jesus and avoid that learning which quenches the spirit.[9] The Franciscan scholastics were open to divine illumination,[10] and the Franciscan radicals called for a renovation of humanity through the coming of the Holy Ghost. The ferment was powerfully assisted by the ideas of Joachim of Fiore, who divided history into three stages, of which the last, the age of the Spirit, was about to be ushered in.[11] We have here a combination of three ideas, namely: return to an ancient norm, that of Jesus or Francis; rebirth in a spiritual sense (*rinascimento*); and the hope of a new age (eschatology).[12] This Franciscan ideal was not extinct in the

[9] D. H. S. Nicholson, *The mysticism of St. Francis of Assisi* (Boston, 1923), chap. vii.

[10] On Augustinianism in the Franciscan order consult Martin Grabmann, *Die philosophische und theologische Erkenntnislehre des Kardinals Matthaeus von Aquasparta. Ein Beitrag zur Geschichte des Verhältnisses zwischen Augustinismus und Aristotelismus im mittelalterlichen Denken* (Vienna, 1906); *Der göttliche Grund menschlicher Wahrheitserkenntnis nach Augustinus und Thomas von Aquin*, Vol. I, Part 4 (Münster in W., 1924).

[11] Ernst Benz, *Ecclesia spiritualis Kirchenidee und Geschichtsphilosophie der Franziskanischer Reformation* (Stuttgart, 1934).

[12] Konrad Burdach, *Reformation Renaissance Humanismus* (Berlin and Leipzig, 1926); "Die seelischen und geistigen Quellen der Renaissancebewegung," *Historische Zeitschrift*, CXLIX (1933–1934), 477–519, in which Burdach reviews the reception given his view of the Renaissance.

sixteenth century. A new branch of the order was founded
in this period, known as the Capuchin. The opposition to
learning was such that some scholars, on joining the order,
threw away their books. The ideal was pious ignorance,
ignorantia sacra.[13]

Another attempt at rejuvenation was that of the
northern mystics. In the Netherlands we find the Brethren
of the Common Life, whose best-known representative is
Thomas à Kempis. They were not hostile to learning, and
we find among them many representatives of the humanist
movement. Nevertheless, their ideal was simplification in
the interest of a practical piety devoted to prayer, education,
and philanthropy. The *Imitatio* well phrased their feeling in
saying that the Trinity is better pleased by adoration than
by speculation.[14] In the Rhine valley we find the Friends of
God, who, following the tradition of Eckhart, were more
deeply mystical than the Brethren. Their ideal was to sink
the self in the being of God. All self-will and self-love should
be overcome. This movement was not so antithetical to
scholasticism as Protestant writers have contended.[15] The
discovery by Denifle of the Latin writings of Eckhart reveals his indebtedness to St. Thomas.[16] Nevertheless, we
have here a change in tone and direction.

The third attempt to find a new grip was that of
humanism, which sought the spiritual rebirth of humanity
through the restoration of classical antiquity. Some have

[13] Frédégand Callaey, "L'infiltration des idées franciscaines spirituelles
chez les frères-mineurs capucins au XVI ᵉ siècle," Estratto dalla *Miscellanea Fr.
Ehrle*, Vol. I (Rome, 1924).

[14] *Imitatio Christi*, Chaps. I–III. On the *fides simplex* of the *Devotio Moderna*
see Paul Mestwerdt *Die Anfänge des Erasmus Humanismus und Devotio Moderna*
(Leipzig, 1917), chap. ii, especially pp. 89 ff.

[15] For example, Wilhelm Preger, *Geschichte der deutschen Mystik im Mittelalter*
(3 vols.; Leipzig, 1874–1893), I, 145.

[16] Heinrich Denifle, "Meister Eckharts lateinische Schriften und die Grun-
danschauung seiner Lehre," *Archiv für Literatur und Kirchengeschichte des Mittelalters*, II (1886), 417–640, especially pp. 421, 526; Martin Grabmann, *Neuaufgefundene
Pariser Quaestionen Meister Eckharts und ihre Stellung in seinen geistigen Entwick-
lungs-gange* ("Abhandlungen der Bayerischen Akademie der Wissenschaften,"
Vol. XXXII, No. 7 [Munich, 1927]). On the continuation of scholastic tradition
in German mysticism: Gottlob Siedel, *Theologia Deutsch mit einer Einleitung über
die Lehre von der Vergöttung in der dominikanischen Mystik* (Gotha, 1929).

regarded the movement as pagan; some as prevailingly Christian.[17] Among the more recent writers, Toffanin contends that humanism, though opposed to scholasticism, was in league with Catholicism, which had long ago incorporated the classical tradition. Catholicism and humanism were both ancient, both Roman, both universal, both Latin. Even the revival of Cicero was a source of strength to the church, for had he not already been employed by Lactantius, Jerome, and Augustine?[18] There is much in this point of Toffanin, for humanism did not produce a system opposed to Catholicism. The danger lay not so much in atheism as in universal deism and neo-gnosticism.[19] Both, too, had in common a willingness on the part of the individual to accept

[17] The classic picture of the egoism of the Renaissance is that of Jacob Burckhardt, *The civilization of the Renaissance in Italy*, tr. S. G. C. Middlemore (London, 1929). His view is defended against Burdach's (*op. cit.*) stress on the spiritual and Christian currents, by H. W. Eppelsheimer, "Das Renaissance-Problem," *Deutsche Vierteljahrschrift für Literaturwissenschaft und Geistesgeschichte*, XI (1933), 477–500. He selects as the main characteristics of the period classicism, rationalism, an anti-metaphysical bias, and a concern for the autonomy of man. He forgets that classicism was equally strong in scholasticism (Aristotle), that the rationalism of the Renaissance is mainly Averroist, that an anti-metaphysical tendency is found also in nominalism. The cult of man alone remains. The whole controversy is reviewed by Arminio Janner, "Individualismus und Religiosität in der Renaissance," *ibid.*, XIII (1935), 357–377. He vindicates Burckhardt, but shifts the emphasis from the braggadocio of the *condottieri* to the cult of the worth of man among the humanists. A strong secularist tendency is unquestionably to be discovered along with the Christian currents of the period. Herein lies the truth of Burckhardt, but he neglected the philosophy and religion of the Florentine Academy. There is an extensive survey of the literature in A. Stubbe, *Naturalistisch of Mystiek? Het Probleem der Renaissance als Aanleiding tot het Probleem der Barok* (Louvain, 1933). He finds "naturalism" to be the kernel of the Renaissance. Another survey is made by Delio Cantimori, *Sulla storia del concetto di Rinascimento*, ("Annali della R. Scuola normale superiore di Pisa," Ser. II, Vol. I [Pisa, 1932], pp. 228–268). Burckhardt receives full length treatment in the three-volume biography by Werner Kaegi (Basel, 1947–1956). His classic work on the Renaissance has received reappraisal on the centenary of its publication in 1860. See *Jacob Burckhardt and the Renaissance 100 Years After* (The University of Kansas, 1960), articles by Robert Kingdon, Lewis W. Spitz, William Gilbert and Klaus Berger. Hans Baron gives an illuminating appraisal in *Renaissance News*, XIII, 3 (Autumn 1960).

[18] Giuseppe Toffanin, *Che cosa fu l'umanesimo* (Florence, 1928); and *Storia dell'umanesimo dal XIII al XVI secolo* (Naples, 1933).

[19] Cf. Wilhelm Dilthey, "Auffassung und Analyse des Menschen im 15. und 16. Jahrhundert," *Gesammelte Schriften*, Vol. II, *Weltanschauung und Analyse des Menschen seit Renaissance und Reformation* (Leipzig and Berlin, 1914), pp. 45–47; and Paul Wernle, *Renaissance und Reformation* (Tübingen, 1912), chap. ii, "Von der Schranken der Renaissancekultur."

the consensus of the experts, a respect for authority.[20] And even with monasticism, humanism had affinities, for both the study and the cell call for withdrawal from active life, and in both may hang the picture of the scholar monk, St. Jerome.[21]

Nevertheless, it would be more exact to say that humanism was in itself neutral precisely because the classical tradition was itself so diverse.[22] It was not necessarily opposed even to scholasticism. There were scholastic humanists and humanist scholastics. There were humanists of the *Via antiqua* and humanists of the *Via moderna*. The Reuchlin controversy divided the humanist camp. In different countries the alignment was different. In Germany humanism fed into the Reformation—witness Melanchthon and Zwingli—and even into the left wing—witness Denck and Franck. In Spain and Italy, on the other hand, humanism made its peace with the Counter-Reformation. Cardinal Ximines is an astonishing figure in this regard. He was thoroughly medieval in his crusade against the Moors and in his monastic reforms. He was a humanist in his edition of the Scriptures in the original tongues and in the foundation of a university with chairs not only in the classical languages but also in Hebrew, as well as in medicine and surgery.[23] In France humanism fed in part the rational tendencies anticipatory of the Enlightenment. Though the Averroist influence was more subversive, nevertheless Cicero was dangerous for the church, as Jerome and Augustine had been aware. He was dangerous partly because he was so near to the kingdom of God, so near that Calvin could quote with approval in the opening books of the *Institutes* the Ciceronian arguments

[20] Erich Seeberg, *Luthers Theologie* (Göttingen, 1929), I, 68, 75.

[21] Compare Hajo Holborn, *Ulrich von Hutten* (Leipzig, 1929), English tr. R. H. Bainton (New Haven, 1937). See the very illuminating article by Hans Baron, "Franciscan Poverty and Civic Wealth in Humanistic Thought," *Speculum*, XIII, 1 (January 1938), 1–37.

[22] Cf. Gerhard Ritter, *Studien zur Spätscholastik*, II, 118 and 134; also Ritter, "Die geistliche Bedeutung des deutschen Humanismus," *Historische Zeitschrift*, CXXVII (1923), 393–453, especially 405, 415, 427.

[23] James Patrick Ronaldson Lyell, *Cardinal Ximenes* (London, 1917).

for the existence of God from the *consensus omnium*.[24] His influence was more insidious than that of Lucretius, whose French editors declared stoutly that they were more interested in his Latinity than in his ideas.[25] Even Lucian stimulated only peripheral criticism, mockery of relics, pilgrimages, and saint-worship.[26] We know from Erasmus how innocuous all this could be for the essential structure of medieval Catholicism. But Cicero's stoic empirical theory of knowledge, his praise of man and of reason,[27] his wistful doubts, and his universal deism made him not improperly the favorite of the French rationalists in the sixteenth century as he was of the English deists in the eighteenth.[28]

But none of these movements—the Franciscan, the mystic, or the humanist—seriously shook the medieval structure. The Franciscan movement in its radical aspects was too nearly spent. The Spirituals, the Fraticelli, the Observants had either succumbed or compromised. The Capuchins soon accommodated themselves to the so-called Counter-Reformation. Heresy in general was played out in Italy. The preceding period had seen the Humiliati, Petro-

[24] *Calvini opera*, II, 36; *Instit.*, Book I, chap. iii, §1.

[25] C.-A. Fusil, "La Renaissance de Lucrèce au XVI⁰ siècle en France," *Revue du seizième siècle*, XV (1928), 134–150. George Depue Hadzsits, *Lucretius and his influence* (New York, 1935), pp. 277–278, concludes: "Fifteenth- and sixteenth-century Europe was far from accepting Lucretius, as thinker, however widely he was read and admired as a poet. . . . Never was he more lonely." Eleanore Belowski, *Lukrez in der französischen Literatur der Renaissance* (Berlin, 1904), finds that among the ideas of Lucretius the most influential was the Venus cult of love as the all-creating force in nature. Less significant were his pessimism, sensualist epistemology, and skepticism as to immortality. Even Montaigne, who was most influenced by the skepticism of Lucretius, was a fideist. See H. J. T. Janssen, *Montaigne fidéiste* (Nimwegen, 1930).

[26] Henri Busson, *Les sources et le développement du rationalisme dans la littérature française de la Renaissance* (Paris, 1922). He finds the Averroists a more potent source of rationalism than the classics. Richard H. Popkin points out that Sextus Empiricus was not published in Latin until the 1560's and in Greek till the next century. Only in the seventeenth and following centuries do we find an extensive impact of his thought. See his "Samuel Sorbiere's Translation of Sextus Empiricus," *Journal of the History of Ideas*, XIV, 4 (1953), 617–621.

[27] On Cicero's contribution to the cult of man in the Renaissance see Giovanni Gentile, *Giordano Bruno e il pensiero del Rinascimento* (Florence, 1920), pp. 135, 169.

[28] Th. Zielinski, *Cicero im Wandel der Jahrhunderte* (Leipzig and Berlin, 1908).

brusians, Arnoldists, Albigenses, Waldensians, Patarenes, and Apostolics.[29] Remnants alone survived. Catholic reform was reduced to corrective discipline.

The mystics were too quietistic either to wreck or to build a church. Mysticism can be content with any outward form or with none, because the inner life alone matters. Hence mysticism was as neutral as humanism and could flower alike on Catholic and Protestant soil.

Humanism was worse than neutral. In some respects it was deadly. As the cult of antiquity it destroyed the living tradition of antiquity. Latin, though plastic for a time in the hands of Erasmus and Hutten, was killed in part by being made a dead language, constricted by the forms of its infancy.[30] And how could humanism as the glorification of reason and man expect to attain a new grip of truth and God? Humility and shame are essential here. That is why humanism lacked a sense of religious compulsion and many devotees could say with Montaigne, "There is nothing for which I wish to break my neck." [31]

As for the scholastics, *antiqui* and *moderni* alike feared to grapple with the problems that had been raised, because they could envisage no adequate substitute for the system of the Church.[32]

A pathetic symbol of the late middle ages is Nicolas of Cusa, persuaded like Occam, that one cannot know, for God has hidden himself. He is a *Deus absconditus*. Philosophy leads only to instructed ignorance, *docta ignorantia*. The bridge from ignorance to prayer is mysticism, but of what comfort is mysticism without assurance? No wonder that a disciple of Cusa said to Luther, "No doubt you are right,

---

[29] G. Volpe, *Movimenti religiosi e sette ereticali nella società medievale italiana* (Florence, 1926); Ellen Scott Davison, *Forerunners of St. Francis* (Boston, 1927).

[30] Étienne Gilson, "Le moyen âge et le naturalisme antique," *Archives d'histoire doctrinale et littéraire du moyen âge*, VII (1932), 5–37.

[31] Albert Thibaudet, ed., *Essais de Michel de Montaigne* (Argenteuil, 1933), Bk. II, chap. x, p. 389.

[32] Compare the judgment of Robert L. Calhoun, *God and the Common Life* (New York, 1935), pp. 42–43.

brother, but you will never get anywhere. Better go back
to your cell and say, 'God have mercy on me.' " [33]

In Martin Luther all these struggles and hopes are
epitomized; but he differs from his predecessors in his
deeper sense of the nothingness of the creature before the
creator, of the impurity of the sinner before the Holy.[34] God
is not merely the hidden God. He is the indignant God, who
hideth himself in his anger. Man has defied him and broken
his law. Nothing that man can do can effect any reconciliation. Here Luther reaches the climax of the feeling of
impotence which obsessed so many. But out of this weakness comes strength; out of negation, affirmation. Man can
do nothing. God can do everything. The hidden God is also
the revealed. He hides himself from the wise and prudent
and reveals himself unto babes. (Here are echoes of the
emphases of the Franciscans and the Brethren on simplicity
and humility.) The wisdom of the world is but folly in his
eyes. Human reason is but a harlot. (Here is Occam's despair
of man's intellectual powers.) How does God reveal himself? In his Word. (This suggests Occam's biblicism.) But
what is God's Word? It is that which goes counter to all the
desires of the natural man.[35] (This sounds like Tauler and
the mystics.) Luther writes:

Repentance which is occupied with thoughts of peace is hypoc-
risy. There must be a great earnestness about it and a deep hurt
if the old man is to be put off. When lightning strikes a tree or a
man, it does two things at once,—it rends the tree and swiftly slays
the man, but it also turns the face of the dead man and the broken
branches of the tree to itself, toward heaven. So the grace of God

---

[33] Rudolf Stadelmann, *Vom Geist des ausgehenden Mittelalters* (Halle, 1929),
chap. ii, §3, and pp. 67, 117.

[34] See the excellent description of Luther's "dark night of the soul" by
Gerhard Ritter, *Luther Gestalt und Symbol* (Munich, 1925). On the "Angst der
Kreatur," p. 29, cf. Rudolf Otto, *Das Heilige* (Breslau, 1920), chap. xiii, "Das
Numinose bei Luther."

[35] Johannes Ficker, *Anfänge reformatorischer Bibelauslegung*, Part I, *Luthers
Vorlesung über den Römerbrief 1515/1516* (Leipzig, 1930), pp. 249, 271. *WA* 56,
423. On these elements in Luther's religion consult Walter von Loewenich, *Luthers
Theologia Crucis* (Munich, 1929). Erich Seeberg, *Luthers Theologie Motive und
Ideen*, Part I, *Die Gottesanschauung* (Göttingen, 1929).

terrifies and pursues and drives a man, but turns him at the same time to himself.[36]

Why did all this happen to Martin Luther? Who can say? The new grip on God and life which he attained did not last. His high hopes for the reformation of the whole church also played out, and a new wave of pessimism swept over men. Witness Sebastian Franck. If the explanation is sought on the human side, perhaps we may say that humanity can stand the strain of defeat only so long, and, thwarted for a decade, will reaffirm itself. From the divine side we can say no more than that the Spirit bloweth where it listeth.

The most immediate, and perhaps important, effect of Luther's new grip was the arrest of secularism for a century and a half. This is speaking roughly, of course. One has in mind the triumph of secularism at the treaty of Westphalia from which the pope was excluded, though, on the other hand, the revocation of the Edict of Nantes came later. Prior to the Reformation, Catholicism itself was suffering secularization. The pope was not unwilling to make an alliance with the Turk, and Machiavelli's ideal prince was a son of the pope. But Luther made religion the dominant concern of man even in politics. Maurice of Saxony, who would betray his coreligionists for the sake of the electoral dignity, was a shocking exception. Typical, rather, was George of Brandenburg, who, when Charles V called on the German princes to participate in a Corpus Christi procession, informed the emperor that sooner than do so he would kneel down and have his head cut off.[37]

Or take the example of Galeazzo Caracciolo, the Marquis of Vico. He was the only son of a Neopolitan nobleman, a relative of the pope, a favorite of Charles V, married to a Carafa. The union, designed to unite domains, served even more to cement hearts. There were six children, four girls and two boys, all devoted to their father. Then Galeazzo was converted to the reform and fled to Geneva,

[36] *WA* VII, 308, translated in Henry Eyster Jacobs (ed.), *Works of Martin Luther*, III (Philadelphia, 1930), 49–50.

[37] *Realencyclopedie*, VI, 537.

summoning his family to join his exile. The confessors of Vittoria would not suffer her to live with a heretic. After fruitless attempts at an interview with his wife on neutral ground, Galeazzo risked a return home. The family was overjoyed until he made plain his resolve not to renounce his faith. Then his father covered him with curses, and his wife with tears. His twelve-year-old daughter threw her arms about his feet. Father had come home. Why did he need to go away again? To stay meant the stake. He returned to the ship and took sail while the family stood on the shore waving to him to remain.[38] "Let goods and kindred go, this mortal life also"—these words of Luther's hymn expressed the mood of thousands of Protestants and Catholics alike.

The immediate outworking of this spirit was the formation of a multitude of sects. The initial impulse came from Luther, however much medieval elements may have been incorporated in the new formations. The radicals of the Reformation almost uniformly went through a Lutheran stage. Anabaptism was an offshoot of the Reformation. Various considerations have been adduced as affecting the growth of the sects. The coincidence of certain churches with national lines is obvious. The coincidence likewise with class cleavages is stressed by some. Lutheranism, Zwinglianism, and Calvinism are interpreted as middle-class movements, and Anabaptism as the religion of the disinherited.[39] There is something in the point, but it must not be overdone. One of the spiritual descendants of the Anabaptists has well remarked that men in the sixteenth century became Anabaptists not because they were disin-

---

[38] Not until this year have we had a scholarly study of Caracciolo. It is from the pen of Benedetto Croce, *Vite di aventure di fede e di passione* (Bari, 1936), 179–281. The almost contemporary life by Balbani was early translated into English. There is a modern reprint of the Italian by Comba and an English translation based upon it, *Life of Galeazzo Caracciolo from the Italian of Nicolao Balbani 1587 republished by Professor Emilio Comba translated by Maria Betts* (London, 1907).

[39] This thesis is persuasively set forth by H. Richard Niebuhr, *The Social Sources of Denominationalism* (New York, 1929).

herited, but were disinherited because they became Anabaptists.[40]

More important, I think, as a factor in sect formation
is the conception which we have already met among the
Spiritual Franciscans and among some of the humanists of
a restitution of original Christianity. Here is a sort of
Christian primitivism. Erasmus was fond of rebuking the
superstition and intolerance of his own day by the example
of the early church. From him, probably Luther, and
Melanchthon in a measure, and more especially Zwingli,
learned this device for combating the church of Rome. But
they were speedily to recoil, having been made aware by the
Anabaptists of the too radical implications of a complete
restoration of primitive Christianity, for the New Testament provides no warrant for infant baptism or the union
of church and state. Calvin discreetly entitled his book the
Institutio, leaving his opponent Servetus to call his work the
Restitutio, a title already utilized by half a dozen Anabaptist
tracts.[41] Precisely as with the Spiritual Franciscans, the

[40] John Horsch, "Was the Swiss Brethren movement an economic and social
class struggle or a religious movement?" Section 1 of the article "The faith of the
Swiss Brethren," *Mennonite Quarterly Review*, IV (1930), 245–254; *The Hutterian
Brethren 1528–1931* (Goshen, Ind., 1931), pp. 3, 4, 6.

[41] Karl Borinski, *Die Weltwiedergeburtsidee in den neueren Zeit* ("Sit-
zungsberichte der Bayerischen Akademie der Wissenschaften," Philos. philol. und
hist. Kl., 1 Abh. 1919). Attention was called to these ideas by Paul Wernle,
Renaissance des Christentums im 16. Jahrhundert (Tübingen and Leipzig, 1904).
Compare J. Huizinga, *Wege der Kulturgeschichte* (Munich, 1930), pp. 124–127.
Borinski calls attention to the significance of the difference between the titles of
Calvin and Servetus, but does not recognize that Servetus drew from Anabaptist
circles. Here are the works or utterances which fall in this category:

An Anabaptist tract addressed to Philip of Hesse in 1528, reprinted in the
Wittenberg edition of Luther's *Works* (1588), II, fols. 240–265*b*.

Johann Campanus, *Göttlicher und Heiliger Schrift vor vilen jaren verdunc-
kelt, und durch unheylsame Leer und Lerer (aus Gottes Zulassung) verfinstert, Restitution und besserung durch den hochgelerten Johannem Campanum . . . 1532*, analyzed
and reproduced in part by Johann Georg Schelhorn, *Amoenitates Literariae*, XI
(Frankfurt and Leipzig, 1729), 78–89. There is a recent analysis and discussion by
Stanislaus Dunin Borkowski, "Quellenstudien zur Vorgeschichte der Unitarier
des 16. Jahrhunderts," *75 Jahre Stella Matutina* (Feldkirch, 1931), I, 91–138, on
this point, pp. 114–115.

Bernhard Rothmann, *Restitution rechter und gesunder christlicher Lehre*
(1534), reprinted in *Neudrucke deutschen Literaturwerke, Flugschriften aus der
Reformationzeit*, Vol. VII (Halle, 1888).

adoption of the primitive as the only norm produced an attitude of intransigent opposition to churches which thought in terms of a developing and comprehensive Christian society. Moreover, the attempt to recover original Christianity of necessity led to multifarious sect formation because the Christianity of the New Testament itself presented diverse types of organization and thought. With equal justice one group selected one point and another another for emphasis. The *reductio ad absurdum* of Christian primitivism was the case of John Smyth, the English refugee in the early seventeenth century in Holland, who thought that the continuity of Christianity had been so completely broken that no one on earth was competent to baptize him. He must therefore baptize himself. For that reason he is called a Se-Baptist, or Self-Baptizer.[42]

Here I must throw in a word about the origin of the English sects which so largely colonized New England. Hall, in his recent work on the religious background of American culture, claims that in England the Reformation produced three types: the Anglican, which was aristocratic and essentially Catholic; the Puritan, which was middle class and based on continental Calvinism; and the Sep-

---

Hendrik Niclaes believed "das Evangelium spreche von einer Wiederherstellung der ersten vollkommenen Gerechtigkeit" (Friedrich Nippold, "Heinrich Niclaes und das Haus der Liebe," *Zeitschrift für die historische Theologie*, XXXII [1862], 323–402; on this point p. 342).

The closing section of William Postell's *Panthenosia* (1547), p. 136, begins "Unde Restitutionis ducetur exordium." The conception is prominent in his letter to Bauhin. See my article "Wylliam Postell and the Netherlands," *Nederlandsch Archief voor Kerkgeschiedenis*, XXIV, Part 2 (1931), 161–172, reprinted in vol. 2 of this series.

David Joris entitled the fourth section of his *Wonderboeck* (1542 and 1551, both editions at Yale), *Dat vierde Deel vant Wonder-boeck: Daer die Restitutie oder wederbringhe Christi . . . gheopenbaerdt werdt.*

Against the Anabaptists, Dirk Philips wrote a tract, "Van de geestelijcke Restitution," *Bibliotheca Reformatoria Neerlandica*, X (The Hague, 1914), 338–376, dated by the editors later than 1559; *ibid.*, pp. 10–11, n. 7.

Likewise against the Anabaptists was the tract of Urbanus Rhegius, *De Restitutione regni Israelitici, contra omnes omnium seculorum Chiliastes* (Zell, 1536). The importance of this theme in Anabaptist thought has been extensively explored by Franklin H. Littell, *The Anabaptist View of the Church*, 2d ed. (Boston, 1958).

[42] Walter H. Burgess, *John Smith, the Se-Baptist* (London, 1911).

aratist, which was lower class and indigenous, going back to
Wyclif and the Lollard movement.[43] Against this view I
would point out that, while the Lollard movement may
have had some underground influence, there was also an
overflow from the continental sects. The Family of Love,
for example, was transplanted from Holland.[44] More to the
point is the analogy of the continent. Just as Anabaptism
broke off directly from Zwinglianism because of disillusionment as to the visible effects of the reform in life, so English
Separatism split off from English Puritanism, itself ad-
mittedly of Calvinist origin, when reform lagged. So soon as
petitions to parliament proved futile, then Robert Browne
came out with his tract, *A treatise of Reformation without
tarying for anie* (1582).

The formation of so many sects had the indirect consequence of necessitating religious liberty. The outstanding
reformers had no intention of moving in this direction.[45] The
early Luther, to be sure, had many liberal moments; but he
soon hardened,[46] and Calvin was flint.[47] But when the church
was definitely atomized, the alternative to religious liberty
was mutual extermination. In the face of this peril many
set themselves to wrestle with the problem. The materials
for the pleas on behalf of freedom were drawn from humanism and mysticism. The humanist scholar desired freedom
for his investigations. The universal theism and wistful
skepticism of Cicero supplied the ground for the intellectual
attack. Deeper was the religious assault drawn from the

[43] Thomas Cuming Hall, *The Religious Background of American Culture*
(Boston, 1930).

[44] Thomas C. Allen, *The Family of Love or the Familists*, "Haverford College
studies," XII (1893), 1–46.

[45] Heinrich Hermelink, *Der Toleranzgedanke im Reformationszeitalter* (Leipzig, 1908); Walther Köhler, *Reformation und Ketzerprozess* (Tübingen, 1901);
Nikolaus Paulus, *Protestantismus und Toleranz im 16. Jahrhundert* (Freiburg i.Br.,
1911); Karl Völker, *Toleranz und Intoleranz im Zeitalter der Reformation* (Leipzig,
1912).

[46] Roland H. Bainton, "The development and consistency of Luther's attitude to religious liberty," *Harvard Theological Review*, XXII (1929), 107–149, reprinted in vol. 2 of this series.

[47] Roland H. Bainton, *Sebastian Castellio Concerning Heretics* (New York,
1935).

mystics, for whom religion is too inward to be created or constrained by the outward sword of the magistrate, for whom also the way of religion is the way of suffering, not of persecution. The ethical approach could be drawn from both sources, since both were more interested in deeds than in creeds.[48] These intellectual, religious, and ethical considerations received reinforcement from others of a more secular character. In France, rising nationalism became the ally of religious liberty. Michel de L'Hôpital, the chancellor of Catherine de Medici, pointed out that the Huguenots could not be exterminated without the loss of Frenchmen.[49] Henry IV with his famous "Paris is worth a mass," had come to the recognition that the welfare of the state is to be preferred to the victory of one religion. In Holland and in England, the interests of commerce and liberty coincided. William the Silent well recognized that "our land is the mart of the world," and religious dissension would be inimical to trade. The English sectarians pointed out the damage to economic life in the exile of so many excellent sheepmen. Even English imperialism lined up for liberty in the seventeenth century, for Britannia could not rule the waves if disturbed by domestic controversies.[50]

These diverse allies of religious liberty are plainly secular, and their prevalence may well be adduced to qualify the earlier statement with regard to the arrest of secularism. On the other hand, we must not forget that the primary cause for the triumph of freedom was the existence of a number of minorities who preferred annihilation to the abandonment of their principles.[51] Secular motives for liberty proved too feeble to resist absolutism.

[48] Johannes Kühn, *Toleranz und Offenbarung* (Leipzig, 1923), has given a very stimulating analysis of the various ways in which diverse religious types make for or against tolerance. He tends, I think, to make the types too precise and the examples too clear cut.

[49] Henri Amphoux, *Michel de l'Hôpital et la liberté de conscience au XVI e siècle* (Paris, 1900).

[50] Leonard Busher, "Religions Peace," in *Tracts on Liberty of Conscience*, Hanserd Knollys Society (London, 1846), p. 64. James Harrington, "Oceana," ed. Liljegren, *Skriften utgivna av Vetenskaps-Societeten* (Lund), pp. 196–197.

[51] John Neville Figgis, "Political thought in the Sixteenth Century," *Cambridge Modern History*, III, 769.

The question of religious freedom has brought us directly into the political area. Here the great change wrought by the sixteenth century was the disruption of that universal society which sought to curb the rising spirit of particularism. Curiously enough, nationalism, which overcame disunity at the bottom of medieval society,[52] destroyed unity at the top. The passing of the canon law left the nations without a law of nations.[53] The Protestant Reformation certainly gave an impetus to this rising nationalism by rejecting the authority of the church universal and making possible the formation of national churches. Nevertheless, the significance of the Reformation at this point must not be exaggerated, for the papacy had lost its international character long before the debacle. French control of the Holy See had caused the disaffection of Louis of Bavaria in the fourteenth century, as Spanish control produced the revolt of Henry VIII in the sixteenth. The Inquisition became an instrument of national consolidation in France and Spain. The Catholic saints are more easily nationalized than is the sovereign God of Calvinism.[54]

The Reformation, however, did minister to the displacement of clerical by lay authority and to the development of a society in which the state has taken the place of the church. Luther sought to vindicate for the magistrate a share in the priesthood of all believers, a calling as divine as that of any monk.[55] Figgis not improperly draws a line straight from Luther's doctrine of the divine vocation of the magistrate to James I's theory of the divine right of kings,[56] and Troeltsch sees affinities between the political thought of

[52] Bernhard Schmeidler, "Die Bedeutung des späteren Mittelalters für die deutsche und europäische Geschichte," *Historische Vierteljahrschrift*, XXIX (1934–1935), 93–108.

[53] R. F. Wright, *Medieval Internationalism* (London, 1930).

[54] The international character of Protestantism is emphasized by Gerhard Ficker, *Das ausgehende Mittelalter und sein Verhältnis zur Reformation* (Leipzig, 1903), p. 19.

[55] Karl Eger, *Die Anschauungen Luthers vom Beruf* (Giessen, 1900).

[56] *Op. cit.*

Luther and Machiavelli.[57] Both did work in the direction of state absolutism, but Luther's conception is thoroughly religious. The right of the magistrate is divine.

And for that very reason it is not absolute. The magistrate is bound by God's Word. He may reform the church on this basis only; and if he transgresses God's Word, he may be resisted. Here the line runs straight from Luther to the regicides, however much he might have recoiled at the suggestion. He had always said that the magistrate must be disobeyed if he goes counter to the gospel, but disobedience should be passive. The sword belongs only to the ruler. But when Charles V contemplated the extermination of Protestantism, Luther discovered that he could pit magistrate against magistrate, the German princes against the emperor. Similarly in France, the Huguenot noble could be set against the crown; and in England, parliament against the king. The step was not far from the resistance of the lower magistrate to the rebellion of the citizen. The successors of Calvin went the full length, even to tyrannicide. John Knox could describe the assassination of Cardinal Beaton as having been conducted with all the gravity of a religious liturgy.[58] The Jesuits coincidently worked out a similar theory to justify attacks upon Elizabeth.[59]

In all these theories, whether of the divine right of kings or of the divine right of rebellion, the one modern note which we miss is the recognition that in the clash between the state and the dissenter both sides may be equally conscientious and, from the subjective point of view, equally right. In the sixteenth century the persecutors and the persecuted were all too convinced of the justice of their

[57] Ernst Troeltsch, *Die Soziallehren der christlichen Kirchen und Gruppen* (Tübingen, 1912), p. 536; English translation, *The Social Teaching of the Christian Churches* (London and New York, 1931), II, 532, 857–858.

[58] John Knox, *History of the Reformation in Scotland*, ed. C. J. Guthrie (London, 1898), pp. 66–69, under the year 1546.

[59] J. W. Allen, *A History of Political Thought in the Sixteenth Century* (New York, 1928). Herbert Darling Foster, "The political theories of the Calvinists before the Puritan exodus to America," *American Historical Review*, XXI (1915), 481–503.

cause to envisage any possibility of right on the other side. Only when the view developed that truth must be wrought out by clashes could the position be taken that the state must suppress even though objectively wrong. and the martyr must suffer even while recognizing that the position for which he now dies may some day appear to him to have been mistaken. Yet to have suffered for it was no mistake. Such a position makes possible mutual respect between persecutor and persecuted. The sixteenth century never reached that point.[60]

The marked development of our period in the field of law was the introduction of the Roman law into Germany. The triumph of the *corpus juris* was neither absolute nor uniform, but nevertheless sufficient to cause an interruption in the cultural traditions of the German people such as did not occur in other lands.[61] The general revival of the Roman law had an incidental effect, which has been little noticed, in providing a theory of religious persecution for Protestants. At the very moment when the Inquisition and the canon law were rejected, the *Codex Justinianus* was embraced, including the ecclesiastical edicts.[62]

In the realm of ethics the Reformation raised some very acute problems. Rabbi Klausner contends that the only possible form of Christianity is Catholicism because the Christian ethic is pitched too high for actual life. Jesus destroyed property, the family, and the state. "Take no thought for the morrow," eliminates property; "Forsake father and mother, wife and child," eradicates the family; and "Turn the other cheek," disrupts the state. The only way in which such an ethic can be realized is by the segregation of certain groups to follow the counsels of perfection while the rest soil their hands in the muck of the world. This explains the frightful contrasts of Christianity. The religion

----

[60] R. H. Bainton, "Academic Freedom," *Proceedings Middle States Assoc. Hist. Teachers,* XXXIII (1935), 37–44.

[61] Georg von Below, *Die Ursachen der Rezeption des Römischen Rechts in Deutschland* (Munich and Berlin, 1905).

[62] See "The Struggle for Religious Liberty" in *Reformation Studies* (Series II of this work).

of kindness brings forth the Inquisition; the religion of love blesses the Great War.[63] Now, without admitting the extremes of this picture, one cannot deny that the Sermon on the Mount is a perpetual embarrassment to the world. Catholicism met the problem by monasticism. Protestantism repudiated this solution, and the difficulty was raised again in acute form. The Anabaptists had recourse to a quasi-monasticism, aloofness from the state with a qualified acceptance of economic and family life. Luther, however, embraced the whole of this present evil world as the sphere of the Christian. The magistrate, the hangman, and the soldier exercise a religious vocation. What, then, becomes of the precepts of the gospel? They are conserved in part by a relegation to private ethics. Here, I suspect, is a partial key to the Protestant exaltation of the home, which offers a substitute for the monastery. The hearth, like the cloister, admits of no eye for an eye, no mine and thine. The other way out is by a distinction between act and attitude. The soldier, even while he slays, must love. The dichotomy now is transferred from groups in society to within the breast of the individual.[64]

Nowhere did the Reformation introduce a greater change than in domestic relations. Religious celibacy was repudiated in favor of marriage. The Middle Ages at its worst vilified marriage, and at its best regarded it as inferior to virginity.[65] Luther reversed the scale of values. For him a

[63] Joseph Klausner, *Jesus of Nazareth* (New York, 1925), pp. 391–393.

[64] The major utterances of Luther on these points will be found in the following tracts: "Treatise on good works," *Works of Martin Luther*, I, 274; "Warning against insurrection and rebellion," III, 211; "On secular government," III, 233 ff.; "On trading and usury," IV, 22–23; "That soldiers, too, can be saved," V, 35; "On war against the Turk," V, 83. See the discussion by Walther Köhler, "Sozialwissenschaftliche Bemerkung zur Lutherforschung," *Zeitschrift für die gesammte Staatswissenschaft*, LXXXV, 2 (1928), 343–353.

[65] The ascetic depreciation of marriage in the middle ages is described by Heinrich von Eicken, *Geschichte und System der Mittelalterlichen Weltanschauung* (Stuttgart, 1887), chap. iii, "Die Familie." Von Hertling complains (*Historiches Jahrbuch*, X [1889], 128–129) that he has taken his examples from fanatics and reformers rather than from popes and doctors. Alfred von Martin, *Mittelalterliche Welt-und Lebensanschauung im Spiegel der Schriften Coluccio Salutatis* (Munich and Berlin, 1913), points out that there was a conflict in the middle ages between

mother out of wedlock was better than a nun, because fulfilling God's law of nature.[66] Carlstadt taught not merely that ministers might marry but that they must.[67] Bigamy was condoned, if not recommended, by Bucer, Melanchthon, and Luther[68]; and the Anabaptists at Münster, under the stress of siege conditions, introduced polygamy.

The speedy and frequent remarriages of the reformers appear to us unseemly. Pellikan, for example, announced to a friend on December 2, 1536, the death of his wife and his intention never to remarry. He had changed his mind by the twenty-third of the same month. On January 16 the Lord pointed out to him a suitable partner, to whom he was united on the twentieth. Castellio waited six months.[69] Wilhelmina Rosenblatt was married in turn to Wibrandis, a layman of Basel and then to the ministers Oecolampadius, Capito, and Bucer.[70] One may doubt whether the Reformation introduced anything new at this point, however, since the middle ages likewise sanctioned speedy remarriage.[71]

The exaltation of matrimony as a religious obligation coincided with secularization on the legal side, since marriage was no longer regarded as a sacrament. Jurisdiction in consequence passed to lay tribunals. Zurich set up a special

---

the monk and the church which opposed extremes. Nevertheless, the extreme remained; and even a humanist like Salutati felt the need of defending marriage with discretion. A well-balanced view is given by Heinrich Finke (*Die Frau im Mittelalter* [Kempten and Munich, 1913], chap. iii, "Die Frauen in der Ehe des Mittelalters") who points out that the introduction of the Roman law hindered the attainment of legal equality by the wife.

[66] Lilly Zarncke, "Die naturhafte Eheanschauung des jungen Luther," *Archiv für Kulturgeschichte*, XXV (1934–1935), 281–305. Cf. Olavi Lähteenmäki, "Sexus und Ehe bei Luther," *Luther-Agricola Gesellschaft in Finnland*, X (1955).

[67] Hermann Barge, *Andreas Bodenstein von Karlstadt*, I (Leipzig, 1905), 265, 289, n. 136.

[68] Hastings Eells, *The Attitude of Martin Bucer to the Bigamy of Philip of Hesse* (New Haven, 1924); William Walter Rockwell, *Die Doppelehe des Landgrafen Philipp von Hessen* (Leipzig, 1903).

[69] Bernhard Riggenbach, ed., *Das Chronikon des Konrad Pellikan* (Basel, 1877), pp. 147–148; Ferdinand Buisson, *Sébastien Castellion* (Paris, 1892), I, p. 253.

[70] *Reformations-Almanach*, III (1821), clxxxvii-cxciv.

[71] Richard Köbner, "Die Eheauffassung des ausgehenden deutschen Mittelalters," *Archiv für Kulturgeschichte*, IX (1911), 136–198, 279–318. On this point, p. 157.

matrimonial court in 1525, and other cities soon followed. The canon law was retained in part with admixtures from Roman and German law. Annulment was superseded by divorce with the possibility of remarriage, and spiritual impediments were abrogated.[72]

The ranking of marriage above virginity made for no advance beyond the middle ages in the association of marriage with romance,[73] since for Luther the purpose of the institution was to satisfy the cravings of one sex for the other, not the attraction of individuals. One wife was as good as another. Jacob showed himself frail in that he worked another seven years for the pretty face of Rachel when he already had Leah. Nevertheless, Luther rejoiced in this failing of Jacob, which clearly showed that he must have been saved by faith and not by works. Love, indeed, there is in marriage, a love flowing from faith and comparable to love for one's neighbor[74]; but the extent of Luther's romance may be inferred from his remark with regard to his wife, "I would not exchange my Katie for France and Venice, because God has given her to me, and other women have worse faults," [75] and John Knox referred to his betrothed as "she whom God hath offered to me and commanded me to love as my own flesh." [76] Compare these statements with the cry of Shylock when Jessica sold the turquoise ring to buy a monkey, "I had it of Leah when I was a bachelor: I would not have given it for a wilderness of monkeys."

One is tempted to wonder whether there is any connection between the coincident decline of chivalry and monasticism and the Protestant emphasis on marriage without

---

[72] Walther Köhler, *Zürcher Ehegericht und Genfer Konsistorium* (Leipzig, 1932). For a summary see the concluding section.

[73] On the lack of romance in the marriage of the middle ages see the article of Köbner, pp. 152–159.

[74] See the article of Lilly Zarncke listed above and also the earlier article, "Der Begriff der Liebe in Luthers Aeusserungen über die Ehe," *Theologische Blätter*, X (1931), 45–49.

[75] Preserved Smith, *The Life and Letters of Martin Luther* (New York, 1911), p. 179.

[76] Henry Cowan, *John Knox* (New York, 1905), p. 101.

romance. One hesitates to press the point because a crass
attitude toward womankind ran parallel alike to chivalry
and to the Neoplatonic idealization of love in the Renaissance,[77] and was not the product of the Reformation,[78] but
merely a survival.[79]

The combination of the courtly tradition of romantic
unwedded love was combined with Christian love in England in the sixteenth century in the poetry of Edmund
Spenser,[80] but is to be found earlier on the continent, in the
twelfth century in Germany in Wolfram von Eschenbach,
in the fourteenth in France in the poetry of Christine of
Pisa, and in the fifteenth in Italy in a tract of Francesco
Barbaro.[81]

The contribution of the Reformation was at the point
of comradeship in marriage and is to be found among those
groups which subordinated the physical side of marriage to
a common commitment to serve God in the rearing of
children and the service of the religious community. This
note appears among Anabaptists,[82] Calvinists, English
Puritans, Quakers,[83] for all of whom affection is nurtured
by "tenderness and a respective heart."[84]

The economic effects of the Reformation have been
greatly debated. The reader is well acquainted with the
view of Weber, Troeltsch, and Tawney that Protestantism,

[77] On the Neoplatonic idealization see Nesca A. Robb, *Neoplatonism of the
Italian Renaissance* (London, 1935). On the two currents see Abel Lefranc, "Le
tiers livre du 'Pantagruel' et la querelle des femmes," in *Grands écrivains français
de la Renaissance* (Paris, 1914), pp. 250–303.

[78] As Johannes Janssen contended, *History of the German People at the Close
of the Middle Ages*, tr. A. M. Christie, XII (London, 1907), chap. iv.

[79] Waldemar Kawerau, *Die Reformation und die Ehe* (Halle, 1892).

[80] C. S. Lewis, *The Allegory of Love, a Study in Medieval Tradition* (Oxford,
1936).

[81] R. H. Bainton, *What Christianity Says about Sex, Love and Marriage*
(New York, 1957).

[82] Ernst Correll, article "Ehe" in *Mennonitisches Lexikon*, ed. Christian Hege
and Christian Neff, I (Frankfurt a. M., 1913).

[83] Marianne Weber, *Ehefrau und Mutter in der Rechtsentwicklung* (Tübingen,
1907). Chapter iv is valuable on this whole development.

[84] Levin L. Schücking, *Die Familie im Puritanismus. Studiën über Familie
und Literatur in England im 16., 17. und 18. Jahrhundert* (Leipzig and Berlin, 1929),
especially p. 65.

and especially Calvinism, provided a morale for capitalism by the removal of the ban on usury, an emphasis on the duty of labor in an earthly calling, and an asceticism which forbade the dissipation of wealth in pleasure.[85] Robertson has lately criticized the theory on the ground that Weber leapt from Calvin to Baxter without regarding the restrictions on gain in the intervening literature.[86] (Weber, of course, recognized that the result was unforeseen and not desired.) Robertson sees economic forces at work to which Protestantism and Catholicism alike succumbed. Brodrick would exculpate the Jesuits at this point.[87]. Now Fanfani has reviewed the whole subject with great richness of bibliographical detail.[88] He defined the spirit of capitalism as that which makes the acquisition of wealth the chief end of man, so that economics displaces politics and religion. The supreme example of this spirit is to be found in communist Russia, where the state and religion have been subordinated to economic ends. The main factors in the rise of this capitalist spirit have been secular, and the lead of Protestant over Catholic countries is largely accidental. England and Holland acquired the colonial market lost by Spain, and trade shifted from the Mediterranean to the Atlantic. Nevertheless, Protestantism contributed in that it divorced salvation from conduct. Since works do not save, economic activity was left to take the course of nature, unhampered by religious restrictions. This, in my judgment, is a funda-

---

[85] Max Weber, *The Protestant Ethic and the Spirit of Capitalism*, tr. Talcott Parsons (London, 1930); Richard Henry Tawney, *Religion and the Rise of Capitalism* (London, 1926); Troeltsch, *Social Teachings*, cited above.

[86] H. M. Robertson, *Aspects of the Rise of Economic Individualism. A Criticism of Max Weber and his School* (Cambridge, England, 1933).

[87] James Brodrick, *The Economic Morals of the Jesuits, an Answer to D. H. M. Robertson* (London, 1934).

[88] Amintore Fanfani, *Catholicism, Protestantism and Capitalism* (New York, 1935); *Le origini dello spirito capitalistico in Italia* (Milan, 1933). More recently the whole field has been surveyed by E. Fischoff, "The Protestant Ethic and the Spirit of Capitalism: the History of a Controversy," *Social Research*, XI (1944), 53–77. Wallace Ferguson has set the entire subject into the wider framework of the economic history of the period of the Renaissance in "Recent Trends in the Economic Historiography of the Renaissance," *Studies in the Renaissance*, VII (1960), 7–26.

mental perversion of Protestant teaching. The doctrine of
the worldly calling was thoroughly religious. If anything,
Catholicism is more in danger of relinquishing religious control over secular enterprises, because the only religious vocation is that of the monk. But the ideal of Catholicism and
Protestantism alike is religious control over every area of
life.

Let us turn now to the more speculative fields of science,
philosophy and theology. In science the sixteenth century is
generally considered an era of marked change, for was not
this the period of Vesalius, Brahe and Copernicus? The dis-
continuity with the preceding period, however, must not be
exaggerated. Thorndike has pointed out to us that the
science of the fifteenth century was by no means despicable.[89]
We are concerned here, however, not with the history of
science as such, but only with its influence upon the ideas
and ideals of the period. The incorporation of the science of
the sixteenth century into the European *Weltanschauung*
was the work only of the generation following. The Coperni-
can theory was slow in finding acceptance and understanding. Luther would have none of it. Montaigne saw in the
new discovery only a confirmation of the skepticism already
derived from the ancients. If the view of Copernicus has displaced that of Ptolemy, "Who knows," he said, "but that a
thousand years from now a third opinion may reverse them
both?" [90] Bruno died for a Copernicus whom he did not
understand. Like the Inquisition, he regarded the new
system as a neo-Pythagorean revival and welcomed it as
confirmatory of his theory of the plurality of worlds; but he
combated Copernicus' retention of the Ptolemaic view of
fixed stars on the confines of the universe, not on scientific
grounds, but because it was in conflict with the Lucretian
doctrine of limitless space.[91]

---

[89] Lynn Thorndike, *Science and Thought in the Fifteenth Century* (New York, 1929).

[90] *Essais*, Book II, chap. xii, p. 552.

[91] Leonardo Olschki, "Giordano Bruno," *Deutsche Vierteljahrschrift für Literaturwissenschaft und Geistesgeschichte*, II (1924), 40–42.

In the realm of philosophy the sixteenth century was not creative. Interest was too centered on theology and ethics for any profound grapplings with the general principles of metaphysics and epistemology. Luther, in so far as he had a philosophy, remained an Occamist. The exception to this generalization is the preservation of the Neoplatonic tradition in living fashion from the Florentine Academy to the Cambridge Platonists. Herein lies the qualification to Gilson's dictum that humanism killed, not only Latin by making it dead, but also classical philosophy by making it history.[92] That might perhaps be said of Cusa, when he introduced historical exactitude by sensing the difference between Platonism and Neoplatonism,[93] but the Florentine Academy kept the tradition plastic and alive.[94] The sixteenth century, except for a diversion of attention, offers no interruption in the continuity of thought. Pomponazzi is in the Averroist tradition; Descartes goes back to Augustine, Anselm and Aquinas[95]; Locke, to Aquinas and Occam,[96] and Bruno to the Florentine Academy.

In theology one would look for the greatest break, but in vain. The essential structure of medieval thought was retained. Even to the end of his life Luther could participate in a discussion of the Trinity along scholastic lines.[97] The great change is in turning theology away from itself and subordinating it to religious interests. Calvin would consider only those questions which bore directly on salvation. The result was a simplification, not an abandonment, of the main lines of scholastic theology. The *Institutes* of Calvin start off with the initial question of Augustine, the Lombard, or Aquinas, whether the pilgrim in this life can attain

[92] See n. 30 above.

[93] Ernst Cassirer, *Individuum und Kosmos in der Philosophie der Renaissance* (Leipzig, 1927), 16.

[94] Robb, *op. cit.*

[95] Étienne Gilson, *Études sur le rôle de la pensée médiévale dans la formation du système cartesien* (Paris, 1930).

[96] Edouard Krakowski, *Les sources médiévales de la philosophie de Locke* (Paris, 1915).

[97] Paul Drews, *Disputationen Dr. Martin Luthers in d.J. 1535–1545 an der Universität Wittenberg gehalten* (Göttingen, 1895).

to the knowledge of God. Calvin's answer is unconsciously
in the tradition of the Augustinianism of the middle ages.
The humanist solution is excluded because, although the
ancient philosophers were marvelously endowed, nevertheless the depravity of human reason is such that even the
most gifted were blinder than bats and moles in matters of
religion. The natural theology of Aquinas is largely excluded, for the evidence of God in the natural world is invisible to corrupt eyes. The immediate revelation of the
Spiritual Franciscans or the Anabaptists is excluded, for
God has spoken only through his Word. But this Word would
be unintelligible apart from the measure of inspiration supplied by the testimony of the Holy Spirit, which performs
for Calvin the same function as the illumination of Alexander
of Hales and Bonaventura.[98]

Thus far the emphasis has been upon the religious
character of the sixteenth century. Secularist forces, however, were concurrently at work. Two ideas, for example,
suffered a transformation, namely primitivism and eschatology. We have already observed a Christian primitivism
which sought to restore the church to the New Testament
model. There was another and even more prevalent type
which looked back to Adam[99] and the garden of Eden, and
sought to recover the golden age in the earthly paradise.[100]
The Renaissance substituted Arcadia for Eden, and the
discovery of America located the earthly paradise in the
New Isles and displaced Adam by the *bon sauvage*.[101] Léry, a
French Calvinist who accompanied Villegagnon to Brazil in
the middle of the sixteenth century, returned with a nos-
talgia for primitive life. He approved of the way in which
the Indian mothers nursed their own babies, and thought

---

[98] Karl Heim, *Das Gewissheitsproblem in der systematischen Theologie bis zur
Schleiermacher* (Leipzig, 1911), p. 279.

[99] Georg Jellenik, *Adam in der Staatslehre* (Heidelberg, 1893), reprint from
Neue Heidelberger Jahrbücher, III, 1 (1893).

[100] Gilbert Chinard, "Le mirage américain," introduction to *Les refugiés
Huguenots en Amérique* (Paris, 1925).

[101] Gilbert Chinard, *L'exotisme américain dans la littérature française au
XVIe siècle* (Paris, 1911).

the shocking nudity of the savages less immoral, after all, than the coquetry of Europeans.[102] All this two hundred years before Rousseau! Montaigne took up the strain in his idyllic picture of the cannibal isles, and quite relished the strictures on European life of some imported Indians who expressed surprise that some men should be content to starve while others stuffed.[103]

Eschatology was similarly secularized into the idea of progress. Both conceptions see relief in the future. One looks to a divine intervention; the other, to a gradual human improvement. Kant discerned the similarity and, when Lessing enunciated the idea of progress, dubbed him a chiliast.[104] The transition from the one idea to the other began in our period. Eschatology still dominated the thought of the Reformers[105]; but the Renaissance had contributed the conception of a becoming in history,[106] and Bodin by the end of the century envisaged a general law of progress.[107]

Primitivism and progress may be combined if progress is a gradual return to a golden age lost by a fall; but if primitivism sees its ideal in the *bon sauvage*, and progress in a mechanized society, conflict is inevitable. The clash came in the eighteenth century.[108] I have referred to both ideas as secular. On the other hand, we must not forget that the American mirage included many dreams of a holy community and that the idea of progress was appropriated by modernist Christianity.

To sum up, the sixteenth century presents new alignments. Gaps are closed, and rifts are opened. Henri Hauser

[102] Jean de Léry, *Histoire d'un voyage faict en la terre du Brésil*, Paul Gafferel (ed.), 2 vols.; (Paris, 1879).

[103] Montaigne, *Essais*, Book I, chap. xxxi.

[104] A. A. Van Schelven, *De Idee van den Vooruitgang* (Kampen, 1927).

[105] Willem Simon Christiaan Deijll, *Het chiliasme ter Tijde der Hervorming* (Amsterdam, 1872); Johannes Köstlin, "Ein Beitrag zur Eschatologie der Reformatoren," *Theologische Studien und Kritiken*, LI (1879).

[106] Pierre Bizilli, "La place de la Renaissance dans l'histoire de la civilization," *Revue de littérature comparée*, XIV (1934), 253–282.

[107] Jules Delaville, *Essai sur l'histoire de l'idée de progrès, jusqu'à la fin du XVIIIe siècle* (Paris, 1910); J. B. Bury, *The Idea of Progress* (London, 1920).

[108] Lois Whitney, *Primitivism and the Idea of Progress in English Popular Literature of the Eighteenth Century* (Baltimore, 1934).

sees in this period the achievement of a new unity of humanity in that the cleavage between the Christian, on the one hand, and the pagan, the infidel, and the heretic, on the other, began to be closed. Even the pope would make a treaty with the Turk, and the Catholic king of France with the Schmalkald League.[109] Yes, and he might have added that the gap between the lay and the monastic was eliminated in Protestant lands. But, on the other hand, the seamless robe of the medieval church was rent. National feeling was intensified, and class and color feeling arose. Most torturing are the rifts created within the individual. The Protestant can no longer be either a monk or a magistrate or a father. He is all at once. He must assume all of the responsibilities of the state, the market place, and the home, and yet remain the disciple of him who lived like the lilies, took no thought for the morrow, and forgave his enemies. Well does Ritter conclude his article on Luther in the *Encyclopedia of the Social Sciences*, "His religion is the religion of the heroic *Willensmensch* who bears in his breast the contradictions of good and evil which rend the world asunder—Its irresolvable internal contrarieties have filled the spiritual life of Germany with ever new tensions."

[109] Henri Hauser, "La modernité du XVIe siècle," *Bibliothèque de la revue historique* (Paris, 1930).

III. Religion and Church in the Renaissance

10 Man, God and Church in the Renaissance

The Renaissance is currently conceived to have been at variance with the Middle Ages and nowhere more so than in the area of religion. The classic contrast was vividly drawn by Symonds. He took, as his type of the Middle Ages, St. Bernard, who rode for an entire day beside the shores of Lake Leman without "noticing the azure of the waters, the radiance of the mountains with their robe of sun and snow, but instead bent his thought-burdened forehead over the neck of his mule, and at the end of the journey, when his companions referred to the lake, inquired, 'What lake?'" Even so were the men of that day pilgrims intent on sin, death, and judgment. They esteemed beauty a snare, pleasure a sin, the world a fleeting show, man as depraved, judgment inevitable, hell everlasting, and heaven best attained by the mortification of the flesh.[1]

The type of the Renaissance was Dr. Faustus, an emancipated Dr. Faustus, for in the original tale the devil played a part and to him the doctor had to pledge his soul in order that blind Homer might sing for him, that at his

First published under the title "Man, God, and the Church in the Age of the Renaissance," by The Metropolitan Museum of Art, New York, in 1953, after having been delivered as an address at The Renaissance, a symposium held at the museum in February 1952. Reprinted in *The Journal of Religious Thought*, vol. XI, 2 (1954).

[1] J. A. Symonds, *The Renaissance in Italy*: "The Age of the Despots" (1935), pp. 9–11.

behest Alexander might rise from the dead with all his
legionaries, and Helen of Troy be given to him as a bride.
That for which Faustus forfeited his soul the Renaissance
appropriated without price. "Homer, no longer by the intervention of a fiend but by the labor of the scholar, sang to
the new age." The legions of Alexander rose again in the
pages of the historians, and Helen was taken to wife in the
recovery of the ineffable beauty of Greek art, of which her
loveliness was the symbol. Not by magic but by the toilsome
devotion to erudition on the part of magnificent Italy was
the guilty dream of the ancient legend given blithe fulfill-
ment; and thereby was ushered in the modern world.[2]

This picture like many another interpretation of the
past has of late been subjected to revision. There are those
who point out that the Middle Ages were not innocent of
the Faustian type. There were Aucassins who, with a
Nicolette and a convivial company of lords and dames, preferred hell to a bored eternity with stuffy saints. There were
roistering vagabond students, throat-cutting outlaws, predatory barons, and wenching bishops. Contemporary with St.
Bernard was Abelard, the troubadour theologian tinctured
with rationalism.

On the other hand, there were Bernards in the age of
the Renaissance. Michelangelo could never dismiss from
memory the reverberations of the diluvian tones of Savonarola as he stunned his hearers with predictions of imminent
doom. Nor should one forget the renown of San Bernardino
of Siena, nor of that other Bernardino, also of Siena, known
as Ochino, the general of the Capuchins of the order of St.
Francis, who toured Italy on penitential missions, barefoot,
meanly clad, emaciated, his long white beard and ethereal
countenance reminiscent of the face of Moses after he had
talked with God. And all this in the very heyday of Renaissance in the Eternal City. Even the humanists, of the first

---

[2] *Ibid.*, "The Revival of Learning" (1935), p. 354. The Faust story emerges
full-blown only at the end of the sixteenth century, and even then not in Symonds'
emancipated form. Stories of compacts with the devil are common in the Middle
Ages.

generation at least, were imbued with the ideals of Franciscan poverty and regarded as their patron saint Jerome,
the monastic scholar.[3]

One is prompted to wonder whether Bernard and
Faust are not perhaps eternal contemporaries existing side
by side in every age and culture. To go so far, however,
would be to abandon differentiation of historical periods;
and some shifts of emphasis and interest certainly are
evident.

These two types afford a contrast all the more striking
because there are so many parallels to be compared. Both
involve man's behavior, his concept of himself, his aspira-
tions declared or unavowed, his belief as to his destiny and
as to those forces which brought him into being and determine or contend for his fate.

We may conveniently begin with man, the way in
which he demeaned himself and the manner in which he
envisaged his place and role in the universe. The classic
portrayal has thought to find in the Renaissance the emer-
gence of the superman, egoistic, ambitious, unscrupulous,
ruthless, and remorseless, consumed with a passion not for
immortality but for fame. The type is seen in the despots of
the Italian city states. Take for example Fondolo of Cre-
mona, who when the Pope and the emperor visited him on
their way to the Council of Constance, took them to the
rampart of a high tower affording a view of the panorama
of the Po. The thought flashed into the mind of Fondolo
that here was a remarkable opportunity to immortalize himself by shoving them both over the parapet, thus attaining
the distinction of having killed a pope and an emperor on
the same day. He resisted the temptation, but when later he
himself was condemned to execution, regretted that he had
let slip the greatest opportunity of his life.[4] And then there
were all the Sforzas, Viscontis, the Medici, and the Borgias,
whose demeanor supplied the models for Machiavelli's

[3] Hans Baron, "Franciscan Poverty and Civic Wealth in Humanistic
Thought," *Speculum* XIII, 1 (January 1938), 1–37.
[4] J. A. Symonds, "The Age of the Despots," p. 233, n. 17.

Prince. Al Capones were they in the methods by which they won and held power, but Carnegies, Rockefellers, and Morgans in the liberality with which they employed it. The distinction of these elegant banditti is less to be found in their buccaneering behavior—that can be matched in other periods—than in their patronage of the arts. Lorenzo de Medici was equally adept in plotting an assassination, making merry at a carnival, or in judging a horse, a sermon, a poem, or a picture, and this it is that marks him off from plain cutthroats.

Perhaps then we should shift from the lust for power to the love of elegance as the primary note of the era. The ideal was the rounding out of man's personality, the development of all his capacities, the subjection of all disciplines to his rational control. The courtier literature draws the picture of the well-rounded man. He can fight, dance, swim, hunt, woo, and warble. His mind introduces system into every field. War becomes strategy, business is bookkeeping, statecraft is diplomacy, art is perspective. Here and now man aspires to bring to bloom his seeded powers and cherishes less a blessed immortality than an imperishable name acquired not by spectacular deviltry but by artistic and literary pre-eminence. One thinks at this point of the burgeoning geniuses of the Renaissance: Leonardo in art and mechanics; Michelangelo in painting, sculpture, and architecture; Rabelais in medicine and literature; Raleigh in exploration and historiography; Servetus in theology and physiology; Postell in statecraft, mathematics, and orientalia; Erasmus in classical and patristic scholarship, not to mention journalism. Many of them were supported by a Maecenas who thought to attain an undying reputation through a dedication. Surely, here we have a contrast to the prevailing anonymity of medieval donors and craftsmen who vied with one another to honor the Blessed Virgin without carving their names into the pediments.

Even more, we are told, is this the period in which man had the temerity first to apply to himself a designation hitherto reserved for God, the title of creator. The sculptors, painters, and poets first commenced to talk of their "creations." To point the comparison, God himself was painted seated at an easel. All of the modern vocabulary of creative art, creative writing, creative painting stems thus from the Renaissance.[5] The Middle Ages would have regarded such terminology as arrogant, if not indeed well-nigh blasphemous. Did not Thomas Aquinas say, "God alone can create, because creation is the bringing of something out of nothing, and that no man can ever do"?[6]

This total picture may not be wholly without warrant. A certain shift of tone is discernible in the Renaissance, but the differences can be grossly exaggerated. The *uomo universale* was for some indeed an ideal, and yet he may also have been simply the result of a lack of specialization, just as in the early nineteenth century Benjamin Silliman handled both chemistry and geology because the sciences were not yet sufficiently advanced to compel a division. Again, the claim of newness for the application to man of the title "creator" calls for considerable qualification. The view of Aquinas was not that which prevailed in antiquity, for the doctrine of creation out of nothing was a scholastic invention. It is not the classical Greek view as expounded in the *Timaeus*, nor even the Hebrew picture of the first chapter of Genesis, where the Spirit of God brooded over the waters and the waters were already there. The Greeks did not hesitate to apply to man two of the words descriptive of God as Creator. The one was *Demiourgos* and the other was *Poetes*. Nor did St. Paul himself disdain this latter term. The position of Thomas Aquinas was not even that of the other scholastics, for he frankly avowed that at this point he was dissenting from the *Magister Sententiarum*. Peter Lombard had said that in the absolute sense, to be sure, creation cannot be predicated of man. No more can the forgiveness of sins; yet in a derivative sense man may be said both to create and to forgive.[7] Aquinas, in taking issue with him,

---

[5] Edgar Zilsel, *Die Entstehung des Geniebegriffes* (1926), pp. 280–283.
[6] *Summa Theol.* I, 45, 8.
[7] Sent. II, I and IV, 5.

objected only to his terminology. He would reserve strictly
for God the designation "creator," and would apply to man
rather the title "concreator." [8] The Renaissance then did
not so much introduce a new view of man as display a distaste for overly refined distinctions.

If one turns to the doctrine of man as expounded by
Renaissance writers, the departure from the classical Christian picture is evident but not glaring. Let us examine three
cases. Take first the passage most frequently cited as mark-
ing the radical departure, namely, Pico's essay "On the
Dignity of Man," where he holds that man is stationed in
the middle of the great chain of being, endowed with freedom either to degenerate to the level of the brute or to
ascend and "be reborn into the higher forms which are
divine." Man is so much "the maker and moulder of himself
that he may fashion himself into whatever shape he shall
prefer." The summit of the ascent is an illumination and
intoxication whereby man is united with divinity. "Roused
by an ineffable love, full of divine power, we shall no longer
be ourselves but shall become He Himself who made us." [9]
The end is thus deification.

This passage has been characterized as Promethean,
but that emphatically it is not. The myth of Prometheus is
the picture of man in defiance of the gods inventing and dis-
seminating technological arts. Such a picture one can indeed
find in the period of the Renaissance. One has it in a little
fantasy of Erasmus, who, finding Colet and some of his
friends somewhat heated over a discussion of the nature of
the sin of Cain, undertook to relate a diverting story which
he professed to have found in some ancient author. In this
version, Cain with guile approached the angel with the
flaming sword guarding the gate of Paradise in order to
wheedle and needle him into passing out some of the luxuri-
ant seeds of Eden. What would God care? inquired Cain.
He had forbidden only the apples on one tree. Besides, did

[8] *Summa Theol., loc. cit.*
[9] Trans. in *The Renaissance Philosophy of Man*, ed. Cassirer, Kristeller and
Randall (1948), p. 225 f.

the guardian relish his task? From an angel God had made him into an executioner performing the duty assigned on earth to dogs. To keep men out of Paradise the sentinel must himself forego the delights alike of Paradise and earth, and earth is wondrous fair with vast oceans, lofty mountains, secluded vales, rivulets leaping down rocky declivities. There are thousands of trees with lush foliage and perennial fruits. Man is indeed plagued by disease, but there is nothing which ingenuity and industry cannot surmount. Why then should the angel brandish his sword against the wind and deprive himself of such charms, and why should he deprive those who already have so many, of a few paltry seeds? The angel is seduced and Cain achieves such an abundant yield that God is jealous and plagues him with ants, weevils, toads, caterpillars, mice, locusts, swine, hail, and tornado, and Cain's propitiatory offering is rejected.[10] This is Promethean and perhaps it is no accident that it should have been penned by one trained among the Brethren of the Common Life, with their insistence on man's ability to imitate the Redeemer. Yet, again, how seriously did Erasmus intend his *jeu d'esprit*, which he related apologetically and with his Mona Lisa smile?

At any rate, Pico's picture is not this. Technological progress is not his aim, and the displeasure of God is not incurred. The point is, rather, that man, situated between the beasts and the angels, has it within his power to descend or to ascend until he be actually united with God. This is nothing other than Neoplatonic mysticism, and it is not alien to the Christian tradition into which it had already been incorporated. The early Greek theologians had declared that God became man in order that man by union in the Eucharist with God might become God. For a parallel to Pico's "Dignity of Man" one may turn to Bonaventura's "Itinerary of the Soul to God," where he asserts that although man can do nothing without divine assistance, he is endowed with faculties enabling him to cooperate with God. Let man then

[10] *Ep.* 116.

bestir himself, open his eyes, unstop his ears, that rising above the terrestrial to the celestial he may be wholly transferred and transformed into God. Not without reason does Bonaventura cite Dionysius the Areopagite, that favorite transmitter of the Neoplatonic tradition to the Christian world.

Take a second example from the age of the Renaissance, the whimsical fantasy of Giambattista Gelli, who conceived a diverting variant of the story of Ulysses and Circe. In the new version Ulysses prevails upon Circe to restore to human form and to permit to return to their native land all of the Greeks upon her island whom she had transformed into beasts. Circe consents with, however, one stipulation. The Greeks must desire to be restored. Ulysses conveys to them one after another the good news, only to be rebuffed. "For what is man," he is asked, "if not a featherless, hideless biped with no roof upon his back like a turtle or a snail?" He must till and toil, whereas nature provides for the animals. Consider, moreover, the diseases to which men are a prey. The serpent, formerly the famous physician Agesimos of Lesbos, is of no mind to return, because the animals do not get sick, and besides physicians know nothing anyway. "How then did you acquire your reputation?" inquires Ulysses, and the candid answer is "By fraud." Men are distraught by fears, racked by passions, and addicted to cruelties. The goat says of his present situation, *Io sono contento*. And the deer is not inclined to return, for she had been the wife of a philosopher who insisted that she talk philosophy, in which men are peculiarly adept. Besides when the children are a bawling nuisance they are left to their mothers, and when they become interesting their fathers take over. Nine of the animals declined. Only the elephant, formerly a philosopher, was willing to listen to the praises of man, who by contemplating the beauty of the heavens may change from the terrestrial to the celestial, and casting off the impediments of the flesh— this is addressed to the elephant—may himself become as it were a god. The elephant is at length so enraptured that he bursts into a hymn.

I sing the first cause of all things corruptible and incorruptible
Who hath weighed the earth in the midst of the heavens
And let fall gentle waters for the nutriment of mortals,
Who hath ordained various kinds of creatures for the services of
    man,
Who hath endowed man with intellect to know him and with will
    to love him;
May all that is within me bless his name.
All ye gifts of my soul sing with me the first cause of all causes.
Join with me, light of my mind and freedom of my will,
O eternal mover without end and without beginning,
It is today man who sings thy praises,
And with all his powers desires that to thee be given glory and
    honor.[11]

Now what shall be said of this rhapsody? Particularly
in the original, it calls to mind, first of all, St. Francis'
"Song of the Creatures." There are besides certain reminis-
cences of the Psalms plus a few Aristotelian phrases already
incorporated into the synthesis of Thomas Aquinas. And
the whole once more is suffused with the mysticism of the
Florentine Platonic Academy.

A third example serves further to reinforce the point.
It is a prayer placed by Castiglione in the mouth of Bembo
and based upon certain passages in his authentic works.

Deign, then, O lord, to hear our prayers, pour thyself upon our
hearts, and with the splendour of thy most holy fire illumine our
darkness and, like a trusted guide, in this blind labyrinth show us
the true path. Correct the falseness of our senses, and after our long
pursuit of vanities give us true and solid good; make us to inhale
those spiritual odours that quicken the powers of the intellect, and
to hear the celestial harmony with such accord that there may no
longer be room in us for any discord of passion; fill us at the inexhaustible fountain of content which ever delights and never sati-
ates, and gives a taste of true beatitude to all who drink its living
and limpid waters; with the beams of thy light purge our eyes of
misty ignorance, to the end that they may no longer prize mortal
beauty, and may know that the things which first they seemed to
see, are not, and that those which they saw not, really are.

[11] Giambattista Gelli, *La Circe* (1548), ed. Severino Ferrari (1897), 139–141.

Accept our souls, which are offered thee in sacrifice; burn them
in that living flame which consumes all mortal dross, to the end that,
being wholly separated from the body, they may unite with divine
beauty by a perpetual and very sweet bond and that we, being
severed from ourselves, may, like true lovers, be able to transform
ourselves into the beloved, and rising above the earth may be admitted to the angels' feast, where, fed on ambrosia and immortal
nectar, we may at last die a most happy and living death, as died
of old those ancient fathers whose souls thou, by the most glowing
power of contemplation, didst ravish from the body and unite with
God.[12]

In this prayer of Bembo, Bonaventura would have
missed one Christian essential, and that is a reference to the
name of Christ. The same observation applies, of course, to
the other two examples. For the Christian mystic, Christ is
the mediator, and only by feeding on him can one taste of
God. In these Renaissance writers the Christian note is
muted, though never definitely denied, and the door is
thereby opened to pass from Christianity, not to irreligion
but rather to universal religion.

This becomes the more evident if one turns from the
Renaissance view of man to the Renaissance view of God.
Immanentism was the kernel of the concept. Now this, of
course, is not definitely anti-Christian, and texts in the New
Testament were not inappropriately found by way of support. Did not the Apostle Paul say of God, "In Him we live
and move and have our being?"[13] Observe, however, that
the apostle was quoting a classical poet. Another favorite
text was the reference in the Johannine prologue to the immanent light,[14] that "light that lighteth every man that
cometh into the world,"[15] because this was interpreted in
terms of the Neoplatonic doctrine of light conceived through

[12] Translated in H. H. Blanchard, *Prose and Poetry of the Continental Renaissance* (1949), p. 380. On the subject of the dignity of man in the Renaissance
compare: Eugenio Garin, "La 'Dignitas hominis' e la Letteratura Patristica,"
Rinascita 1 (1938), 102–46; Herschel Baker, *The Dignity of Man* (1947).

[13] Acts 17:28.
[14] John 1:9.
[15] John 8:12.

metaphysics rather than physics. Light was held to be a
form which has to be united with all matter if it is to be
capable of visibility. If God is identified with light and if
Christ is the light of the world, then God and Christ themselves permeate all reality. In science this meant a vitalistic
view of nature, everywhere vibrant, tingling, surging with
the energy of God.

Such a view of God, though recurrently appropriated by
Christians, is essentially at variance with the main tradition
derived from Judaism. Indeed, the Renaissance may be
viewed as another of the perennial upsurges of the Hellenic
against the Hebraic spirit. For Judaism, God is the trans-
cendent Lord, who from Mount Sinai delivers his commandments to Moses. If this God is brought down from the
Mount and made to dwell in every stream and blade, then
man finds it easier to discover God everywhere, and the
necessity for a unique revelation is less acutely felt. A basis
is then discovered for the blending of all religions and the
tolerance of all cults.

This process was facilitated in several ways. One was
to discover confirmation of Christian doctrines in other religions. The Florentine Academy, for example, discovered in
all systems traces and confirmations of the doctrine of the
Trinity, whether in Plotinus or in the occult lore of the
East: the Zoroastrian Oracles, the Hermetic literature, and
the Jewish cabala, in which strands of Pythagorean nu-
merical speculation afforded a presumed vindication of the
Christian doctrine. So Pico and so Reuchlin in his *De Verbo
Mirifico*. Much of the borrowing from classical mythology
aspired to be no more than a restating in a new set of symbols of the traditional affirmations.

The second method was the reverse, namely, to purge
Christianity of those elements which could not be found in
other religions. Servetus, for example, being a Spaniard, was
deeply concerned for the problem of the conversion of the
Moors and the Jews. To him it appeared that the sole
obstacle was the Christian claim that God is both three and
one. What, then, was his relief when, on examining the
Scriptures, he could find no mention of the word trinity nor

of the related formula of the one substance and the three persons, nor of the key word *homoousios*! He jettisoned the doctrine in the high hope that unity of religion might thereby be facilitated.

The same general objective was achieved, perhaps unwittingly, by those who, averse to speculation, sought to reduce Christian doctrine to the simplest affirmations. A non-dogmatic piety had characterized the Brethren of the Common Life and their disciple Erasmus, whose patron saint was the penitent thief, since saved with so little theology. This only he believed: that Christ could get him to Paradise. All other beliefs, therefore, are non-essential for salvation. The outcome of such an approach was to reduce Christianity largely to ethics, a blend of Stoicism and the Sermon on the Mount. Little wonder that, when in the Enlightenment this position became dominant, a similarity was discovered between Christianity and Confucianism!

Still a third way of fostering the concord of all religions was to divest Christianity of its historical core and, by allegory, to impose upon all religions identical meanings. This device was congenial to the mystics who held that religion involved a beginning from within rather than a point of departure from some event without. Such a view negates the essential character of Christianity, resting upon what God did in the fifteenth year of Tiberius. The affirmation that at a point in time God became flesh, suffered, died, and rose, became simply a symbol of the birth of Christ in the soul of man, the dying to sin, and the rising to newness of life. Such was the view of Sebastian Franck. Tolerance for all religions was an inescapable corollary. Highly congenial to such a position was Boccaccio's story of the three identical rings bestowed by a father upon three sons, each of whom supposed his ring to be unique. On the father's death the three proved to be indistinguishable. Now, these are Christianity, Judaism, and Islam.[16]

---

[16] Jacob Burckhardt, *The Civilization of the Renaissance in Italy* (English, 1933), p. 475, asserts that the story of the three rings, though much older than Boccaccio, is first used by him to place Christianity on a par with the other religions (*Decam.* 1, Nov. 3).

Our next inquiry is to ask what bearing these develop-
ments had upon the church, and the answer is that there
was very little overt clash between the exponents of the
positions delineated above and the church of Rome. If the
advocates of the New Learning suffered at the hands of the
church, it was only in the second half of the sixteenth
century, during the period of the Counter-Reformation. In
the heyday of the Renaissance Pico was merely looked upon
askance, whereas the thoroughly medieval Savonarola went
to the gallows. The reason was partly that the popes were
themselves the patrons of the new learning and the new art,
and they were not passionately concerned about religion.
Moreover, the humanists lacked the temper of martyrs.
They were ready to go just up to the edge of the fire, since
to die for an idea is to put too high a price upon a conjecture.

Skepticism was not rife, and such as we do find is to be
understood rather as a heritage from the Middle Ages than
as a new development of the age of the Renaissance. It consisted in a dualism between philosophy and theology, two
disciplines capable of arriving at contradictory conclusions.
Two Christian doctrines were in this way called into question. The first was personal immortality and the second was
the doctrine of the Trinity. The difficulty with regard to immortality stemmed from the Arabic influence, for the Arabs
interpreted Aristotle as meaning that at death the individual
soul is absorbed into the world soul. The energy is not lost,
but the identity is submerged. In the Renaissance period,
Pomponazzi stood in this tradition and in his work on immortality endeavored to demonstrate by a more acute
examination of the mind-body problem that no evidence
and no analogy point to continuance of personal conscious-
ness after the dissolution of the body. One may wonder why
no action was taken against Pomponazzi, and the answer is
that he was perfectly covered by the doctrine of double
truth, or at least of double logic, which held that philosophy
and theology, far from being related as maid and mistress,
are divergent and often contradictory quests for truth.
What is philosophically indefensible may be theologically
sound. Pomponazzi was quite prepared, therefore, to believe

in personal immortality, although he could not bolster his conviction by physiological or philosophical underpinning.

A similar position arose out of late scholasticism which called itself Modernism. This view made difficulty for the doctrine of the Trinity, that God is both three and one, because these philosophers took an atomistic view of reality which, according to them, is made up of individual components which are not held together by any comprehensive entities. The state, for example, cannot be regarded as a corporate entity but only as an agglomeration of citizens; likewise, the church. If this theory be applied to the three persons in God, that is to say, if they cannot be held in unity by the entity of the one substance, then there must be three gods. The doctrine of the Trinity becomes thereby the doctrine of tritheism. But once again, tritheism was not affirmed, because theology rules otherwise. Here, likewise, one kind of logic compels the conclusion that there are three gods, whereas another points to monotheism. The decision rests with the church. When, however, the authority of the church was undercut by the Protestant Reformation, then Servetus employed all of these late scholastic arguments to reinforce his objection to the doctrine of the Trinity.

Beyond this there was little skepticism. But one or two examples of a somewhat flippant criticism of biblical miracles can be discovered in the same number of centuries. Luigi Pulci suggested that Moses might have unloosed the floodgates of a fishpond and drowned a few of Pharoah's men, that Samson carried off the door of a summer booth, and that Peter walked on a frozen sea.[17] Indirect ridicule was poked at Joshua's exploit by relating that Charlemagne for three days stopped the sun in order to complete a victory, and thereby gravely inconvenienced the people on the other side of the earth. Pietro d'Abano, as early as 1300, is credited with a rationalistic explanation of the resurrection of Lazarus. But serious skepticism is scarcely discoverable prior to the very end of the sixteenth century, in Bruno,

---

[17] Ernst Walser, "Die Religion des Luigi Pulci," *Die neueren Sprachen,* Beiheft X (1926).

Campanella, and Vanini, and they expiated their temerity at the stake after the manner of the high Middle Ages.[18]

Satire and ridicule of the church were common enough. Although serious in intent, they were not revolutionary in objective. The authors were minded to correct abuses but not to destroy the structure of the church. Witness the Pasquinades and Facetiae. Take, for example, the anecdote related by Poggio Bracciolini that a certain priest buried his pet dog in consecrated ground. The bishop remonstrated. The priest explained, "Father, if you knew the cunning of this dog, his intelligence was more than human in his lifetime, and especially manifest at his death, for he made a will and, knowing that you were needy, left you fifty golden ducats. Here they are." The dog was undisturbed. The relater of this tale was a papal secretary and he also was undisturbed.[19]

More subversive to the church was the literary criticism of documents and the exposure of forgeries undertaken by Lorenzo Valla. He demonstrated that the Donation of Constantine, which claimed that this emperor had conferred upon the pope temporal sovereignty over the whole of the West, could not have arisen in the days of Constantine, because of variations in the Latin and certain historical allusions which necessitated a date not much in advance of the time of Charlemagne. The Apostles' Creed was shown by Valla not to have originated with the Apostles. Likewise, the letter of Christ to Abgar of Edessa was proved not to have been genuine. On this letter rested an elaborate superstructure. In the letter Christ promised to send Abgar his portrait. So many portraits came to be extant, each claiming to be genuine, that the church selected one as the true image, the Veron-Ikon, whence the name Veronica, and the legend of her napkin. Valla likewise wrote critical notes on the New Testament text which, after his death, were published by Erasmus. Yet Valla held a post as papal secretary.

---

[18] G. Spini, *Ricerca dei Libertini* (1950).

[19] In translation in Merrick Whitcomb, *A Literary Source Book of the Italian Renaissance* (1900), p. 35.

The church was sufficiently entrenched that the loss of a few documents did not unsettle her foundations.

Only one serious clash occurred between the humanists and the church. It was the Reuchlin affair and had to deal with freedom to pursue Semitic studies. Reuchlin, a layman, was invited to give a judgment because a converted Jew named Pfefferkorn was displaying the zeal of a convert in clamoring for the destruction of Jewish books. Reuchlin, who believed that the Jewish cabala offered a confirmation of the doctrine of the Trinity, rallied to the defense. The upshot of the affair was a tacit victory for the humanists. Reuchlin was indeed saddled with the costs of the trial, but he never paid them, and Semitic studies went valiantly on. Was it not Cardinal Ximenes who published the Complutensian Polyglot containing the Hebrew text of the Old Testament?

The Renaissance then was rather subversive by the subtle transmutation of values noted above: syncretism, allegorization, moralization, the reduction of dogma, the spiritualizing of everything external. These exercised a corrosive influence so imperceptibly that none took fright until the Reformation commenced the exposure of the Renaissance and then the Counter-Reformation turned upon them both.

By way of gathering up the themes, we may inquire as to the mood of the Renaissance. Commonly, it is represented as exuberant, unconcerned, blithe, without twinges of conscience, pangs of remorse, or tremors of anxiety. Again, there is some measure of truth in this generalization, but the change in tone from the Middle Ages can easily be overdone. The exuberance of the Renaissance is not to be exaggerated. There was at the same time a strain of melancholy, and Petrarch suffered from *accidie*,[20] the typical monkish slough of despond, a doubt not only as to the vocation but with regard to the central affirmations of the faith. Renaissance man was not so sure of his knowledge. Nicholas of Cusa

[20] Giulio A. Levi, "Accidia e Dubbio nel Petrarca," *Rinascita* 1 (1938), 40–47.

pushed to the upper limits the reach of the human understanding and eventuated in learned ignorance, *docta ignorantia*. Agrippa of Nettesheim wrote on "The Uncertainty
of All the Sciences" (*De Incertitudine Omnium Scientarium*).
Some even made a virtue of necessity and acquiesced in
ignorance on the ground that knowledge puffed one up. A
docta ignorantia was matched by a *sacra ignorantia*.

Neither did Renaissance man feel so certain that he was
the master of his fate. Pico held that man was the moulder
of his destiny and could descend and ascend in the scale of
being, because Pico did not believe in astrology; but many
did. And one of the great problems of the Renaissance was
whether *Virtu* was able to impede the wheels of the goddess
Fortuna.

Expressions of despondency are not uncommon. Erasmus indulged in wistful scoffing at the very endeavors to
which he had consecrated the unremitting toil of a lifetime.
"Why inflict upon oneself," he inquired, "invalidism, sore
eyes, and premature age in the making of books when per
chance wisdom lies with babes?" Dürer, in his *Melancolia*,
poignantly displays the plight of man, the exuberant, confronted by the unresolved decisions of destiny. A woman of
high intelligence broods torpidly amid all the symbols of
man's highest skills. Only the little cherub scribbling at her
side is insouciant of the forces at play—for in the sky a rain-
bow, the sign of God's covenant with man, contains a
comet, the symbol of impending disaster. Until the conflict
in the heavenly places be resolved, what is the meaning of
man's endeavor?

Where did man turn for solace? Erasmus looked to traditional Catholic Christianity. He is sometimes regarded as
religiously shallow because he wrote only in a foreign tongue.
This was true perhaps until the final hour. As he lay dying he
murmured, first in Latin, *Miserere mihi*, and then in Dutch,
Liefe Godt. Dürer found his resolution in the rediscovery of
the gospel by Martin Luther, the man who had released him
from great anguish of spirit. Michelangelo, in accord with

the forms of traditional medieval piety, took his stand at
the foot of the cross.

> Freed from a burden sore and grievous band,
>   Dear Lord, and from this wearying world untied,
>   Like a frail bark I turn me to Thy side,
> As from a fierce storm to a tranquil land.
> Thy thorns, Thy nails and either bleeding hand,
>   With Thy mild gentle piteous face, provide
>   Promise of help and mercies multiplied,
> And hope that yet my soul secure may stand.
> Let not Thy holy eyes be just to see
>   My evil past, Thy chastened ears to hear
>   And stretch the arm of judgment to my crime:
> Let Thy blood only lave and succour me,
>   Yielding more perfect pardon, better cheer,
>   As older still I grow with lengthening time.[21]

If then the Renaissance was so near to the Kingdom of
God, why the conflict with the Reformation? Here it is striking to observe that the most intense clash occurred not with
the least but with the most Christian representatives of the
Renaissance. Luther attacked not the ribald Aretino or the
trifling Boccaccio, but, rather, the great restorer of primitive
Christianity, Erasmus of Rotterdam. And Calvin came to
grips not with the scoffing Luigi Pulci, but with the passionate herald of the new day of the Lord, Michael Servetus.

The reason was that the Reformation marked a return
to the Judaic element in Christianity, to the concept of God
as high and lifted up, who is known to man not because
everywhere and obviously immanent, but because, normally
veiled in obscurity, he has, in a point of time, disclosed himself, in Jesus Christ, and in him enacted a great drama of
redemption upon Calvary, only by believing in which—and
not by beginning from within—can man be saved. No moral
achievement can ever give any claim upon God, and no
ascending of the ladder of the chain of being can ever unite
man with God and make him into God. Man, who is no clod

---

[21] Translated by J. A. Symonds, *The Sonnets of Michel Angelo Buonarroti*
(1902).

or clay or lump, is nevertheless dust and ashes before God. Not by achievement but by trust is man saved, and morality itself is only the by-product of religion, the behavior springing from gratitude to God for his unspeakable gifts.

The Renaissance was marked mainly by an exaggeration of the Hellenic elements in the Christian synthesis, with an ever-present tendency to destroy the distinctiveness of the Christian revelation. And in some quarters there was a secularistic tendency which relegated religion to the periphery of life.

11 The Religion of the Renaissance

The religion of the Renaissance is as much controverted as the Renaissance itself. The classic treatments of the nineteenth century considered it to have been essentially pagan. Such was the view of Burckhardt, Monnier and Symonds, who believed the spirit of the Middle Ages to have been epitomized in St. Bernard and that of the Renaissance in Faust. A similar point of view is evident more recently in the works of Croce, Gentile and Cassirer who stressed the shift from God to man and from heaven to earth. The cardinal notes of the Renaissance are held to have been freedom, emancipation, individuality, and the capacity of man to mould his destiny. The Renaissance was Promethean. At the other pole of opinion is Toffanin with his contention that the humanism of the Renaissance was a reinforcement of Catholicism and that the real subversion of the Church and of Christianity emanated from the sects. A middle ground is represented by Walser, Garin and Kristeller, who acknowledge secularism only in the sense that the Renaissance introduced a number of new interests not specifically religious in character.

If one equates the Renaissance with humanism this movement itself is complex and its religious emphases correspondingly diverse. Humanism meant on the one hand the cultivation of *litterae humaniores*, a concern for form and poetry, nurtured by a revival of the literature of classical

Published in German in *Die Religion in Geschichte und Gegenwart*.

antiquity, including that of the fathers of the Church. At the same time humanism was a way of life, *Humanitas*, the ideal of the cultivated man, rich in interests, urbane and magnanimous in spirit.

As the cult of form through the revival of antiquity, humanism was as varied as were the religions and philosophies of antiquity. Classical paganism was of course not Christian and its mythology was used by the humanist as a garment for Christian themes purely as a matter of form, for no one thought of reviving paganism. The varied philosophies of antiquity were fused with Christianity quite after the manner of the Church Fathers. Early Christianity had long since appropriated the Stoic doctrine of natural law, grounded in the structure of a rational universe and marked by a cosmic concord in accord with which the heavenly bodies do not collide and animals do not destroy each other. Men ought therefore to find a reasonable resolution of their disputes or if they fight, should observe humanity. These concepts had early been incorporated into Christian thinking, notably by Augustine. They became again the staple of the peace literature of the Renaissance, in conjunction with strains from the Old Testament and the New with which they are not incongruous.

The Epicureanism of antiquity, on its vulgar side as carnal enjoyment, had no representative in the Renaissance, if some modern interpreters are correct that Lorenzo Valla was not voicing his own opinion in the third section of his *De Voluptate*. The refined Epicureanism of the *beata tranquilitas* is to be found in the works of such men as Conrad Celtis and Mutianus Rufus. It is not incompatible with the *pax dei* and the *vita contemplativa*. The political ethic of the Sophists had a representative in Machiavelli, but he was an isolated figure and the great bulk of the political writing of the sixteenth century was in the moralistic tradition.

Neoplatonism was the most characteristically new element in the religious life of the Renaissance; new particularly because this Neoplatonism included the occult lore of the Orient: the Sybilline Oracles, the Zoroastrian Oracles, the

Cabala and the Hermetic literature. The latter was the more readily received because believed by reason of interpolations to have been a Christian document. The core of this religion was that man, standing at the center of the great chain of being, is not chained but may descend or ascend until united with God. These concepts had been appropriated early by the Christian Fathers, for whom the end of religion was that man should be made God. There was the difference that Neoplatonism felt no need for a mediator, whereas the fathers insisted that God became man in order that man through the God-man might become God. At this point the piety of some of the Christian Neoplatonists of the Renaissance was closer to Plotinus than to the Gospel. Yet one is not to think of these elements in the Renaissance as fundamentally new, because for centuries the writings of Dionysius the Areopagite had profoundly influenced Western thought, and one may well compare Pico's *De Dignitate Hominis* with Bonaventura's *Itinerarium Mentis ad Dominum*.

There was no skepticism in the Renaissance deriving from humanism. The skepticism which did exist stemmed rather from two medieval movements. One was Occamism, which denied the possibility of rational demonstration for theological tenets, particularly the doctrine of the Trinity, but at the same time believed on the basis of revelation and of the authority of the Church. The position has been described as one of "double truth." It was rather one of double logic. So long as the authority of the Church was retained, the theological logic prevailed. But when authority collapsed during the Reformation this Occamist position led to Antitrinitarianism, as in the work of Servetus. The other movement was that of Averroism which interpreted Aristotle to mean that the soul is not immortal but at death is absorbed in the world soul. Pomponazzi defended this view, but failing to find rational grounds for immortality, believed nevertheless on authority. Once again this position might and eventually did end in skepticism. But this skepticism did not issue in atheism. Systems in opposition to Christianity first appear at the end of the sixteenth century with

Bruno, Campanella and Vanini whose contemporaries visited upon them the same penalties which they would have incurred in the high Middle Ages, namely, prison and the stake.

Yet there was an element subversive to Christianity in the religion of the Renaissance, namely, that syncretism which tended to make of Christianity only a religion among the religious of the world after the manner of Boccaccio's and Lessing's story of the three identical rings signifying Judaism, Christianity and Mohammedanism. Cusa found that even opposites can be true and can find a place in ultimate harmony. Aquinas thought that the pre-Christian heathen could be saved by implicit faith in the necessary dogma but Erasmus considered only minimal dogma to be necessary. The Florentine Neoplatonists thought to find the doctrine of the Trinity in non-Christian religions, whereas Servetus eliminated the doctrine of the Trinity from the Christian religion. Sebastian Franck by the use of allegory caused all religions to mean the same thing.

As for the exuberant this-worldliness of the Renaissance one must bear in mind that the concept of nature as refulgent with the glory of God was not irreligious and is more nearly expressed in St. Francis' "Song of the Creatures" than in Petrarch's account of climbing Mont Ventoux. The cult of fame in the Renaissance was reduced by Petrarch and Colucci Salutati to willingness to submit one's work to the corporate judgment of one's colleagues. And along side of the exuberance there was also an intense preoccupation with death during the fourteenth and fifteenth centuries. To be sure, the humanists turned from the Virgin and the saints as protectors to confidence that no harm could befall him who was *integer vitae*. Yet the terror of death was by no means exorcised, witness the experiences of Luther and Loyola. As for the claim that man was emancipated from the depressing fatalism of astrology not by science but by virtù, one may claim with greater plausibility that the victory was due to Christian theology. One notes that Luther, who was less of a humanist than Melanchthon, denied astrology, and

Melanchthon, who was more of the humanist than Luther, accepted it.

The Renaissance was subversive mainly by way of syncretism, relativism and the tolerance of all religions. That it was not anti-religious may be inferred from the behavior of the humanists in the religious upheavals of the sixteenth century. The older generation remained with the Church. At the end of the period a very few went to the stake like medieval heretics. The younger generation abandoned non-dogmatic syncretism for the flaming dogma of Wittenberg and Rome.

Selected Bibliography

The literature is reviewed in the following surveys:

ANGELERI, CARLO, *Il Problema del Rinascimento*, Florence, 1952.

CHABOD, FEDERICO, "Il Rinascimento," in *Problemi storici e orientamenti storiografici*, ed. E. Rota, Milan, 1948; English trans. in *Machiavelli and the Renaissance*, London 1958.

Among general treatments may be noted:

CASSIRER, ERNST, *Individuum und Kosmos in der Philosophie der Renaissance*, Berlin, 1927.

HUIZINGA, J., "Das Problem der Renaissance," in *Wege zur Kulturgeschichte*, Munich, 1930.

KRISTELLER, PAUL OSKAR, "Paganism and Christianity," in *The Classics and Renaissance Thought*, Cambridge, Mass., 1955.

STADELMANN, RUDOLF, *Vom Geist des ausgehenden Mittelalters*, Halle, 1929.

WALSER, ERNST, "Studien zur Weltanschauung der Renaissance," in *Gesammelte Studien zur Geistesgeschichte*, Basel, 1932.

WERNLE, PAUL, *Renaissance und Reformation*, Basel, 1912.

On skepticism:

KRISTELLER, PAUL OSKAR, "El Mito del Ateismo Rinacentista y la Tradicion Francesa del Librepensamiento," *Notas y Estudios de Filosofia*, IV, 13 (1953).

SPINI, G., *Ricerca dei Libertini*, Rome, 1950.

On the relations of humanism, scholasticism and Hermeticism:

KRISTELLER, PAUL OSKAR, "Florentine Platonism and its Relations with Humanism and Scholasticism," *Church History*, VIII, 3 (1939).

———, "The Scholastic Background of Marsilio Ficino," *Tradition*, II (1944).

———, "Marsilio Ficino e Lodovico Lazzerelli," *Annali della R. Scuola Normale Superiore de Pisa* (Lettere Storia e Filosofia, Ser. II, VII, ii–iii, 1938).

On the cult of death:

TENENTI, ALBERTO, *Il Senso della Morte e l'Amore della Vita nel Rinascimento*, Turin, 1957.

On Aquinas and Erasmus as to the salvation of the heathen:

THOMPSON, CRAIG, *Inquisitio de Fide*, New Haven, Conn., 1950, rev. Hans Baron, *ARG*, XLIII, 2 (1952).

On classical themes in the Renaissance peace literature:
BAINTON, R. H., "The *Querela Pacis* of Erasmus," *ARG*, XLII (1951).
There are excellent introductions to the works of individuals in:
CASSIRER, E., ed., a.o., *The Renaissance Philosophy of Man*, Chicago, 1948.
On two northern humanists:
HALBAUER, FRITZ, "Mutianus Rufus," *BKGMAR*, XXXVIII (1929).
SPITZ, WILLIAM L., *Conrad Celtis*, Cambridge, Mass., 1957.

12 Biblical Scholarship in the Renaissance and Reformation

The age of the Renaissance and Reformation gave, if possible, an even greater stimulus to Biblical than to classic studies, because the Bible as a document of antiquity and a textbook of religion enlisted the interest alike of the humanist and of the reformer. Commentaries on the Sentences gave way to commentaries on the Bible, to which one must still turn for much of the political and social as well as for the religious thinking of the day. Yet despite the importance of the subject no adequate work on the field of Biblical scholarship and influence in the period has ever appeared, nothing comparable, for example, to the work of Hans Rost for the Middle Ages.[1] A partial attempt was indeed once made by Berger, and his work is still useful especially for the account of the editions of Ximines and Erasmus.[2] Farrar's work is likewise useful, but scarcely goes beyond summary sketches of the work of Valla, Erasmus, Luther, and Calvin.[3]

An adequate treatment should begin with the text and even prior to the text with the philological tools available for its study. Greek, of course, can be taken for granted, but

First published under the title of "Biblical Scholarship in the Age of the Renaissance and Reformation" in *Church History*, X, 2 (1941). The first two paragraphs have been omitted here.

[1] Hans Rost, *Die Bibel im Mittelalter* (Augsburg, 1939). The bibliography of printed Bibles in many European tongues runs well into the sixteenth century.

[2] Samuel Berger, *La Bible au seizième siècle* (Paris, 1879).

[3] Frederick W. Farrar, *History of Interpretation* (New York, 1886).

Semitic scholarship outside of Jewish circles was largely in-spired by Biblical interests. The Cabala did indeed intrigue Pico and Reuchlin, but the Bible even more, and the only serious clash between humanism and the church was over freedom to prosecute Semitic studies. The *viri obscuri* lost the battle and Hebrew continued to be cultivated as an integral part of a theological education.[4]

The printing of the Bible in the original tongues is covered by Copinger.[5] The translations into Latin and the vernaculars have attracted a great deal of attention. Brief introductions to the subject are to be found in *Die Religion in Geschichte und Gegenwart (I Bibelübersetzungen)* and in the useful little handbook by Guppy.[6] The Latin Bibles are described by Copinger,[7] whose collection is now housed in the library of the General Theological Seminary (Chelsea Square, New York). The German translation of Luther has given rise to an extensive literature which is covered in Taylor's admirable manual of problems.[8] The English Bible also has received considerable attention. An excellent ac-count of how divergent estimates of the Reformation in general have affected appraisals of Tindale as a translator is given by Knappen in an article on Tindale.[9] The Tudor translations as a whole and individually have been the sub-

---

[4] On the Biblical interests of the humanists we have: J. Lindeboom, *Het Bijbelsch Humanisme in Nederland* (Leiden, 1913), and H. J. Hak, "De Humanis-tische Waardeering van de H. Schrift in het bijsonder bij Marsilio Ficino en Faber Stapulensis," *Archief voor Nederlandsche Kerkgeschiedenis*, N. S. XXIX (1937), 77–90. Semitic studies, in general, are admirably covered in the bibliography of Karl Schottenloher, *Bibliographie zur deutschen Geschichte* (Leipzig, 1933–39), under the rubric *Hebräisches Sprachstudium*.

[5] Walter Authur Copinger, *The Bible and its Transmission* (London, 1897).

[6] Henry Guppy, *A Brief Sketch of the History of the Transmission of the Bible* (Manchester, 1936).

[7] Walter Arthur Copinger, *Catalogue of the Copinger Collection* (Manchester, 1893, with many facsimiles). Descriptions are given in the work by him listed above.

[8] Archer Taylor, *Problems in German Literary History* (New York, 1939), pp. 35–36. See also Schottenloher's *Bibliographie* under Luther and for the whole subject under "Bibel-Ausgaben," "Bibelglossar," "Bibelillustrationen."

[9] M. M. Knappen, "William Tindale—First English Puritan," *Church History*, V (1936), 201–205.

ject of numerous monographs.[10] So too have the versions into
various European tongues.[11]

The theory of translation occasioned controversies in
the sixteenth century. Tindale was accused by More of a
Protestant bias when *priest* became *presbyter* and *church* became *congregation*.[12] Castellio was reproached for a humanist
bias when for the sake of linguistic purity he substituted
lavare for *baptizare* and *respublica* for *ecclesia*. His classical
periodic sentences ruined the parallelism of the Hebrew. In
his French version, to avoid Greek roots like *holocauste*, he
invented *brulage*. Yet his work was not without merit.[13]

The concept of Biblical inspiration has not been pursued to my knowledge systematically through the reformers

[10] Francis Fry, *A Bibliographical Description of The New Testament* (London,
1878), covers forty editions of Tindale with 73 plates. Francis Fry, *A Description
of the Great Bible* (and of other editions down to 1640. Half the volume consists of
facsimiles. London, 1865). Alfred William Pollard, *Records of the English Bible:
The documents relating to the translation and publication of the Bible in English,
1525–1611* (London, 1911). John Rothwell Slater, "The sources of Tyndale's
Version of the Pentateuch." (Diss., Chicago, 1906). Albert H. Gerberich, "Luther
and the English Bible." (Diss., Johns Hopkins, Lancaster, Pa., 1933). Henry Guppy,
William Tindale (Bull. John Rylands Lib., IX 2 [1925]). Henry Guppy, *Miles
Coverdale*, (Bull. John Rylands Lib., XIX, 2 [1935]). Elizabeth Whittlesey Cleave-
land, "A study of Tindale's Genesis compared with the Genesis of Coverdale
and of the Authorized Version," *Yale Studies in English*, XLIII, (New York,
1911). Grace F. Swearingen, "Die englische Schriftsprache bei Coverdale," (Diss.,
Berlin, 1904). Harold Rideout Willoughby, "A Census of the Extant Coverdale
Bibles," (n. d. n. p. mimeographed).

[11] French translations are covered by Willem J. Van Eys, *Bibliographie des
Bibles et des nouveaux Testaments en langue française des XV. et XVI siècles* (2
vols., Geneva, 1900 and 1901). Consult also Horst Kunze, "Die Bibelübersetzungen
von Lefèvre d'Étaples und von P. R. Olivetan," *Leipziger Romanistische Studien*
(Leipzig, 1935). Dutch translations are treated by H. van Druten, *Geschiedenis der
Nederlandsche Bijbelvertaling* (2 vols., Leiden, 1895–98), a work which I have not
been able to consult. For the Spanish translator, Cassiodore de Reina, there is still
no better study than the old one by Edward Boehmer in *Bibliotheca Wiffeniana*,
II, (Strassburg, 1883). Samuel Berger deals chiefly with the manuscript versions,
but also with the printed translations of the sixteenth century into Spanish and
Portuguese in his "Les Bibles Castillanes," *Romania*, XXVIII (1899). For bibliography of works dealing with translations into Italian and the Slavic tongues see
Hans Rost, *Die Bibel im Mittelalter* (Augsburg, 1939), 376–78.

[12] Compare S. L. Greenslade, *The Work of William Tindale with an essay by
C. D. Bone comparing the translations of More and Tindale* (London, 1938).

[13] See the articles by Douen in the appendix of volume I of Ferdinand Buisson,
Sébastien Castellion (Paris, 1892).

as through the doctors of the Middle Ages by Holzhey,[14] but the monographs devoted to the views of individuals are numerous. Luther's attitude to the authority of Scripture is crucial and puzzling. The key lies in his Christology. A word of Christ he dared not tamper with, however irrational it might appear, but with Christology as a touchstone he could move otherwise through the Bible with royal freedom. He was quite ready to discard traditional views of authorship, though not to reject from the canon anything beyond the Old Testament Apocrypha.[15] Calvin, too, though more systematic and sober than Luther, was no narrow Biblical literalist. He, too, would relinquish traditional theories of authorship, yet stoutly rejected Castellio's attempt to expunge the Song of Solomon from the canon.[16] Paternity for the doctrine of verbal inspiration in Protestantism has usually been assigned to Matthias Flacius Illyricus, but this view has been contested by Moldaenke.[17] Yet Flacius certainly did talk sometimes in terms of verbal inspiration.[18] The controversy in the Reformation period over the relative authority of the outer and the inner word, so dear to the Protestant sectaries, has been well covered by Maronier and Grützmacher.[19]

Biblical criticism, whether higher or lower, was not far advanced in the fifteenth and sixteenth centuries, and what there was has not been adequately canvassed. Luigi Pulci mocked some of the Old Testament miracles. Lorenzo Valla raised problems with regard to the text. Erasmus at first re-

[14] Karl Holzhey, *Die Inspiration der hl. Schrift* (Munich, 1895).

[15] Paul Schempp, "Luthers Stellung zur heiligen Schrift," *Forsch. zur Gesch. und Lehre des Prot.*, III (1929), stresses the Christological interest, but neglects the older literature. This can be found by consulting Schottenloher under *"Luther"* and then under *"Schriftprinzip."* Luther's early lectures on Romans and Hebrews have been made available in critical editions in the series *Anfänge reformatorischer Bibelauslegung*, edited by Johannes Ficker, now in WA.

[16] See J. A. Cramer, *De heilige Schrift bij Calvijn* (Utrecht, 1906).

[17] Günter Moldaenke, "Schriftverständnis und Schriftdeutung im Zeitalter der Reformation. Teil I. Matthias Flacius Illyricus." *Forsch. z. Kirchen- und Geistesgeschichte*, IX (1936).

[18] See *Church History, VII* (1938), 183.

[19] J. H. Maronier, *Het Inwendig Woord* (Amsterdam, 1890). Richard H. Grützmacher, *Wort und Geist* (Leipzig, 1902).

jected the "three witness" passage. Michael Servetus was critical of the current typological interpretation of the Old Testament as foreshadowing Christ. Carlstadt attacked the Mosaic authorship of the Pentateuch,[20] and Francis David, the Anti-trinitarian, questioned the genuineness of the command, "Go ye into all the world and baptize all nations in the name of the Father, Son and Holy Ghost." [21]

The Biblical commentaries of the Reformation are an inexhaustible mine not only for religious but also for political and social ideas. If Baron is looking for the sources of Calvinist republicanism, he is driven to Bucer's commentary on Judges.[22] If one desires a ready touchstone to views about religous liberty the key passages under which to look are Deuteronomy 13 and Titus 2:10. The parable of the tares is the clue to the theory of the church and its relations to the states, because the sectaries identified the tares with the heretics who were not to be weeded out, whereas the representatives of the established order saw the tares in moral offenders only.[23] Certain passages of Scripture in fact constituted rubrics under which to discuss all manner of topics. Suicide would go under Samson; theft under the despoiling of the Egyptians; bigamy under Lamech and polygamy under Abraham or some other patriarch; Judith was the figure for tyrannicide; pacifism and the rejection of the oath of course went back to the Sermon on the Mount, and the stock passage for Christian recognition of the state was always Romans 13. The proof text for the contract theory of government was II Kings 11:17.

The problem of the relation of the New Testament to the Old had long troubled Christian exegetes. The difficulty was in part that the church rejected the Jewish law but canonized the book which contained the law. A deeper dis-

[20] His tract on the canon is reprinted by Karl August Credner, *Zur Geschichte des Canons* (Halle, 1847).

[21] Matt. 28:19. Frederick W. Farrar's *History of Interpretation* (New York, 1886), though still useful in its way, by no means covers all of this territory.

[22] Hans Baron, "Calvinist Republicanism," *Church History, VIII* (1939), 30–42.

[23] See chapter 6.

crepancy appeared when the church, on making its peace with the empire, filled up the gaps in a deficient political ethic out of the Old Testament despite its divergence from the Sermon on the Mount. Calvinism in particular did this in the age of the Reformation, even going to the length of reviving the tyrannicide of Judith. And the Münsterites brought back the polygamy of the patriarchs. No little discussion in consequence arose as to the relation of the new dispensation to the old.[24]

The Biblical commentary of the common man was the drama and the picture book. A bibliography of the dramatizations of the Bible all the way from the mysteries to the present has been prepared by Coleman,[25] and Philip Schmidt has pointed out that Biblical illustration is valuable not only as art but also as exegesis.[26]

The primary need in this whole field is for a comprehensive work covering all aspects of the subject. Less tangible but ultimately more important would be a realization on the part of scholars in related areas of the stores of relevant material deposited in Biblical commentaries. Particularly is this true of social and political thought, and even theologians have not always been aware that Luther's theology can better be gleaned from his commentaries on Psalms, Romans, and Genesis than from more direct treatises.[27]

[24] See chapter 7.

[25] Edward D. Coleman, *The Bible in English Drama* (New York, 1931). Attention may be called also to Erwin Kohler, "Entwicklung des biblischen Dramas des 16 Jhr. in Frankreich." (Diss., Naumburg, a. S., 1911). Joseph Herrlich, "Das englische Bibeldrama zur Zeit der Renaissance und Reformation." (Diss., 1907) which gives particular attention to Udall, but adds bibliography on Bale, Buchanan, etc. Ernst Nahde, "Der reiche Mann und der arme Lazarus." (Diss., Jena, 1928), adds bibliography on works treating the dramatization of Susanna, the Prodigal, Esther and Tobias. Cf. also Archer Taylor, *Problems in German Lit. History*, 108–109. Joseph E. Gillett, "The German dramatist of the sixteenth century and his Bible," *Publ. Mod. Lang. Ass.*, XXXIV (1919), 465–493.

[26] Philip Schmidt, "Die Bibelillustrationen als Laienexegese," *Festschrift Gustav Benz* (Basel, 1935), 228–239. A guide in general to the Biblical illustrating of the period will be found under the caption "*Bibelausstattung*" in *Die Religion in Geschichte und Gegenwart*.

[27] Cf. also: Smalley, Beryl, *The Study of the Bible in the Middle Ages* (Oxford, 1941).

Selected Bibliography

Among the more recent works one may note:

On translation:

BLUHM, HEINZ S., "Recent American Research on Luther's German Bible," *The Germanic Review*, XVIII, 3 (October 1943), 164–171.

———, "Luther's Translation of Luke 22:15," *Modern Language Notes* (June 1950), 405–408.

———, "Luther and the First Printed English Bible," *Anglican Theological Review* (October 1958), 3–32.

SCHWARZ, W., *Principles and Problems of Biblical Translation* (1955).

On Luther as an exegete:

BORNKAMM, HEINRICH, *Luther und das Alte Testament* (1948).

EBELING, GERHARD, *Evangelische Evangelienauslegung* (1942).

———, "Die Anfänge von Luthers Hermeneutik," *Zeitschrift für Theologie und Kirche*, XLVIII, 2 (1951), 172–230.

———, "Luthers Auslegung des 44 (45) Psalms," in *Luther Forschung Heute* (1958).

LOEWENICH, WALTHER, VON, "Luther und das johanneische Christentum," *Forschungen zur Geschichte und Lehre des Protestantismus*, VII, 4 (1935).

———, "Luther als Ausleger der Synoptiker," *ibid.*, X, 5 (1954).

PELIKAN, JAROSLAV, "Luther the Expositor," *Luther's Works* (St. Louis, 1959).

QUANBECK, WARREN A., "Luther's Early Exegesis," in *Luther Today* (1957).

On the problem of Word and Spirit:

For Luther:
GERDES, HUGO, *Luthers Streit mit den Schwärmer* (1955).

PRENTER, REGIN, *Spiritus Creator* (1954).

RUPP, GORDON, "Word and Spirit in the First Years of the Reformation," *Archiv für Reformationsgeschichte*, XLIX, 1/2 (1959), 13–26.

For Zwingli:

BURCKHARDT, ABEL E., *Das Geistproblem bei Huldrych Zwingli* (1932).

For Calvin:

KRUSCHE, WERNER, *Das Wirken des Heiligen Geistes bei Calvin* (1957).

For Franck:

HEGLER, ALFRED, *Geist und Schrift bei Sebastian Franck* (1892).

13 The *Complaint of Peace* of Erasmus, Classical and Christian Sources

Erasmus' *Querela Pacis* is one of the classics of the literature of peace, which has enjoyed a widespread and continuous hearing. In the sixteenth century there were thirty-two dated editions, not to mention many without date, and some seven translations into French, Spanish, Dutch, and Swiss German at Zurich and at Basel, High German, and English, the latter by Thomas Paynell in 1559.[1] This translation has been several times reprinted and notably on the occasion of great wars. The Yale Library has an edition printed in London in 1802 at the time of the Napoleonic conflict, another printed in Boston in 1813 during the War of 1812, and another printed at Chicago in 1917, the year in which the United States entered World War I. At the termination of World War II, William J. Hirten brought out a facsimile of the original together with Paynell's translation in the Scholars' Facsimiles (New York, 1946). And in the midst of the cold war the Beacon Press issued a new translation by José Chapiro.[2]

The original was composed in the year 1516 and first

First published under the title, "The *Querela Pacis* of Erasmus, Classical and Christian Sources," in *Archiv fur Reformationsgeschichte,* XLII (1951).

[1] Elise Constantinescu Bagdat, *La Querela Pacis d'Erasme* (Paris, 1924).

[2] *Erasmus and Our Struggle for Peace* (1950).

published in 1517,[3] at the instance of a counselor of Charles
of Burgundy, later to be Charles V of the Holy Roman
Empire. Some modern writers have been disposed in consequence to question the sincerity of Erasmus, who might
conceivably have written on the other side if the interests of
the court had so dictated. Such a suspicion might be war-
ranted were it not that the plea for peace in the *Querela* was
no more than the gospel which Erasmus reiterated in season
and out of season all his life long, in the *Adages*, the *Col-
loquies*, the *Letters*, the *Praise of Folly*, the *Institution of the
Christian Prince*, the *Panegyric on Philip*, the tract on *War
with the Turks*, and in many other places.[4] His advice,
whether requested or spurned, palatable or unpalatable, was
always the same.

There is a more serious question as to whether he may
not unwittingly have been voicing merely provincial politics.
He was by birth a Hollander, a citizen of a land which de-
pended for its very existence upon peace among the great
powers or at least the maintenance of its own neutrality.[5]
No accident can it be, argue some, that pacifist sentiments
emanated from Erasmus of Holland, a small state, and
Thomas More of England, an island begirt by a sea wall,
whereas the philosophy of power politics was espoused by
Machiavelli, the Italian, caught inescapably in the maelstrom
of power politics amid the great powers. Such a picture is
difficult to assess or refute because it lies in the area of the

[3] *EE*, ed. P. S. Allen, III (1913), p. 13.

[4] *Epistolae*, especially *EE* I, 551–554; III, 65, 29–34; IV, 373, 13–15; VII,
452, 3–6; 509, 7–8; VIII, 193.

   Opera: I *De Rerum Copia* 87 B-E; *Colloquia: Charon*, 822–24; *Militaria*,
641–43; *Militis et Carthusiania*, 708–10. II *Adagia*, 551D–555D. 591 B–C. 775 D–F.
951–70. IV *Stultitiae Laus*, 493–94; *Ad Philippum*, 534B–540C; *Institutio Principis*,
607–612; V. *De Bello Turcico*, 353D–355E; *Symboli Catechesis*, 1193 D–E; IX *Ad
Stunicam*, 360E–361A; *Supputatio Errorum*, 635 A–B; X *Responsio*, 1752 C–D.
Professor Craig Thompson has supplied me with numerous references in the letters.
Ampler discussions together with citation of sources will be found in the following:
Adriana Wilhelmina de Jongh, *Erasmus Denkbeelden over Staat en Regeering* (Am-
sterdam, 1927); Ines Thuerlemann, *Erasmus von Rotterdam und Joannes Ludovicus
Vives als Pazifisten* (Freiburg, Switzerland, 1932).

[5] Cf. concerning this problem: Gerhard Ritter, *Erasmus und der deutsche
Humanistenkreis am Oberrhein* (Freiburg, 1937).

intangible. But it at least is evident that Erasmus was more than a Hollander. He was a European deeply concerned for the maintenance of Christendom. His arguments for peace did not take the form of advising Holland to rely not on the horsemen of France or on the chariots of the Empire, but of counseling both France and the Empire to recall their common brotherhood in Christ. To reinforce his argument Erasmus blended in an artistic weave the great themes of peace which came down from the classical heritage and the Christian tradition. His method, of course, was altogether typical of the Renaissance, nor was it any innovation inasmuch as St. Augustine long before had effected to some degree a similar fusion. But Erasmus by fresh delving in the literature and by a zeal quickened through circumstance fashioned a new whole so well integrated that the sources are lost to view and the plea sweeps to an impassioned climax as if springing unpremeditated from the author's mind and pen. To break up the argument into its components and lay bare the sources may appear a fruitless exercise, but partly because of the inherent importance of the theme and partly as a study in methodology there is an interest in seeing how traditions can be blended in mutual reinforcement.

Before engaging, however, in analysis we must have in mind the content of Erasmus' plea. For that reason a brief digest is in order. Peace enters, speaking in her own person and lamenting that she is so little received among men. She marvels at this the more because the heavenly bodies, though inanimate, preserve a happy equilibrium: the very plants cling to each other and the irrational animals do not devour those of the same species. The boar does not bury his tusk in the boar, the lion shows no fierceness to the lion, nor does the serpent expend his venom on the serpent. The wolf is kind to the wolf. And if animals do fight it is only to assuage their hunger. Why then should not man of all creatures be at peace with man? The more so because he is endowed with reason and gifted with speech, the instrument of social intercourse and reconciliation, and with tears which in a shower dissolve the clouds and suffer the sun again to shine. Man depends for his very existence upon co-operation. He could not be born without the union of partners or survive without a helping hand. The human being, unlike the animals, arrives physically defenseless. Why then should man prey upon man?

Peace, not yet disillusioned, assumes that when she hears the name of man and Christian, there she will find a reception. She approaches hopefully a city begirt by walls and living in accord with laws, only to discover factions. She turns from the common rout to kings and finds them embracing with obsequious flattery while conniving at mutual destruction. The learned men, the philosophers, are little better with their wrangling schools. Nor even are the religious orders superior though they bear the name of brother, dress in white, and carry the cross, for they are continually contentious. The home is indeed better, yet not without discord, and even in the breast of a single individual the passions are at war with reason.

All this is the more amazing when one examines the precepts of the Christian religion. In the Old Testament Isaiah foretold the coming of the Prince of Peace and in the New Testament Christ bequeathed peace as his legacy. The mark by which his disciples should be known is love one for the other. The Lord's Prayer addresses Our Father, but how can they who call upon a common Father drive steel into the bowels of their brethren? Christ compared himself to a hen, Christians behave like hawks. Christ was a shepherd of sheep, Christians tear each other like wolves. Christians have the same supper of the Lord, the same heavenly Jerusalem, but they are less peaceful than the Jews who fight only with foreigners and the Turks who keep the peace among themselves.

And who is responsible for all this? Not the common people, but kings, who on the strength of some musty parchment lay claim to neighboring territory or because of the infringement of one point in a treaty of a hundred articles, embark on war. Not the young, but the graybeards. Not the laity, but the bishops. The very cross is painted on their banners and cannons are christened and engraved with the names of the apostles, so that Paul, the preacher of peace, is made to hurl a cannon ball at the heads of Christians.

Consider the wickedness of it all, the breakdown of laws which are ever silent amid the clangor of arms. Debauchery, rape, incest, and the foulest crimes are let loose in war. Men who would go to the gallows in peace are of prime use in war, the burglar to rob, the assassin to disembowel, the incendiary to fire an enemy city, the pirate to sink his vessels.

Consider the cost of it all. In order to prevent the enemy from leaving his town one must sleep for months outside of one's own. New walls could be built for less than is required to batter down old ones. When all the damage is taken into account the most brilliant success is not worth the trouble.

Consider the folly of it all. What is man but an insect of a summer day, and what is a king but a crowned animalcule, soon to vanish like smoke into the air? At the very portal of the palace, at the very entrance to the pavilion, death hovers, and will you then fume over phantoms of a waking dream?

How then is peace to be secured? Not by royal marriages, but by cleansing the human heart. Why should one born in the bogs of Ireland seek by some alliance to rule over the East Indies? Let a king recall that to improve his realm is better than to increase his territory. Let him buy peace. The cheapest war would be more expensive. Let him invite the arbitration of learned men, abbots, and bishops. Let the clergy absent themselves from silly parades and refuse Christian burial to those who die in battle. If we must fight, why not go against the common enemy, the Turk? But wait. Is not the Turk also a man and a brother?

Above all else let peace be sincerely desired. The populace is now incited to war by insinuations and propaganda, by claims that the Englishman is the natural enemy of the Frenchman and the like. Why should an Englishman as an Englishman bear ill will to a Frenchman and not

rather good will as a man to a man and a Christian to a
Christian? How can anything so frivolous as a name out-
weigh the ties of nature and the bonds of Christianity? The
Rhine separates the French from the German but it cannot
divide the Christian from the Christian. The Pyrenees lie
between the French and the Spaniards but cannot break the
indissoluble bond of the communion of the church. A little
strip of sea cuts off the English from the French, but though
the Atlantic rolls between, it could not sever those joined by
nature and still more indissolubly cemented by grace. In
private life one will bear with something in a brother-in-law
only because he is a brother-in-law, and cannot one then
bear anything in another because he is a brother in Christ?

Let us then repent and be wise, declare an amnesty to all
past errors and misfortunes, and bind up discord in adaman-
tine chains which can never be sundered till time shall be no
more. *Haec ille.*

Is this plea essentially classical or Christian? The
recent editor of the facsimile counts but three classical
quotations and pronounces it therefore Christian. But the
classical influences cannot be so readily assessed. There are
few quotations but abundant allusions. Erasmus knew his
classics too well to require annotations or even quotation
marks. The work is an intricate blending of the classical
with the Christian tradition.

To begin with, the *mise en scène* is classical. The per-
sonification of Peace comes from the side of Greece and
Rome with her *ara pacis*, and the device of having Peace
assume the word is adapted from Seneca's *De clementia*
where Clemency appears in a like role.[6]

But deeper than any such superficial device are the
themes. The first is the harmony of the cosmos. It is the
Stoic faith that all the universe is pervaded with the immanent principle of reason which bestows even upon the
inanimate a certain rationality so that the heavenly bodies
do not collide in their courses, and even the brute beasts do

---

[6] *De clementia,* I, 2–4.

not prey upon those of the same species. The theme, of course, was not universal. In antiquity Hesiod looked upon the animals as warlike in comparison with man.[7] And commonly the fishes were considered an exception to the rule of peace within the species,[8] though Pliny sought to conserve the formula by distinguishing varieties among the fish.[9] Apart, however, from all qualifications the theme was very prevalent that the animals keep the peace among those of their own kind and therefore the anomaly is all the more glaring that man the rational should destroy his fellow man.

Two examples will suffice by way of illustration. The first from Dion of Prusa celebrates the concord of the heavenly bodies. "The sun graciously gives way at night to the weaker stars and moon and even by day suffers himself to be eclipsed or shrouded by cloud and mist. The stars in turn show each other consideration and preserve their orbits without collision. Likewise in the lower world, the birds nest beside the birds, the ants assist the ants and the bees do not quarrel over the same flower." [10]

Erasmus, versed as he was in classical literature, would almost surely have known this passage though he need not have done so in order to employ the theme, because it was appropriated early in Christian literature, and Clement of Rome in the same vein besought the Corinthian church to avoid faction in imitation of the harmony of the heavenly bodies.[11]

On peace among the animals, classical citations could be multiplied. The one closest to Erasmus is from the Satires of Juvenal who affirmed: "Wild beasts are more merciful to beasts spotted like themselves. When did the stronger lion ever take the life of the weaker? In what wood did a boar ever breathe his last under the tusk of a boar bigger than himself? The fierce tigress of India dwells in perpetual peace

[7] Hesiod, *Erga*, 276f.

[8] Cf. Irenaeus, *Adv. Haer.*, V, 24, 2.

[9] *N.H.*, VII, 1, 5.

[10] *Oratio*, XL, 35, Arnim, II, p. 55. Cf. Harald Fuchs, "Augustin und der antike Friedensgedanke," *Neue philologische Untersuchungen*, III (1926), 101–103.

[11] For this and numerous examples in the Fathers consult Fuchs, *op. cit.*

with her fellow; bears live in harmony with bears. But man
finds it all too little to have forged the deadly blade on the
impious anvil; for whereas the first artificers only wearied
themselves with forging hoes, harrows, spades and plough-
shares not knowing how to beat out swords, we now behold
a people whose wrath is not assuaged by slaying some one,
but who deem a man's breasts, arms and face afford a kind
of food." [12]

One observes incidentally in this passage the theme of
the fall of man from the Golden Age without war to the age
of Iron and conflict, a very prevalent theme in classical
literature from Hesiod to Ovid, but not appropriated by
Erasmus for whom the fall was rather from the pacifism of
the Gospels.

The modern reader may be disposed to smile at these
passages as utterly unrealistic and to sympathize rather
with Hesiod in his picture of the animal world in conflict.
Here one must recall that the discussion in antiquity was
not motivated by an interest in zoology but rather by a
concern for human nature. The real question was as to the
character of man. Was Plautus right that man to man is a
wolf, homo lupus homini?[13] Or Seneca that man is sacred to
man, homo res sacra homini?[14] The whole question in
modern times has taken on a new pertinence with the
doctrine of organic evolution. If man is thus linked to the
lower forms of life, then it is highly relevant to inquire
whether nature is red in tooth and claw and man by nature
will devour his kind, or whether even on the animal level
co-operation and maternal sacrifice are rather the key to
nature.

The ancient proponents of peace like Erasmus were
insistent that man by warring upon man is violating his own
nature and doubly so because his qualities and endowments
should make him even more peaceful than the beasts. Like

---

[12] *Sat.* XV, Loeb translation. Cf. Cicero, *De Fin.*, III, 19, 61–62; Horace,
Ep., VII; Seneca, *De clem.*, I, 26, 4; Lactantius, *De ira*, c. 12; Fuchs, *op. cit.*, p.
107, note 4.

[13] Plautus, *Asinaria*, Act. III, 1. 495, cited by Erasmus, *Opp.*, II, 55D.

[14] *Ep.*, XCV, 33.

them he shares the implicit rationality of the universe making for concord, but unlike them he is equipped with the faculty of active reason and unlike them he is gifted with the power of speech, the agent of reconciliation and the gift of tears with which to dispel the mists of disaffection. These themes are all distinctly classical. Cicero eloquently voiced the praises of reason and inculcated rational behavior. Man, he pointed out, has in common with the beasts animal courage but man alone has a sense for equity and goodness because he alone is endowed with reason and the capacity for communication.[15] Juvenal presumably supplied Erasmus with his observation on the gift of tears in the passage:

When nature bestowed the gift of tears she proclaimed the tenderness of man. This is his best quality. She bids us weep for a friend on trial . . . for what good man believes that any human woe concerns him not? Tenderness alone separates us from the dumb herd. To us alone has been granted a nature worthy of reverence, capable of divine things.[16]

This passage already introduces us to the second great theme which Erasmus appropriated from antiquity, that of humanity. When he represented Peace as expecting hospitality the moment she heard pronounced the words man and Christian, he was in this very phrase combining the classical and the Christian strains. The concept of humanity was elaborated by the Stoic Panaitios and popularized in the circle of Scipio Africanus. The ideal was that of the integrated life lived in conformity with the true nature of man defined in terms of dignity and excellence inspiring reverence. In the Scipionic circle of ruling aristocrats humanity at first connoted the code of gentlemen characterized by decorum, civility, refinement, and polish. Hellene and barbarian came to signify cultivated and uncouth. But humanity did not as yet extend to the common herd. Progressively the concept of humanity became humanitarian.

[15] *De Off.*, I, 4, 16. On speech as the promoter of intercourse; *De Leg.*, I, 6, 27.

[16] *Sat.*, XV.

The change is evident in the sense with which Cicero invested the term *magna anima*. The great soul had originally been regarded as the soul mighty in battle. Cicero fastened upon the term an imperishable meaning when in appealing to Caesar to spare his conquered foes he exhorted him to display the quality of the great soul, magnanimity; and the response of Caesar was exemplified in his statue holding hands with the goddess Clemency. The ultimate sense was conveyed to the term humanity by Seneca when he declared that man is sacred to man.[17]

Humanity then became the ally of peace. More than once in her name the appeal was made for a cessation of hostilities. Two examples will suffice. The first is a speech composed by a Platonist of the fourth century B.C. who may well have been voicing his own ideas,[18] in what he attributed to Nikolaus the Aged, of Syracuse, who opposed the slaughter of the defeated Athenians. Mounting the rostrum the tottering statesman said, that

none could accuse him who had lost two sons in the war of any softness toward Athens. How did he envy those who had died gloriously for their country leaving him to a childless old age! Nevertheless mercy should be shown to Athens, partly because the common usage of the Greeks forbade the slaughter of the vanquished, and partly for the sake of humanity. To crush a bruised reed is to despise the common weakness of mankind. Why did the ancients set up their trophies in wood rather than in stone if not that the memory of their victories might be short? Let Athens, who first erected an altar to mercy find mercy in Syracuse. In the fluctuations of fortune the victor of today may be the vanquished of tomorrow, and how can he expect to find mercy if he refuses it? Magnanimity will be the best way to establish peace and to make the Athenians ashamed

---

[17] Rudolf Pfeiffer, "Humanitas Erasmiana," *Studien der Bibliothek Warburg*, XXII (1931); Richard Harder, "Nachträgliches zu Humanitas," *Hermes*, LXIX (1934), 64–74; Max Pohlens, τὸ πρέπον, "Nachrichten von der Gesellschaft der Wissenschaften zu Göttingen," *Philol. Hist*. Kl. LXXXIX I (1933), 63–92; ders. Antikes Führertum, "Cicero de Officiis und das Lebensideal des Panaitios," *Neue Wege zur Antike*, II, 3 (Berlin, 1934), 137f; R. Reitzenstein, *Werden und Wesen der Humanität im Altertum* (Strassburg, 1907); Grace H. Macurdy, *The Quality of Mercy, the Gentler Virtues in Greek Literature* (New Haven, 1920); Max Muehl, *Die Antike Menschheitsidee in ihrer geschichtlichen Entwicklung* (Leipzig, 1928)

of their unjust war. Recall their contributions to Greek culture and
the common loss which will be sustained in the destruction of their
citizens. Confound not men like Alcibiades the fomenter (who
saved himself by flight) and Nicias the restrainer (who had been
captured) and forget not the common soldier who has not to reason
why. Above all let humanity be exercised toward those of the same
stock.

In this speech humanity is blended with pan-Hellenism,
but it appears unalloyed in Seneca when he remarks:

"We punish murders and what shall we say of wars and mas-
sacres which we laud because they destroy whole nations? . . . That
which would be visited with death if done privately is vaunted
when committed publicly. . . . Shameful it is that men, the mildest
breed, should delight in mutual bloodshed, even handing on their
wars to their children, whereas animals devoid of reason are at
peace. Man who is sacred to man is even killed for sport."[19]

The prudential considerations against war and in favor
of peace in Erasmus find their anticipation chiefly on the
classical side. He was deeply mindful of the horror of war,
the devastation which it wrought, the crimes which it un-
leashed, the recession of law and reason which it entailed.
His feeling was summed up in that maxim of Pindar, "Sweet
is war to those who have had no taste of it." [20] The Latin
version, *Dulce bellum inexpertis*,[21] was taken by Erasmus as
the text for one of his longest commentaries in the *Adages*.
There even more than in the *Querela* he lamented that in
war cities are burned, cattle are driven off, virgins are raped,
laws are abrogated, and religion is held in contempt.[22] Erasmus was fond of the observation of Cicero, "*Silent leges
inter arma.*" [23]

For the sheer horror of a siege there is even in Erasmus
nothing so vivid and moving as the lines of Aeschylus,

[18] Ephoros (fl. 341 B.C.), Diodoros Siculus, *Hist.*, XIII, 20–27.
[19] *Ep.*, XCIX.
[20] *Frag.*, 110.
[21] Vegetius, *De Re Mil.*, III, 12. "*Inexpertis enim dulcis est pugna.*"
[22] *Opp.*, II, 951–70, especially 953.
[23] Milo, XI, cited by Erasmus, *Opp.*, IV, 536C.

Groaning within: without
A net is spread
Gripping the towers about:
Man strikes man dead;
And inarticulately,
Like beasts in dread,
Mother and infant cry,
And blood runs red.
Running, they rob, they fly.[24]

As for the wickedness of war, the ancient polemic
against the military education of Sparta provided a model.
Plato caused the Spartan to say: "We are trained in hardy
endurance by means of contests and robberies carried out at
the risk of a drubbing." [25]

The uncertainty of the outcome in war was not infrequently urged in antiquity as a reason for being exceedingly
slow to commence hostilities. Thucydides presents Archi-
damus of Sparta as seeking to dissuade his countrymen from
an attack on Athens on the ground that "When a great con-
federation in order to satisfy private grudges undertakes a
war for which no man can foresee the issue it is not easy to
terminate it with honor." [26] That the chances were weighted
against any genuine advantage was suggested by the remark
of the Emperor Augustus that "War is like fishing with a
golden hook." Any fish that is caught is not equal to the
value of the hook and the fish may go off with the hook.[27]
Cicero was more emphatic in his declaration that an unjust
peace is better than the most just war.[28]

The folly of mutual slaughter when life itself is so
fragile and brief was voiced alike by Greek and Latin.
Pindar speaks of man as but the creature of a day.[29] And
Seneca inquired:

[24] *Seven Against Thebes*, lines 345–51, tr. Gilbert Murray (1935).
[25] *Laws*, 631C–633B.
[26] Thucydides, IV, I, 82.
[27] Suetonius, *Oct.*, XXI. Cited by Erasmus, *Opp.*, II, 966B.
[28] *Fam.*, 6. 6. 5. Cited by Erasmus, *EE*, IV, 373, 13–15; *Opp.*, II, 966A.
[29] Pindar, ed. Farnell, p. 129.

Why do the restless perturb life? Fate stands above our heads and every day brings us nearer to the hour of perishing.[30]

Why did God give the winds? Not that we should equip ships with arms and seek our enemies upon and beyond the seas. What madness impels us that we rush to mutual destruction? We risk an uncertain future, a tempest beyond human power and death without burial. Why do we impel the people to arms? Why infest the seas? For what are we seeking? Death, which is everywhere.[31]

The ancients had also their alternatives to war. Cicero commended the prudence of concession, at any rate in private relations, for, said he, it will often befit a gentleman to yield much of his own right and to keep out of litigation as far as his interests will permit and perhaps even a little farther.[32] Philostratus goes further when he tells the story of an Indian prince who obtained peace by purchase. "I share," said he, "my wealth with my enemies. When the barbarians who border this country were perpetually raiding us I controlled them with money, so that my country is patrolled by them, and instead of invading my dominions they themselves keep off more remote barbarians." [33]

Arbitration was a device to which Erasmus made frequent appeal. In the main he looked to the popes to serve as the mediating power. Certainly since the death of the bellicose Julius, by whose triumphal entry into Bologna he had been so shocked,[34] one could, he believed, look with confidence to the peaceful Leo[35] and to a pope well named Clement[36] to pacify the nations in conflict. For precedent nowhere better could one look than to the Greeks who alone in antiquity were so situated as to make arbitration feasible. It seldom succeeds when there is too great a discrepancy of power. The Jews were not able to arbitrate because they were too feeble, and the Romans declined to do so because they

[30] *De Ira*, III, 42.
[31] *Nat. Quaest.*, V, 18, 4f.
[32] *De Off.*, II, 18, 64.
[33] *Vita Apoll.*, II, 26.
[34] *Opp.*, IX, 361A.
[35] *EE*, II, 82; *Opp.*, II, 970.
[36] *EE*, VIII, 193.

were too strong. But Athens, Sparta, Corinth, and the other Greek city states were more evenly matched and could for that reason the more readily have recourse to the council table. As a matter of fact, nearly one hundred cases of successful arbitration are recorded.[37] Among the pleas for arbitration one may note the lines of Euripides,

> O foolish men
> Who strain the bow beyond the mark, and suffer
> Much harm at justice's hand, and yield at last
> Not to friends' mediation, but stern facts!
> O foolish states, which might by parley end
> Feuds, yet decide them in the field of blood![38]

One argument adduced on the classical side for peace was incapable of use unchanged by a Christian, yet in altered form was often adduced by Erasmus. This was the argument from pan-Hellenism. It was at variance of course with the broader concept of humanity. The consideration that animals of the same species should not devour each other was narrowed from all men to all Greeks. Plato voices the idea in the Republic where he says that the Hellenes should quarrel as those who have the intent to compose their differences. They should seek to correct in love rather than fight as enemies. They should not suppose that the entire population on the other side is equally their enemy for they know that the guilt of war is always confined to a few persons, and that the many on the opposing side are their friends. And for that reason the Hellenes should be unwilling to waste the lands and raze the houses of each other. Enmity should be maintained only until the innocent sufferers have compelled the guilty few to give satisfaction. These were the rules which the Greeks should observe with each other, though in fighting with the barbarians they would follow the practice now in vogue among the Greeks.[39] To reinforce his point Plato would apply the term war only to conflicts with

---

[37] Anton H. Raeder, *L'Arbitrage international chez les Hellènes* (1912); Coleman Phillipson, *The International Law and Custom of Ancient Greece* (1911).

[38] *Suppliants*, lines 744–49, Loeb translation, pp. 557–559.

[39] *Rep.*, V, 471.

outsiders. Strife among the Greeks was not war but simply faction.[40]

When this type of thinking was transferred to the situation of Erasmus the Hellene became the Christian and the barbarian the Turk. Erasmus constantly reiterated that Christian should not fight with Christian. Often enough he went further and deplored that man should fight with man. But what then about war with the Turk? Is not the Turk also a man and a brother? inquired Erasmus in the *Querela*. There is grave danger lest in fighting the Turks we degenerate into Turks.[41] If the first preachers of the gospel had exhibited toward our ancestors the attitude which we display toward the Turk, how should we ever have been christianized?[42] Such passages led to the charge that Erasmus would under no circumstances resist the Turk, a view which he felt constrained to disclaim. His own stand, he explained, was intermediate between that of those who would kill the Turk like a dog and those who would not resist at all, a position which curiously he attributed to Luther, and which Luther then felt obliged to disavow. According to Erasmus, Luther regarded the Turk as a scourge of God for our sins, so much so that to resist the Turk would be to resist God. And to this Erasmus replied that diseases may also be a visitation for sins but we are not for that reason to decline the services of a doctor.[43]

Thus far our concern has been with the classical sources of Erasmus. In no sense did he consider the themes appropriated from the Hellenes as anything other than a groundwork and reinforcement of his Christian approach, and he was all the more ready to borrow unreservedly because Augustine had done so before him. The *Civitas Dei* likewise adduced the cosmic harmony and peace among the animals of the same species as examples shaming the quarrel-

[40] *Ibid.*, 470. Quoted by Erasmus in the *Querela* E, IV verso (1517).
[41] *EE*, III, 365.
[42] *Opp.*, 967A.
[43] *Opp.*, V, 353D–355E.

someness of man.[44] If one turns to that which is specifically
Christian in Erasmus there is scarcely need for any extended
indication of the sources because they are so obvious, the
precepts of the Sermon on the Mount and the Pauline injunctions to a peaceable demeanor. More to the point is to
place the position of Erasmus within the stream of Christian
thinking. Three main views have emerged in Christian
thought with regard to the problem of participation in warfare: pacifism, the just war, and the crusade. These are not
strictly parallel. Pacifism renounces all participation in war,
the other two are variant attitudes toward participation.
The just-war theory allows Christians to engage provided
the war has as its object the vindication of justice conceived
usually in terms of the defense of the rights of person and
property. The war can be fought only under the authority of
government and must be conducted in accord with certain
rules of good faith and humanity. The crusade has as its
object the defense of the faith or of some ideal. It may be
fought under the auspices of the Church or of some inspired
leader. And because of the fanaticism engendered by the
holy war the restraints on violence tend to go by the board.[45]

Of these three attitudes the last for Erasmus was definitely excluded. Much of his polemic against war was an
attack upon the crusading ideal. The faith for Erasmus
could not be extended and should not be defended by arms.
The Church should never sponsor a war and churchmen
should not appear in armor. The figure of Pope Julius in
helmet and cuirass was to him an abomination. And certainly the restraints should never be relinquished. Nor was
the first position precisely that of Erasmus. He was never a
pacifist in the full sense of the complete repudiation of all
and any participation in warfare. His thinking moved
within the framework of the traditional just-war theory,
and his uniqueness lies in the discernment of the incompatibility of the wars of Europe as he knew them with the

[44] *Civ. Dei,* XIX, 11–14.
[45] Roland H. Bainton, "The Churches and War: Historic Attitudes toward
Christian Participation," *Social Action* (January 15, 1945).

theory of the just war. Above all else he had the acumen
to perceive the central weakness in the theory itself. In his
hands the just war came very close to disintegration, and
that is the point at which he was certainly on the verge of
becoming a full-blown pacifist.

The traditional just-war theory as formulated by
Augustine required that the war have as its object the
vindication of justice and for that reason he assumed that
a war could be just only on one side at a time. Erasmus was
confident that the conditions were not being fulfilled in his
day. He could not find it in his heart to condemn the sort of
war for the sake of which Augustine had formulated the
theory, namely a war to defend Christian peace against the
barbarians.[46] "But," said Erasmus, "although I do not
condemn all war—there is sometimes necessity—yet it
cannot be denied that wherever there is war there is crime
either on one side or the other and sometimes on both." [47]
Wars are actually fought for private grievances of princes.[48]
These princes call it a just war when they clash to exhaust
and oppress each other's kingdoms and they call it peace
when they connive together for the same end.[49] Conceivably
a war might be just, but a pretext can always so readily be
found.[50]

Another condition of the just war is the observance of
the rules. Non-combatants were to be spared. "This condition," said Erasmus, "is not regarded, for the ills of war fall
on those who have the least to do with it." [51] In the *Querela*
he declared that if one considers the wars of the last ten
years, one observes that they have been undertaken by
kings to the detriment of the people who for the most part
have not known what they were all about.

So far Erasmus was saying that the conditions of the
just war in practice were not actually fulfilled. On occasion

[46] *EE*, I, 554.
[47] *EE*, VII, 452.
[48] *EE*, I, 554.
[49] *Opp.*, II, 775 D–F.
[50] *Opp.*, IV, 610 B–C.
[51] *EE*, I, 552.

he raised the still more devastating query as to whether they ever could be fulfilled, because the just war rests on the analogy of government in which force is exercised in accord with law and is administered by impartial judges, not themselves parties to the dispute, and is directed against the guilty. But in war there is no international law, no international judge, and violence falls indiscriminately upon entire populations. A critic of his argument is represented by Erasmus as saying that if a criminal may be executed, why may not a state be defended by war? Erasmus replies that to answer this question would take too long, but he would say this, that a criminal pays the penalty resulting from his conviction according to the laws, but in war each one holds the other as the accused. Moreover, the greatest ill comes to those who are not participants, farmers, old people, matrons, children, virgins. To vindicate the few we bring misery upon thousands. Some on our own side and the innocent among the enemy are indiscriminately affected.[52]

Erasmus still clung to the framework of the traditional theory and would often throw in parenthetically a disclaimer of total objection to all war and then he would so define the conditions as to make them practically incapable of realization. In the dialogue of Charon an interlocuter inquires whether those who die in a just war do not go straight to heaven. Charon replies that he is unable to answer the question, but this he does know, that whenever there is a war so many souls come to hell that he marvels any remain on earth.[53]

One is entirely in the spirit of Erasmus in combining as a conclusion a passage from Euripides with a benediction from the Apostle Paul.

> O Peace, to all wealth-giver,
> Thou fairest of the Blest,
> I pine for Thee forever.
> Thou loveliest and best.

[52] *Opp.*, II, 964.
[53] *Opp.*, I, 823E.

I fear me that in sorrow
Old age shall come apace,
Ere on some glad tomorrow
I see thy glorious face.
And hear the hymns outringing
Which chorused voices raise,
The dancing and the singing
Of maidens in Thy praise.
Keep from us hate that slayeth
And faction's fires abhorred,
All maddened strife that playeth
With the two-edged sword.[54]

"And the peace of God which passeth all understanding shall keep your hearts and minds through Christ Jesus." [55]

[54] *Cresphontes*, Nauck, Frag., 453, tr. Macurdy, op. cit., p. 139.
[55] *Phil.* 4, 7.

14 Freedom, Truth and Unity

I

The confluence of two tributaries has produced the stream of freedom in the Western world. These two have run parallel in several periods. In antiquity the one was Hellenism, the other Hebraism. In the fifteenth and sixteenth centuries the two were the Renaissance and the Reformation, which at this point was not essentially different from medieval Catholicism. In the seventeenth and eighteenth centuries the copartners were Puritanism and the Enlightenment. The line which runs through Hebraism, the Reformation, and Puritanism has contributed to freedom only indirectly. The cardinal tenet was the absolute duty of man to conform to the sovereign will of God. Rather than transgress, he must defy all earthly powers and suffer all earthly torments even unto death. This creed made martyrs, rebels, and regicides. It contributed to liberty because a government had either to exterminate such men or grant them the freedom of their faith. In the end this proved to be the more acceptable alternative. At the same time this creed contained a terriffic core of intolerance because the performance of God's will was so imperative that not only should one die rather than falter, but also one should constrain the recalcitrant. Hence the Hebrew stoned the apostate. Catholic and Protestant burned and drowned the heretic. And the Puritan imprisoned, banished, and even hanged the dissenter.

First published in *Theology Today*, XII, 1 (April 1955); reprinted with permission of the publishers.

Liberty grew out of such premises only when a situation emerged in which a number of groups, each passionately committed to doing the will of God, differed as to what that will entailed. They were then confronted with the alternative either of exterminating or of tolerating one another. They began with efforts at constraint and ended with the truce of toleration, but this could become tolerance only if a degree of relativism were introduced, if not with regard to the will of God, at least with reference to man's ability to know that will. Conceivably each of the differing groups might be partly right and partly wrong. A certain shift was imperative also from the objective to subjective concept of rightness so that sincerity came to be prized equally with correctness, at least as a stage whereby to arrive at correctness.

One may doubt whether these modifications of the rigorous line would ever have taken place solely through the pressure of circumstance had there not been also a confluence with the other strain. Hellenism, the Renaissance, the Enlightenment mellowed the Hebraic Reformation and Puritan attitude. But in the view of the Renaissance there was also a belief in an absolute duty on the part of man who was committed less to doing the will of the sovereign God than to the proclamation of the unadulterated truth. And whereas God's will was commonly assumed to be given through revelation recorded in sacred Scripture, truth was deemed rather to be discovered alike from Scripture and from nature by observation and the exercise of critical faculties. Witness the concern for natural science and the acute critical inquiry into the nature and accessibility of truth on the part of Greek philosophy. The quest for truth in this stream of thought required that the searcher be unimpeded and the elucidation of truth demanded that all findings be made accessible. This is the point at which the Renaissance made a most notable contribution. For during this period emerged the ideal later formulated as *Freie Forschung* or, in modern terminology, academic freedom.

II

One of the great pioneers in the age of the Renaissance was Lorenzo Valla. He had the temerity to subject to critical scrutiny some of the documents on which the claims of the Church were based. In the year 1451 he composed a manuscript which did not appear in print until 1517. The title was *Declamatio de falso credita et ementita Constantini donatione.*[1] The tract investigated the authenticity of a document which had played a great role in advancing the temporal claims of the Church during the Middle Ages. The treatise purported to emanate from the time of Constantine and related that this emperor, having been cured of leprosy by Sylvester, the Bishop of Rome, thereupon embraced Christianity and conferred upon the Pope temporal dominion over the whole of the West. The document today is believed to have originated in France in the ninth century. Lorenzo, by acute historical investigation, undertook to demonstrate its spuriousness. He pointed out the extreme improbability that Constantine would have immediately relinquished control over territory so recently and so arduously won. Equally improbable was it that an estimable Pope like Sylvester would have accepted from the hands of the Emperor that which Christ refused when proffered to him by the prince of darkness. Had the transfer actually been made, one would have expected to find some subsequent reference, but there is no mention of it in Gratian, Gelasius, or Jacob of Voraigne. Moreover, if such power ever had been exercised by the Pope, when was it lost? For certainly it cannot be discovered in succeeding centuries. There are in the *Donatio* a number of historical ineptitudes. The Bishop of Rome at the time of Constantine's conversion was not Sylvester but Miltiades. Reference is made in the work to the city of Constantinople, whereas at that time Constantine had not yet rechristened Byzantium after himself. Roman senators are referred to as "satraps," a term not then in use. Again the Latinity of the *Donatio* betrays its

---

[1] Ed. W. Schwahn (Leipzig, 1928).

later origin, because there are a number of barbarisms which would never have been perpetrated in the classical period. This penetrating criticism proved to be irrefutable, and today all Catholic scholars recognize that the *Donatio* is a forgery.

But at the time Valla's attack was hardy. He knew it and said there were those who were avid to do him to death "because I have attacked not the dead but the living, not merely the ruler but the highest ruler, namely the supreme pontiff against whose excommunication the sword of no prince can afford protection. But if I should be deterred by what the Pope may do, should I not rather consider what He may do of whom I may rightly say, 'Whither shall I flee from Thy presence?' Did not Paul rebuke the High Priest, and did he not withstand Peter to his face in the presence of the congregation? There may be no tribune or king to deliver me from the hand of the Pope. But this is no reason why I should falter. And the Pope has no right to bind me for defending the truth. Rather I should be deemed worthy of reward. In any case when there are many who will endure death for the defense of an earthly fatherland, should I not incur the danger for the sake of the heavenly home? Be gone then tremor and trepidation. With a stout heart, a firm trust and a good hope let us defend the cause of truth, the cause of justice and the cause of God. That man is not a good orator who knows how to speak unless also he open his mouth." So spoke Valla.

As a matter of fact, he was unmolested, perhaps because his work was little known. It was first published by Ulrich von Hutten in the year of Luther's attack upon indulgences. The following year Luther himself got hold of it and put it to good use. Another work of Valla was even more radical because in his annotations on the New Testament he undertook to investigate the true text. This work of Valla remained unprinted until edited by Erasmus in 1505, who in his preface pointed out that the discrepancies between the different versions of the New Testament prove obviously that some readings must be in error. Erasmus himself pro-

duced in 1516 the first published edition of the Greek New
Testament together with a translation into Latin made
directly from the Greek without conformity to the Vulgate.
Both the edition and the translation contained startling
changes. The famous passage, used throughout the Middle
Ages in support of the doctrine of the Trinity, was gone.
The passage occurred in I John 5:7, where the genuine text
speaks of three witnesses on earth—the water, the spirit and
the blood—but the spurious edition says that "there are
three that bear witness in heaven—the father and the word
and the spirit." So read the Vulgate, but the Greek manu-
scripts did not contain the reference to the heavenly witnesses, and Erasmus therefore left it out. He was subject to
such a storm of outraged remonstrance that he promised to
restore it, could a single Greek manuscript be discovered in
which it occurred. When one was found in Dublin, perhaps
manufactured for the purpose, perhaps previously accommodated to the Latin, Erasmus ruefully fulfilled his promise,
but he could not be dislodged with regard to his translation
of Matthew 3:2 where the Vulgate reads "do penance"
(*poenitentiam agite*), whereas the Greek means simply
repent. Erasmus translated *resipiscite*. This caught the attention of Luther and served him powerfully in his attack
on the penitential system.

III

Authors were prepared to risk reputation, convenience,
and life itself to declare what they deemed to be true.
Equally intrepid were the publishers who likewise incurred
grave risks. Oporinus in Basel, for example, suffered imprisonment in 1542 for having printed the Koran. Strictly
speaking he was penalized for evading censorship. Six years
earlier a fellow publisher of Basel had envisaged the publication but had been impeded by the censors. Oporinus resolved to be beforehand and had the entire text already in
print when a rival publisher tipped off the authorities. They
then promptly sequestrated the issue and imprisoned the

printer. Several influential persons interceded, including Luther, who declared that no more damaging blow could be dealt to the Turks than the publication of their Koran that all might see what a farrago it was of lies, fables, and abominations. The censors at Basel relented. Oporinus was released, and the book appeared with a preface by Luther.[2] But all publishers could not be sure of coming off so well.

The authors and the printers of that age had no itch for martyrdom. They desired not to die for the truth but to speak for it and did not hesitate to employ all manner of subterfuges in order to insinuate their findings and their ideas without imperiling either their books or their bodies. Sometimes they used pseudonyms and sometimes employed a dialogue in which an unpalatable opinion was placed in the mouth of one interlocutor and refuted by another. The author really endorsed the offensive view but if taxed with sympathy would declare himself on the side of the refutation. Lorenzo Valla, Hutten, and Erasmus all utilized this device. It is characteristic rather of the Renaissance than of the Reformation. Luther and his followers were much more disposed to be forthright, but deception as to the place and circumstances of publication was not deemed improper. Bibliographers, for example, were long puzzled by the publication of a work of Castellio at "Medinae." One supposed that it might be Medina-del-Campo in Spain until it was observed that Medinae is a transliteration of the Greek μήδενι, meaning "nowhere." Again printers issued controversial tracts with no mark of identification whatever. There is, for example, a sixteenth century attack on the Bishop of Constance for tolerating and taxing priests' bastards. The paper and the type make it possible to identify two hundred other works as emanating from this press, and yet to this day no one has discovered the identity of the printer.

To discover the truth and to declare the truth when discovered, for this the scholars of the Renaissance were ready to labor, suffer, resist, evade, and if need be to die. But this

---

[2] *WA*, LIII, 563 f., and X, 160–163.

does not mean that they were therefore devoted to the ideal
of liberty for its own sake. Their truth was as much an
absolute as the God of the reformers. Liberty they demanded for what was so, not for error, and they, too, could
invoke censorship against what they considered false or
offensive. Erasmus did so, though there is this to be said
by way of palliation, that his person had been assailed.
Sebastian Franck had published a sort of world history including the emperors, the Popes and the heretics from the
point of view of the Roman Catholic Church. Among the
latter was listed Erasmus. The analysis given of his opinions
was objective, and the statement that many in the Catholic
Church considered him a heretic was true, but Erasmus
was of no mind to have this advertised and secured not only
the suppression of the book at Strassburg but also the expulsion of its author from the city.[3]

IV

One may doubt whether the humanists any more than
the reformers would have arrived at tolerance of divergent
views unless they had been driven to concede a certain relativity as to truth or at least as to man's ability to know it.
This Erasmus did and notably in his controversy with
Luther. In the opening section of the tract on "The Freedom
of the Will" Erasmus contended that the whole subject was
extremely obscure and that Luther could by no token be as
certain on the subject as he claimed. Said Erasmus, "If
Scripture is clear, why is there any need for an interpreter?
If the sense is obvious, why have so many excellent men desiring to see the light been enshrouded by darkness? If there
were no cloud in Scripture, why should there have been any
need in the days of the Apostles that God should confer the
gift of the Spirit, and if the Spirit made all plain, why did
Paul enjoin a proving of spirits? By what test can they be
proved? By learning? Are not both sides learned? By

---

[3] Eberhard Teufel, *"Landräumig." Sebastian Franck* (Neustadt an der Esch,
1954).

righteousness? Are not both sides sinners? You say that philosophy does not help. Does ignorance? You say that a council may be wrong. Yes, but is not the same true of a conventicle? You reject the interpretation of the ancient and orthodox fathers on the ground that they were men. So are we all, and how did it come to pass that they should have lacked the gift of the Spirit? You reply that the Gospel has been hidden for thirteen hundred years. If we demand as proof of the Spirit a worthy life, the reply is that we are saved by faith and not by works. If we ask for miracles, the answer is that there is no need for a miracle since Scripture is perfectly plain. If we reply that this cannot be since so many men are beclouded in their interpretation, then we are back precisely where we began. As for myself I am a learner, willing to listen to anyone who will instruct me with civility. And if it be true that I am an old bottle incapable of the new wine of the Spirit, I reply that Christ did not spurn Nicodemus." The sum of it all is that controversy is the proof of uncertainty.[4]

This point of Erasmus was remorselessly pressed by an Erasmian in the Protestant fold. After Servetus had been executed for heresy at the instigation of Calvin and with the applause of all the leading reformers, Sebastian Castellio lashed out that Calvin spoke with as great assurance as if he had been in paradise and yet wrote huge tomes to explain what he affirmed to be absolutely clear. The points which Calvin considered certain, said Castellio, could not be indisputable because they were subject to dispute.

> Nobody ever defended homicide and murder, but the affair of religion and of the knowledge of the Sacred Scripture is altogether different, for the things contained in it are given obscurely and often in enigmas and inscrutable questions, which have been in dispute for more than a thousand years. . . . The questions commonly controverted are obscure. This point can be readily established. No one doubts whether there is a God, whether He is good and just, whether He should be loved and worshipped, whether vice should be avoided and virtue followed. Why? because these points are

---

[4] "De Libero Arbitrio," *Opera*, IX (Louvain, 1706), 1215–1220.

clear. But concerning baptism, the Lord's Supper, justification, predestination, and many other questions there are capital dissensions. Why? because these points are not cleared up in Scripture.

Castellio proceeded to inquire more precisely into the question of religious truth and its limits, for, said he, to recognize the limits of what one can know is as important as to affirm what one does know, and mischief as great may arise from failing to doubt what should be doubted as from failing to believe what should be believed.

Castellio to my knowledge was unique in addressing himself to the problem of knowledge in relation to the problem of liberty. To be sure, John Locke wrote a treatise on toleration and another on the human understanding, but he did not bring the two into such direct relation, because the English government in his day was exercising coercion in religion, not in the interest of truth but for the sake of uniformity. The Church of England did not pretend that its liturgy or its polity was any more grounded upon immutable truth than were the simpler forms of Puritanism, but in the interests of a national Church a single mode of worship was demanded throughout the nation. But in Castellio's day persecution was based on the claim to truth.

The principles which Castellio formulated harked back to the Stoics and anticipated the Enlightenment. He recognized revelation and sense-experience as the sources of knowledge. Error in observation he could not deny but contended that it could be corrected by critical intelligence. Man, he said, is endowed with reason, and reason has not been vitiated by the fall. Reason is able to judge of matters of religion and even with regard to the matter of the consistency and accuracy of the sacred Scriptures. Yet reason was not deemed competent to construct an elaborate, comprehensive, and integrated theological system. What reason afforded was mainly simple propositions, clear, universally intelligible, strongly ethical in content, and only in a broad sense theological. Plainly this was the program of the Enlightenment, and it never did become the basis of toleration among the Puritans. Nevertheless, they approxi-

mated its relativity to this extent: that the many sects of
the Cromwellian era came to believe that at least the points
on which they differed from each other were neither so
certain nor so important as to preclude fellowship.

V

There were other considerations in the age of the
Renaissance which likewise ministered to an ultimate
tolerance. One was individualism. This is a very complex
concept, and one cannot speak of it simply as a product of
the Renaissance. Several types of individualism were in
evidence in the fifteenth and sixteenth centuries, and these
in varying degrees coalesced. There was a philosophical
individualism derived from late Scholastic thinking, which
defined reality in terms of an infinite number of unrelated
particular objects or persons. From this point of view the
state and the Church were not, as the realistic philosophy
held, entities in the mind of God antecedent to particular
Churches or states, but rather the state is an aggregate of
its individual citizens, and the Church is the sum of its
individual members. Neither is humanity so integral a whole
that every individual child born into the world can be held
to be involved in and responsible for the sin of Adam. In its
extreme form this philosophy of individualism destroyed
the solidarity of the human race and of human institutions.
The state became simply a social compact to be easily dissolved, the Church a covenant which might be repudiated
and marriage a contract which could readily be abrogated.
Grave dangers obviously lurk in an individualism so extreme. Yet it may contribute to freedom on the ground that
the individual should not be forced to conform to the
patterns of institutions.

There was another variety of individualism more
indigenous to the Renaissance. This was the picture of the
ideal man who develops all of the gifts bestowed upon him
by the Creator. If man has the capacity to be an artist, a
poet, a musician, a statesman, a banker, and so on, he should

be given the opportunity to develop all of his powers and should not be impeded by financial stringency, ecclesiastical censure, or political interference. This view may lead to sheer irresponsibility with regard to social obligations, but it may also contribute to emancipation from social constraints.

There is a third individualism which is purely religious and is more characteristic of the Reformation than of the Renaissance. This is the view that every man must stand for himself alone in naked confrontation with the Judge of all the world. No man can die for another, as Luther said, and no man can believe for another. The inevitable corollary is that no man should be forced to faith nor impeded in its expression. There were debates as to precisely what constituted faith, and this Protestant principle did not have as its immediate issue the removal of all constraints. Yet in the long run so individualistic a picture of the life of religion was bound to point the lesson of liberty.

Another strand in Renaissance thinking was mysticism. Of course, one is not to associate mysticism exclusively or even primarily with the Renaissance. Yet mystical movements flourished in that age and were not unassociated with the tendencies more specifically labeled "The Renaissance" in the sense of the cultivation of antiquity and of the humanities. The mysticism of the Brethren of the Common Life profoundly affected Erasmus, and the mysticism of the revived Neoplatonism of Florence had also its impact upon him and upon the entire generation.

Mysticism as such is the view which sees the essence and the end of religion in absorption into the godhead, whereby all that is carnal and earthly is cast aside, and spirit is united with spirit. The rungs in the ladder of ascent are marked by a progressive emancipation from the external and the ephemeral and a growing absorption into the eternal. Here plainly is an experience too inward to be helped or hindered by the sword of the magistrate. Erasmus did much to foster the view that God must be worshipped in spirit and in truth, and the external forms are to be prized only if they minister to a spiritual experience. It was Erasmus who so spiritualized the Lord's Supper that Melanchthon called in question the doctrine of transubstantiation, and Melanchthon acutely remarked that the radicalism of Erasmus would have been much more subversive of medieval Catholicism had not Luther arisen to arrest the dissolution. Erasmus plainly saw and often enough pointed out that the religion of the heart cannot be constrained, and his disciple Castellio remarked that one can no more build faith by force than construct a wall by blasting at it with cannon balls.

Another consideration derived also from the mystical tradition reinforced the conclusion, though on the basis of a different assumption. The emphasis was upon the imitation of the suffering of Christ. Now this was actually external. Yet the appeal to the imitation of the meek and dying Redeemer was frequent among those who like Erasmus sought coincidently to remove Christianity from the region of outward observance. In so doing, one should not go so far, said they, as to forget that Christ in reality did not revile, did not retaliate, and did not avail himself of legions of angels. Therefore, it was pertinent to appeal to his example against persecution.

One cannot but wonder why Castellio should have deduced religious toleration from the suffering of Christ, whereas Calvin, who was fully as familiar with the Gospels and equally devoted to Christ, should not have felt the cogency of the appeal. Can it perhaps be that the men of the Reformation were primarily interested in truth and the men of the Renaissance in unity? One recalls all of the tracts on the reunion of Christendon from Nicolas of Cusa to Erasmus himself. Until the very verge of the Diet of Augsburg, Erasmus was indefatigable in his efforts to heal the breach. Likewise he dreamed of a European unity in which the nations should remit their claims and be ready even to suffer wrong at the hands of Christian brethren than have recourse to war. A man who so wrote was deliberately in quest of harmonistic devices, ready to minimize differences, eager to discover common ground. There is always the implicit danger here that peace may be won at the price of a sacrifice of truth, but equally great is the danger that truth may be held at the expense of charity. The Renaissance was striving to combine truth, unity, and freedom.[5]

[5] Consult my *Sebastion Castellio Concerning Heretics* (New York, 1935), *The Travail of Religious Liberty* (Philadelphia, 1951) and the material in Series II of this collection.

Selected Bibliography of Roland H. Bainton

1922   "Church History and Progress," in *Education for Christian Service,* by Members of the Faculty of the Divinity School of Yale University (New Haven, Yale University Press, 1922), pp. 243–266.

1923   "Basilidian Chronology and New Testament Interpretation," in *Journal of Biblical Literature* XLII (1923), pp. 81–134.

1925   "What is Calvinism?" in *Christian Century* XLII (March 12, 1925), pp. 351–352.

1929   "The Development and Consistency of Luther's Attitude to Religious Liberty," in *Harvard Theological Review* XXII (1929), pp. 107–149.

1930   *Debtors to God,* Westminster Departmental Graded Materials. Teacher's Edition (Philadelphia, Westminster Press, 1930), 64 pages. Pupil's edition (Philadelphia, 1930).

      "The Immoralities of the Patriarchs According to the Exegesis of the Late Middle Ages and of the Reformation," in *Harvard Theological Review* XXIII (1930), pp. 39–49.

1931   "Sebastian Castellio and the Toleration Controversy of the Sixteenth Century," in *Persecution and Liberty,* Essays in Honor of George Lincoln Burr (New York, Century, 1931) pp. 183–209.

      "The Smaller Circulation: Servetus and Colombo," in *Sudhoffs Archiv für Geschichte der Medizin* XXIV (1931), pp. 371–374.

      "William Postell and the Netherlands," in *Nederlandsch Archief voor Kerkgeschiedenis* XXIX (1931), pp. 161–172.

1932   "Methods of Great Religious Teachers," in *International Journal of Religious Education* IX (1932) September, pp. 7–8; October, pp. 6–7; November, pp. 6–7; December, pp. 19–20.

      "The Parable of the Tares as the Proof Text for Religious Liberty to the End of the Sixteenth Century," in *Church History* I (1932), pp. 57–89.

      "The Present State of Servetus Studies," in *Journal of Modern History* IV (1932), pp. 72–92.

1935   "Academic Freedom in the Light of the Struggle for Religious Liberty," in *Proceedings of the Middle States Association of History Teachers* XXXIII (1935), pp. 37–44.

Bibliography of the Continental Reformation: Materials Available in English (Chicago, The American Society of Church History, 1935), 54 pages. (Monographs in Church History, No. 1.)

Concerning Heretics, by Sebastien Châteillon: Now First Done into English, by Roland H. Bainton (New York: Columbia University Press, 1935), xiv, 342 pages. (Records of Civilization.)

1936   "Changing Ideas and Ideals in the Sixteenth Century," in *Journal of Modern History* VIII (1936), pp. 417–443.

"Servetus and the Genevan Libertines," in *Church History* V (1936), pp. 141–149.

1937   *David Joris, Wiedertäufer und Kämpfer für Toleranz im 16. Jahrhundert* (Leipzig: M. Heinsius Nachfolger, 1937), vi, 229 pages. (Archiv für Reformationsgeschichte. Texte und Untersuchungen. Ergänzungsband, VI.)

Ulrich von Hutten and the German Reformation, by Hajo Holborn, translated by Roland H. Bainton (New Haven: Yale University Press; London, H. Milford, Oxford University Press, 1937), viii, 214 pages. (Yale Historical Publications. Studies, XI.)

1938   "New Documents on Early Protestant Rationalism," in *Church History* VII (1938), pp. 179–187. Review of *Per la Storia Degli Eretici Italiani del Secolo XVI in Europa,* Testi Raccolti da D. Cantimori e E. Feist (1937).

"Refugees of Other Days," in *Bulletin of the Story Behind the Headlines* II (December 13, 1938), pp. 14–20.

"Servet et les Libertins de Genève," in *Bulletin Société de l'Histoire du Protestantisme Français* LXXXVII (1938), pp. 261–269.

"Straightforward Speech," in *Yale Divinity News* XXXIV (May 1938), pp. 1–3.

"Technology and Pacifism," in *Christian Century* LV (May 18, 1938), pp. 618–619.

"Unity, Utrecht and the Unitarians," in *Christian Century* LV (October 5, 1938), pp. 1189–1190.

1940   *Bernardino Ochino, Esule e Riformatore Senese del Cinquecento,* 1487–1563, Versione dal Manoscritto Inglese di Elio Gianturco (Firenze: G. C. Sansoni, 1940), x, 213 pages. (Biblioteca Storica Sansoni. Nuova Serie IV.)

"Christian Conscience and the State," with Robert L. Calhoun, in *Social Action* VI (October 15, 1940), pp. 4–42.

"Congregationalism: The Middle Way," in *Christendom* V (Summer 1940), pp. 345–354.

1941   *The Church of Our Fathers* (New York: Charles Scribner's Sons, 1941), vi, 248 pages. Also, an English edition; a special edition for Sunday Schools by the Westminster Press; translations into Spanish, Japanese, Siamese, Hebrew and Chinese.

"The Left Wing of the Reformation," in *Journal of Religion* XXI (April 1941), pp. 124–134

"The Struggle for Religious Liberty," in *Church History* X (June 1941), pp. 95–124.

1942   "Christian Views of Human Destiny," in *Religion in Life* XI (Winter 1941–1942), pp. 96–105.

"A Communication for a More Explicit Declaration of Peace Aims," in *Christian Century* LIX (September 16, 1942), pp. 1122–1124.

"Individualism, Christian and American," in *Vital Speeches of the Day,*
VIII, No. 19, pp. 590–592.

"Teaching Church History," in *Journal of Bible and Religion* X, 2 (1942),
pp. 103–107.

1943 "Bossuet and Leibnitz and the Reunion of the Church," in *The Chronicle,*
Protestant Episcopal XLIII (February 1943), pp. 102–103.

"The Churches Shift on War," in *Religion in Life* XII (Summer 1943),
pp. 1–13.

"Congregationalism: From the Just War to the Crusade in the Puritan
Revolution," in *Andover Newton Theological School Bulletin* XXXV
(April 1943), Southworth Lecture Number, pp. 1–20.

George Lincoln Burr: His Life, by Roland H. Bainton; Selections from His
Writings, edited by Lois Oliphant Gibbons (Ithaca, N Y., Cornell University Press; London, Oxford University Press, 1943), xi, 505 pages.

"Reconciliation and Reality," in *Fellowship* IX (December 1943), pp. 208–
210.

1944 "The Christian and the War," in *Christian Century* LXI (May 3, 1944), pp.
559–561.

Pacifism Under Fire. *The Historic Church and Modern Pacificism,* by Um-
phrey Lee. Review by R. H. Bainton in *Fellowship* X (June 1944), pp.
113–114.

1945 "The Amistad," in *Highroad* (September 1945), pp. 4–6, 47.

"The Churches and Alcohol," in *Quarterly Journal of Studies on Alcohol,*
VI (June 1945), pp. 45–58.

"The Churches and War: Historic Attitudes Toward Christian Participation," in *Social Action* XI (January 15, 1945), pp. 5–71.

"The Cohesive Power of Protestantism," in *The Intercollegian* LXII (January 1945), pp. 8–9.

1944, 45 *The Panorama of the Christian Church in Kodachrome Slides* (Boston,
Pilgrim Press, 1944, 1945).

1946 "Early Christianity as a Youth Movement," in *Highroad* (February 1946),
pp. 35–37.

"The Early Church and War," in *Harvard Theological Review* XXXIX
(July 1946), pp. 189–212. Reprinted without notes in *The Church, the
Gospel and War,* ed. Rufus Jones (New York, Harper, 1948), pp. 75–92.

"Our Debt to Luther," in *Christian Century* LXIII (October 23, 1946),
pp. 1276–1278.

"Eyn Wunderliche Weyssagung, Osiander—Sachs—Luther," in *Germanic
Review* XXI, 3 (October 1946), pp. 161–164.

1947 "Dürer and Luther as the Man of Sorrows," in *The Art Bulletin* XXIX
(December 1947), pp. 269–272.

"Let's Agree on the Reformation," in *Christian Century,* LXIV (1947),
pp. 237–239.

"Road to Reformation, by Heinrich Boehmer," in *Church History* XVI
(September 1947), pp. 167–176. Book review.

1948 "The Churches and Alcohol," in *Social Progress* XXXIX (November 1948),
pp. 13–15, 18–19. Reprinted.

"Luther's Struggle for Faith," in *Church History* XVII (September 1948),
pp. 193–206. Printed by mistake in advance of its appearance in the
Festschrift für Gerhard Ritter (Tübingen, 1950), pp. 232–243.

"Marriage and Love in Christian History," in *Religion in Life* XVII (Summer 1948), pp. 391–403.

The Martin Luther Christmas Book, with Celebrated Woodcuts by His Contemporaries; translated and arranged by Roland H. Bainton (Philadelphia, Westminster Press, 1948), 74 pages.

"Our Protestant Witness," in *The Pulpit*, XIX (December 1948), pp. 272–274.

1949   "Christianity and Russian Communism," in *Journal of the Industrial and Social Order Council of the Society of Friends* VI (March, April 1949), pp. 6–11.

"Christmas in 1949," in *American German Review* (December 1949), pp. 3–4. (Philadelphia, Carl Schurz Memorial Foundation, 1949.)

"Luther and the *Via Media* at the Marburg Colloquy," in *The Lutheran Quarterly* I (November 1949), pp. 394–398.

"The Puritan Theocracy and the Cambridge Platform," in *The Minister's Quarterly* V, 1 (February 1949), pp. 16–21. Also in: *The Cambridge Platform of 1648*, Tercentenary Commemoration (Boston, 1949), pp. 76–86.

"Sebastian Castellio and the British-American Tradition," in *Het Boek* XXX, 4 (1949–1951).

"Die Stellung der Quäker zu Krieg und Frieden," in *Der Quaeker*, Monatshefte der deutschen Freunde, 23. Jahrg. 1949 (January, February 1, 2), pp. 1–7.

"Without Despairing of the World, The Quaker Attitude Toward Peace and War," in *Friends Intelligencer* 106, 7 (Second Month 12, 1949), pp. 87–89.

1950   "The Genius of Protestantism," in *The Minister's Quarterly* VI (February 1950), pp. 13–18.

Here I Stand; a Life of Martin Luther (New York, Abingdon-Cokesbury Press, 1950), 422 pages. Reprinted (New York, New American Library of World Literature, 1955), 336 pages. Paperback. Translated into German, Greek, Italian, Japanese, Spanish and Swedish. Portions of this book have been delivered as the Nathaniel Taylor Lectures at the Yale Divinity School (1946–1947), the Carew Lectures at the Hartford Seminary Foundation (1949), and the Hein Lectures at the Wartburg Seminary and Capital University.

1951   "Ernst Troeltsch—Thirty Years Later," in *Theology Today* VIII, 1 (April 1951), pp. 70–96.

"Michael Servetus and the Pulmonary Transit of the Blood," in *Bulletin of the History of Medicine* XXV, 1 (January–February 1951), pp. 1–7.

"The Querela Pacis of Erasmus, Classical and Christian Sources," in *Archiv für Reformationsgeschichte* XLII (1951), pp. 32–48.

"Sebastian Castellio, Champion of Religious Liberty, 1515–1563," in *Castellioniana: Quatre Études sur Sébastien Castellion et l'Idée de la Tolérance*, par Roland H. Bainton, Bruno Becker, Marius Valkhoff et Sape van der Woude (Leiden, E. J. Brill, 1951), pp. 25–79.

The Travail of Religious Liberty; Nine Biographical Studies (Philadelphia, Westminster Press, 1951), 272 pages. The James Sprunt Lectures (1950). Also, an English edition and Harper Torchbooks (paperback).

1952   "Documenta Servetiana," in *Archiv für Reformationsgeschichte*, XLIV (1953), pp. 223–234; XLV (1954), pp. 99–108.

Forschungsberichte und Besprechungen, in *Archiv für Reformationsgeschichte* XLIII (1952), pp. 88–106.

"Luther in a Capsule," in *Bulletin of the American Congregational Association* III (May 1952), pp. 1–9.

The Reformation of the Sixteenth Century (Boston, Beacon Press, 1952), xi, 276 pages. Also, Beacon paperback and translations into Italian and Hebrew.

1952–53 "Christianity and Sex, an Historical Survey," in *Pastoral Psychology* III, 26 (September 1952), pp. 10–26, 82; IV, 21 (February 1953), pp. 12–29. Reprinted in *Sex and Religion Today* (New York, Association Press, 1953), pp. 17–96.

1953 "The Beginnings of Anabaptism," in *Mennonite Life*, five articles commencing in 1953.

"Burned Heretic: Michael Servetus," in *Christian Century*, LXX (1953), pp. 1230–1231.

Hunted Heretic; the Life and Death of Michael Servetus, 1511–1553 (Boston, Beacon Press, 1953), xiv, 270 pages. Reprinted 1956, Beacon paperback; translated into German. For French see below.

"Man, God and the Church in the Age of the Renaissance," in *Journal of Religious Thought* XI (1953–1954), pp. 119–133. Issued also in mimeographed form in *The Renaissance*, A Symposium (New York, Metropolitan Museum of Art, 1953), pp. 41–62a.

"Michael Servetus and the Trinitarian Speculation of the Middle Ages," in *Autour de Michel Servet et de Sébastien Castellion; Recueil*, ed. Bruno Becker (Haarlem, H. D. Tjeenk Willink, 1953), pp. 29–46.

Michel Servet, Hérétique et Martyr, two editions within a few months (E. Droz, Geneva, 1953), the first with inadequate correction to be in time for the commemoration, the second with care as *Travaux d'Humanisme et Renaissance* VI, 148 pages.

They Built for Eternity, by Gustav-Adolf Gedat, translated by Roland H. Bainton (New York, Abingdon-Cokesbury Press, 1953), 175 pages.

"War and Christian Ethic," in *The Church and Social Responsibility*, ed. J. Richard Spann (New York, Abingdon-Cokesbury Press, 1953), pp. 201–219.

1954 *The Covenant in the Wilderness* (1954).

"Friends in Relation to the Churches," The Ward Lecture, Guilford College (November 12, 1954), 16 pages.

"Man, God, and the Church in the Age of the Renaissance," in *The Journal of Religious Thought* XI (Autumn-Winter, 1953–1954), pp. 119–133.

Protestant–Catholic Relations in the U.S., in *Advance* CXXXXVI (October 18, 1954), pp. 13–24.

"What About Catholic-Protestant Relations in the U.S.A.?" in *Messenger* XIX (October 1954), pp. 14–17.

1955 "Freedom, Truth, and Unity: Reflections on the Renaissance," in *Theology Today* XII (April 1955), pp. 85–96.

"Freedom's Religious Foundations," in *Christian Century* LXXVI (January 26, 1959), pp. 106–109.

"Patristic Christianity," in *The Idea of History in the Ancient Near East*, ed. Robert C. Dentan (New Haven, Yale University Press; London, Geoffrey Cumberlege, Oxford University Press, 1955), pp. 215–236.

"The School of Divinity," in *A Study of A Generation in Transition* (1955).

"This Grand Errand," in *Yale Alumni Magazine* (October 1955), pp. 22–23.

1956   *The Age of the Reformation* (Princeton, N.J., Van Nostrand, 1956), 192 pages. An Anvil Original paperback.

"The Ministry in the Middle Ages," in *The Ministry in Historical Perspectives*, ed. by H. Richard Niebuhr and Daniel D. Williams (New York, Harper, 1956), pp. 82–109.

"Religious Biography," in *Writing for the Religious Market*, ed. by Roland E. Wolseley (New York, Association Press, 1956), pp. 185–191.

"Yale and German Theology in the Middle of the 19th Century," in *Zeitschrift für Kirchengeschichte*, Bd. 65, Heft III.

1957   "The Anabaptist Contribution to History," in *The Recovery of the Anabaptist Vision*, ed. by Guy F. Hershberger (Scottdale, Pa., Herald Press, 1957), pp. 317–326.

"Luther's Simple Faith," in *Luther Today* (Decorah, Iowa, Luther College Press, 1957), pp. 1–33. (Martin Luther Lectures, 1.)

"The Universal Ministry of All Believers," in *Encounter* XVIII, 2 (1957), pp. 131–140.

Vignettes of Men Memorialized in the Buildings of the Yale Divinity School; with Drawings by the Author (1957), 11 pages. Condensed from *Yale and the Ministry.*

What Christianity Says about Sex, Love and Marriage (New York, Association Press, 1957), 124 pages. (An Association Reflection Book.)

Yale and the Ministry; a History of Education for the Christian Ministry at Yale from the Founding in 1701, Line drawings by the Author (New York, Harper, 1957), xiii, 297 pages.

1958   "Christian Pacifism Reassessed," in *Christian Century* LXXV (July 23, 1958), pp. 847–849.

"The Making of a Pluralistic Society—A Protestant View," in *Religion and the State University*, ed. by E. A. Walter (Ann Arbor, University of Michigan Press, 1958), pp. 42–57.

Pilgrim Parson, the Life of James Herbert Bainton, 1867–1942 (New York, Nelson, 1958), 166 pages.

"Probleme der Lutherbiographie," in *Lutherforschung Heute*, Hrsg. von Vilmos Vajta (Berlin, Lutherisches Verlagshaus, 1958), pp. 24–31. Internationaler Kongress für Lutherforschung, Aarhus, 1956.

"Sex and Religion," in *Ladies Home Journal* LXXV (August 1958).

"Thomas Hooker and the Puritan Contribution to Democracy," in *Bulletin of the Congregational Library* X, 1 (October 1958).

"Total Abstinence," in *Christianity Today* II, No. 20 (July 7, 1958), pp. 3–6.

1960   "Alexander Campbell and Church Unity" (pp. 81–94) and "Alexander Campbell and the Social Order" (pp. 117–129), Two articles in *The Sage of Bethany; a Pioneer in Broadcloth*, by Perry E. Gresham (St. Louis, Bethany Press, 1960).

"The Bible and the Reformation," in *Five Essays on the Bible* (New York, 1960), pp. 20–29. Paper read at 1960 annual meeting of the American Council of Learned Societies Devoted to Humanistic Studies.

Christian Attitudes to War and Peace: an Historical Survey and Critical Reevaluation (New York, Abingdon Press, 1960), 299 pages.

Constantine and Religious Liberty, by Hermann Dörries, translated by Roland H. Bainton (New Haven, Yale University Press, 1960), 141 pages. (The Terry Lectures.)

Early Christianity (Princeton, N.J., Van Nostrand, 1960), 192 pages. An Anvil Original paperback.

1961 *El Alma Hispana y el Alma Sajona* (Buenos Aires, Argentina), 143 pages.

Index